D1046879

Effective Leadership Communication

Effective Leadership Communication

A Guide for Department Chairs and Deans
for Managing Difficult Situations and People

Mary Lou Higgerson
Baldwin-Wallace College

Teddi A. Joyce
The University of South Dakota

ANKER PUBLISHING COMPANY, INC.
Bolton, Massachusetts

Effective Leadership Communication
A Guide for Department Chairs and Deans
for Managing Difficult Situations and People

ISBN 978-1-933371-19-1

Composition by Lyn Rodger, Deerfoot Studios
Cover design by Borges Design

Anker Publishing Company, Inc.
563 Main Street
P.O. Box 249
Bolton, MA 01740-0249 USA

www.ankerpub.com

Library of Congress Cataloging-in-Publication Data

Higgerson, Mary Lou.
   Effective leadership communication : a guide for department chairs and deans for managing difficult situations and people / Mary Lou Higgerson, Teddi A. Joyce.
      p. cm.
   Includes bibliographical references and index.
   ISBN-13: 978-1-933371-19-1
   1. College personnel management. 2. Conflict management. 3. Departmental chairmen (Universities) 4. Deans (Education) 5. Communication in management. I. Joyce, Teddi A. II. Title.

   LB2331.66.H54 2007
   378.1'1—dc22
                              2006033511

Table of Contents

About the Authors

Mary Lou Higgerson is vice president for academic affairs and dean of the college at Baldwin-Wallace College. She also serves on the board of trustees at Elmhurst College. Since the 1980s she has used her knowledge of organizational communication and more than 25 years of experience in higher education administration to help other college administrators. Dr. Higgerson is a regular presenter at the American Council on Education Chairing the Academic Department Workshop series and the Kansas State University Academic Chairpersons Conference. She has consulted at numerous institutions and is known for publications and presentations that offer immediately useful insights to practicing administrators. The recipient of eight prestigious teaching awards, including the Distinguished Teacher Award at Southern Illinois University Carbondale and the Bill Cashin Award for outstanding research contribution to the study and practice of higher education administration, Dr. Higgerson brings a hopeful clarity to complex issues that pose stressful conditions for chairs and deans.

Teddi A. Joyce is vice president for marketing, enrollment, and student services at The University of South Dakota. She previously served as associate academic dean and director of academic planning and research at Baldwin-Wallace College. With more than 16 years in various administrative capacities, her foci include using research to inform planning and decision-making processes, facilitating communication to help strengthen institutional planning, and understanding the role of public relations in the development of image. Prior to joining Baldwin-Wallace, Dr. Joyce worked in private industry. Her experiences with and insights into organizational issues in higher education provide a broad, practical understanding of today's challenges.

Introduction

For those who serve or aspire to serve as chair or dean in higher education, this book was written especially for you. It is designed as a personal resource and as a text for leadership development programs.

National changes in higher education bring new and difficult challenges for chairs and deans. For example, new accrediting criteria place greater accountability on institutions to demonstrate program quality. However, presidents and governing boards cannot assure program quality without effective leadership at chair and dean levels because acceptable measures of program quality reside at the program level. Successful institutions need faculty to engage in ways that enhance the institutional mission, and this cannot be achieved without effective chair and dean leadership.

The leadership demands on chairs and deans are varied and significant. Regardless of the type of institution, chairs and deans are expected to be both the catalysts for and implementers of needed change. This dual responsibility would be demanding in any organization, but chairs and deans must navigate change with faculty who are accustomed to working with considerable autonomy and at a pace that fits comfortably within an academic year calendar. As part of the institution's leadership team, chairs and deans are expected to understand the context and reasons for change—and persuade others about the need for certain changes. At the same time, faculty and staff rely on chairs, and in many cases deans, to acknowledge and, perhaps more importantly, respect certain longstanding traditions within the academy.

With leadership responsibilities to both faculty and administration, chairs and deans often find themselves considering both perspectives. If, for example, faculty and staff perspectives are to influence the central administration, it is typically because chairs and deans have effectively communicated the views held by faculty and staff to the central administration. Similarly, if faculty and staff work constructively to implement change directed by the central administration, it is effective because they have persuaded faculty and staff to understand the importance of the change.

This important but in-the-middle position means that a significant portion of a chair's or a dean's job is to manage conflict. Conflict can appear with varying degrees of intensity or hostility, but unless it is managed effectively, it can slow or jeopardize the institution's success. At professional meetings, sessions on managing conflict are well attended, and it is our considered opinion that one's ability to manage conflict tends to be a primary factor in deciding to hold an administrative position as chair or dean. Rare is the person who enjoys managing conflict. Most of us find it unappealing to live and work very long with the tension knot in our stomach that conflict produces. That's why the effective management of conflict is the central theme of this text.

Conflict can be especially difficult to manage unless chairs and deans are able to practice one central leadership communication skill—the ability to consider both first-person and third-person perspectives. This skill serves as an underlying premise for much of what is presented in this text. One strategy for managing conflict more effectively is to develop the proficiency of moving between the first-person and third-person perspectives. If viewing and attempting to manage conflict occurs from only the first-person perspective, it will be virtually impossible to understand the perspective that created the existing conflict or to identify areas of common ground that may permit a resolution to destructive conflict. It is the ability to consider the third-person perspective that provides the insight absolutely essential to effective conflict management. This particular leadership communication strategy will also afford chairs and deans increased comfort in managing conflict. Consequently, mastering this leadership communication strategy can dramatically influence one's comfort and willingness to serve in a leadership position.

To be effective leaders, chairs and deans must manage the inevitable tensions that develop between faculty and staff and the central administration. To manage conflict they must exercise effective leadership communication that is designed to help individual constituencies understand the perspectives held by other constituencies as well as the external conditions that make strategic change essential for all institutions. Because the current conditions require faculty to think and behave in new ways, chairs and deans must inform, motivate, counsel, persuade, critique, facilitate, and build consensus. They must also manage resistance, conflict, change, workloads, student academic achievement, and program quality. More than ever, professional and institutional success demand effective communication with faculty, staff, students, parents, alumni, areas business leaders, accrediting agencies, granting agencies, and, of course, the central administration.

As institutional expectations for chair and dean leadership evolve and increase, the challenge becomes more complex and difficult. The more effective leadership communication strategies may be actions that are counterintuitive to how a chair or dean might typically act or respond. This text is written to help chairs and deans become more proficient in identifying those instances in which a counterintuitive action will more likely be effective. As chairs and deans learn to implement counterintuitive leadership communication strategies, their comfort and skill in managing conflict will improve.

By discussing leadership expectations for chairs and deans, we do not mean to suggest that chairs and deans have similar duties. They do not. Chairs occupy the front-line position of leadership. They work side by side with faculty and staff in gathering evidence that documents program effectiveness and student success in implementing necessary change. Deans occupy a middle position of leadership. They translate between senior leadership and front-line leadership and therefore become the voice for how what is desirable meshes with what is feasible. But to be successful, both chairs and deans must possess the communication skills essential to effective leadership, even though their specific role responsibilities differ.

This book addresses the specific communication skills and strategies needed by chairs and deans to manage conflict as they carry out assigned responsibilities in ways that yield both institutional and professional success. The essential communication strategies are reviewed within the context of chair and dean leadership. In doing so, this text offers a guide for those who appreciate help on how best to execute their duties for more effective outcomes. Consequently, while this book is designed to improve chair and dean leadership, it also is a book about leadership communication. We hope it is helpful to any individual seeking to improve the communication aspect of leadership.

Leadership communication focuses on those responsibilities which inherently involve and depend on open, collaborative communication with others. The focus on leadership communication will also explain what cannot be found in this text. Specifically, no guidance is provided on anything other than communication strategies that support effective leadership. For example, chairs and deans typically have responsibility for reviewing faculty performance. Portions of this book will address the communication involved in counseling faculty performance but will not offer guidance on how to design or purchase an assessment instrument that might be used for this task. Similarly, some institutions need faculty participation in student recruitment which is not a traditional faculty responsibility. This book will not offer guidance on when or how to involve faculty in student recruitment. It will, however, coach chairs and deans on what communication strategies might be used to engage faculty in tasks that are beyond the scope of the traditional faculty role.

The chapters are organized into three parts: establishing a foundation for effective leadership communication; developing a fair and effective leadership communication style; and using leadership communication to manage especially difficult people. However, the chapters do not need to be read sequentially to be helpful. This text is designed to permit the reader to pick and choose among the various communication leadership scenarios. Each chapter encourages chairs and deans to cultivate and practice the first-person participant and third-person observer roles. This skill permits chairs and deans to have more strategic control over the communication in a particular situation and therefore empowers chairs and deans to feel and to be more in control in every situation.

There are several advantages to working through this text. First, the examples are real in that they describe situations that chairs and deans on every campus encounter. Aside from the obvious benefit of commiseration, this text affords the reader with a risk-free opportunity for brainstorming approaches to specific instances. Consequently, a second advantage is the opportunity to accelerate the type of learning that typically derives from real work experience. You don't have to live it to learn it. Moreover, the design of the text permits the reader to custom-fit his or her readings according to personal need and interest. Third, working through this text provides the reader with a credible but safe way to try on the various demands of chair and dean leadership. These jobs are not for everyone, and this text allows the reader to obtain a firsthand sense of what serving as chair and dean is like, to explore the personal comfort associated with exercising effective leadership communication and to envision how to successfully lead through specific situations experienced by chairs and deans on any campus.

You are in control of how much you gain from reading this book. Each chapter contains a series of questions or prompts to help guide you through a hypothetical but realistic situation. It would be easy to empathize with the faculty member, chair, or dean portrayed in these scenarios. However, you will gain more insight into your own style of managing conflict and understanding of leadership communication if you move your vantage point from the comfortable third-person observer perspective to a first-person participant perspective. Using the first-person perspective, imagine yourself in the role of the chair or dean leading the department through the conflict described. This shift in perspective means that rather than a cursory reading, you may need to step back and reflect as you encounter a question or prompt to gain the full benefit intended in this text.

If you have decided to work though this book, you are serious about improving your leadership communication to enhance institutional and personal success. Enjoy the journey.

Part I

Establishing a Foundation for Effective Leadership Communication

This section addresses the communication strategies that serve as a foundation for effective leadership communication. How chairs and deans articulate the institutional mission, share decision-making criteria, set precedents, establish their credibility, and build relationships ultimately helps to set the tone and foundation for their leadership effectiveness. These strategies should become part of the operational fabric of one's daily leadership communication. Unlike some of the leadership communication strategies discussed in Parts II and III of this book, the strategies covered here are meant to be applied consistently and pervasively over time. When these leadership communication components are in place, chairs and deans will find that they possess an advantage in managing difficult issues, situations, and people.

1 Using the Institutional Mission to Empower Performance

2 Setting Precedents Carefully

3 Sharing Decision-Making Criteria to Inform Requests

4 Establishing Your Leadership Credibility

5 Building Relationships

Using the Institutional Mission to Empower Performance

When chairs and deans explain individual goals and performance expectations in relation to the institutional mission, they help clarify which behaviors are valued and empower others to be positive contributors. This chapter provides chairs and deans with leadership communication strategies for linking individual goals and performance expectations to the institutional mission in a way that eliminates the perception of favoritism and removes the frustration that develops when individuals believe they are working hard but not sensing progress or positive recognition.

Faculty members have long enjoyed a significant degree of autonomy. Except for teaching at a set time for assigned classes, faculty have considerable control over their day. They can determine when to hold office hours, grade papers, prepare for class, or engage in scholarly pursuits. In some departments, faculty members are even asked which classes they wish to teach and when they wish to have them scheduled. Faculty can say when they are or are not available for a meeting. This is not to suggest that faculty do not work hard. Most work very hard. Faculty, however, are accustomed to being in control of their daily and weekly schedule, and they are accustomed to working with minimal, if any, oversight or accountability. Faculty members work independently to prepare syllabi, class activities, assignments, and exams. Faculty determine their own areas of scholarly interest and exercise considerable control over the way in which they serve the department and institution by accepting or rejecting committee and other service assignments.

Many of the recent changes in higher education challenge the autonomy enjoyed by faculty. In light of these changes, chairs and deans have needed to engage faculty in new and different tasks and involve them in decision-making in new ways. While specific tasks may vary with the type of institution, faculty on virtually every campus lament that they have more work to do. It is rapidly becoming the norm to have faculty engaged in institutional initiatives such as student recruitment and retention activities, expanded student and colleague mentoring programs, fundraising efforts, strategic planning, and campus facility planning. Chairs and deans involve faculty in these efforts and in other new tasks for good reason. They want the various institutional projects informed by faculty voice. Yet there is also no practical way to complete the changing institutional tasks without help from faculty.

The need to respond to external pressures for increased accountability in higher education has produced several changes that further challenge the individual faculty member's autonomy and create more and different work for faculty. Chairs and deans have needed faculty to accept these new tasks that impose on faculty autonomy. For example, faculty members are expected to assess student academic achievement to obtain reliable and valid evidence of course and program quality. To meet the expectations of today's students, faculty must also be more intentional in linking the course content and the specific discipline to the various career aspirations of students. Faculty find themselves involved in efforts to both affirm the value and market need for their disciplines. Again, chairs and deans involve faculty in this work because the faculty perspective and voice are critical to shaping the process and outcome. But, doing so alters the traditional role and responsibilities of faculty.

Even good-natured faculty can resent new tasks that crowd their day and increase their workloads. Fatigue and resentment can turn ugly if faculty members do not understand the importance of the new responsibilities and why the tasks require their perspective and participation. How might you go about demonstrating the value of new tasks to faculty? Would assuring faculty of the tasks' importance to the department and the institution be sufficient to obtain faculty buy-in? It might be, if as chair or dean you are a highly credible voice with the faculty. However, it is likely that you will need more than just your word as chair or dean to persuade faculty that the new work is important and worthy of their time and attention. What types of information might you provide to faculty to assist them in understanding the mission as a way to help clarify priorities? Because the answers may vary with the situation and with the campus culture, you need to consider what evidence would be credible with the faculty on your campus.

With new initiatives, faculty morale can seem like it is undermining their work. Worse yet, chairs and deans run the risk of appearing arbitrary and demanding when faculty are left to believe that the new tasks are assigned to make life easier for chairs and deans or the central administration. When such misperceptions are permitted to exist, they can fester and eventually surface in ways ranging from a passive-aggressive lack of cooperation to open hostility. Effective leadership communication links new work or initiatives to the institutional mission, and this application will correct misinterpretations and help defuse resentment before it begins to fester or escalate.

To help keep faculty constructively engaged in new tasks that could easily be resented and resisted, chairs and deans need to establish the relationship between individual performance expectations and the institutional mission. Placing individual tasks in the larger context of the institutional mission will elevate their importance and help debunk any misconception that the extra work is generated by the chair or dean to satisfy a personal whim. By framing the work in terms of the institutional mission, there exists a clear understanding of what actions are valued as central to the mission. It then empowers individual faculty to act more independently and in ways that enhance the institutional mission. When faculty members possess this level of understanding, they need less direction from the chair or dean, and their performance will enhance departmental and institutional effectiveness.

Unfortunately, using the institutional mission to empower performance is not intuitive. Often chairs and deans responsible for completing tasks and meeting deadlines are understandably focused on what needs to be done and by when. A focus on deadlines and task completion eliminates the benefit of linking performance expectations to the institutional mission because faculty and staff are not empowered to understand the relationship between their work and achieving the institutional mission. Further, unless faculty and staff understand how their work supports the mission, they are less able to identify tasks that might be eliminated or given a lower priority in relation to new demands on their time.

CONNECTING FACULTY WORK AND THE INSTITUTIONAL MISSION

The institutional mission should provide the context for individual work. When chairs and deans issue directives and set deadlines without establishing the context for action by linking the request to the institutional mission, they will likely encounter more resistance than that which typically accompanies change. Chairs and deans can facilitate institutional and personal success by clarifying the relationship between individual performance expectations and the institutional mission.

Suppose a small private liberal arts college has expanded its mission to incorporate an emphasis on global learning. This emphasis was initiated to achieve its commitment to prepare students for life and work in a global society. Success in meeting this mission is determined by faculty and staff commitment to the new mission. And, to meet the mission, faculty must rethink learning objectives and course content for the core curriculum and every academic major and minor offered at the college. The expectation to emphasize skills for working in a global society will not be automatically understood or easy for faculty in all disciplines as some programs focus on discipline learning without consideration of a global context.

Consider the study of physics or English literature. It is possible for students to study these fields without giving much thought to how the knowledge is relevant to life and work in a global society. Hence, the new mission cannot be realized without effective chair and dean leadership. In your role as chair or dean, do the programs you lead evidence and advance the institutional mission? Do faculty and staff recognize the connection between their work and the institutional mission? If you answer these questions with "no" or "not sure" then it may be helpful to consider the following situation.

A new mission that incorporates global learning suggests that the curriculum will connect discipline study with life and work in a global society. However, when a new mission is approved by an institution's board of directors, typically no direction is provided for the resulting changes that should take place within each department. As chair or dean, how would you lead this change? Since curriculum is typically owned by the faculty, it is important that they understand the implication of the new mission for the curriculum. In physics, for example, an understanding of the new mission might result in faculty helping students understand how their knowledge of physics will enable them to assess government reports about U.S.

military defense and the ramifications of using nuclear weapons. Faculty teaching English literature might help students understand how literature informs us about a period in history and a particular culture. These changes in the curriculum will not occur unless faculty understand the mission and its implications for their work. Faculty have responsibility for developing the curriculum, so for a new mission to influence curriculum development they need to possess an operational understanding of the mission. As chair or dean, how would you facilitate this understanding? Would you rely on discussion or memorandum? Would you involve external sources? Would the existing climate within your department influence how you approached this task?

Consider how you typically announce and implement a new initiative. Do you rely on one-way communication that informs faculty and staff of what needs to be done and by when? Or, do you engage faculty and staff in conversations that permit them to develop an operational understanding of the initiative's objective and empower them to participate in shaping the response? It is likely that on occasion you use both approaches. But, it may be that the particular approach used is dictated by convenience; however, it is preferable to select an approach with consideration of the desired outcome.

One way chairs and deans can facilitate understanding of the institutional mission is by framing questions and revising routine report formats to encourage faculty to think about their individual and collective responsibility for moving the mission to action. For example, an annual achievement report required of each faculty member might be revised to ask for information on how global learning is addressed in each course the faculty member teaches. Also, brainstorming sessions might be held to permit faculty to think out loud within or across disciplines about what the new mission means for curricular development. Teams of faculty might be sent to conferences on innovative pedagogy for the purpose of sharing information with other faculty back on campus. The ideas for how to involve faculty are unlimited, but the leadership communication strategy that chairs and deans should employ is more precise. Specifically, chairs and deans need to help faculty acquire an operational understanding of the institutional mission so that faculty are empowered to carry out their responsibilities in ways that advance the mission.

When faculty and staff understand the institutional mission, they are empowered to go beyond minimum performance expectations in ways that enhance the campus. Many faculty members are, by nature, creative and inventive. These traits can be positive if faculty possess an operational understanding of the institutional mission. If they do not, chairs and deans will find that requests for resource support are more likely to be off target in terms of the mission. If the mission is unclear to faculty and staff, then their requests for resources are less likely to relate to advancing the mission. No matter how reasonable it is to deny requests that do not support or advance the mission, denied requests for resource support can contribute to animosity between faculty and the chair or dean and lower morale among faculty and staff. However, when faculty and staff have an operational understanding of the current institutional mission, they are empowered to contribute new solutions to existing problems, and their requests for resources will more likely support the overall purpose of achieving the institutional mission.

Consider a situation in which faculty believe that the institutional mission requires them to demonstrate institutional quality by imposing academic rigor when, in realty, the institution aspires to evidence quality by documenting student achievement. Faculty performance directed at weeding out students based on initial academic preparation and ability could undermine the institution's objective to demonstrate the value added through instruction.

Possessing an operational understanding of an institution's mission is important in higher education because without a clear sense of the institutional mission faculty and staff will act in accordance with their personal mission and priorities. Suppose a campus is attempting to increase the number of pre-professional experiences for undergraduate students. This objective requires support from faculty to help secure internships, professional mentors, and other discipline-related connections to the real world. Yet faculty will not likely think to spend time on this activity unless they understand the operational mission of the institution and comprehend how their individual actions are needed to achieve the desired outcome. However, if chairs and deans make the institutional mission clear, faculty and staff become empowered to think of new ways that they might carry out the mission. Are you able to think how you might help to develop an operational understanding of the institutional mission among faculty and staff on your campus? What actions have you taken in the past that contributed positively to this objective? What else might you do? If it is difficult to delineate specific action steps, perhaps reviewing another example will help.

REINFORCING NEW MISSIONS THROUGH DECISION AND ACTION

Suppose a doctoral-granting research institution wishes to emphasize a renewed commitment to undergraduate education. This commitment represents a shift in the institutional mission requiring a corresponding change in faculty and staff performance. A research institution cannot deliver on a new promise to undergraduate students unless faculty and staff understand the revised mission and permit it to guide individual performance. Faculty and staff must be willing to change how they spend their time, and this will require more than an announcement about the new mission.

Chairs and deans are accountable for transforming the mission into action, and this requires that individual work be perceived in relation to the institutional mission and that new tasks be perceived as important to the institution. The chair and dean must persuade the faculty at a research institution to spend more time teaching and mentoring undergraduate students outside of class. Faculty entrenched in the stereotypic mission of a research institution will likely perceive the request as counterproductive, if not suicidal, to the performance expectation that faculty must "publish or perish." And, chairs and deans will not likely persuade faculty to spend time on tasks that are perceived as irrelevant to performance expectations unless the new desired behaviors are valued in some tangible way.

As chair or dean, what would you do to systematically reinforce the value of new behaviors? Should work with undergraduate students be recognized as part of tenure and promotion review? Should work with undergraduate students be valued when allocating merit pay? What else night be done to make the new mission credible and real in the eyes of faculty and staff? It is of little use to persuade an operational understanding of the institutional mission if the desired behavior is not recognized, rewarded, and reinforced in every possible decision.

To be credible in moving a new mission to action, chairs and deans must be consistent and pervasive in reinforcing the new mission in every decision and action. Faculty and staff are not likely to take ownership of the new mission or engage in the behaviors needed to support the change in the institutional mission unless they are convinced that their work will be recognized and rewarded. Return for a moment to the example of a large research institution that has incorporated as part of its mission a greater emphasis on undergraduate instruction. Communication about the new mission will be ineffective unless faculty and staff also understand how the new direction is reinforced through decisions and actions. Thus, everything from the awarding of tenure and promotion to the allocation of merit pay and other resources must support and reinforce the importance of quality undergraduate instruction. Unless the new mission is supported through decisions and actions, it will be perceived as empty rhetoric.

COPING WITH FACULTY RESISTANCE TO CHANGE

Consider Dr. Schmidt, a senior faculty member who serves as the program director for an interdisciplinary program in public relations. Although this professor is known for being somewhat set in his ways, he is also well known for working very hard. He is credited with building the program into one that boasts a healthy enrollment and a strong record of placing graduates. Dr. Schmidt has a strong sense of personal ownership for the program and typically insists on managing many of the details himself. For example, he retains a hard-copy log of all internship sites rather than making use of available software and staff support to track information, which would save his time and permit the institution to gather aggregate data more effectively.

Dr. Schmidt also openly resists externally imposed requirements for documenting program quality and student learning. For example, he perceives the task of assessing student learning as an unnecessary bureaucratic exercise imposed by the administration. He resents the time it would take and perceives assessment as something that would actually detract from the program's quality as it would force him to spend less time with students. Somehow Dr. Schmidt has thus far managed to get by without implementing an assessment program. Now, the institution is preparing for its next regional accreditation visit and, in your role as chair or dean, you realize that an otherwise strong program is vulnerable only because its program director remains unconvinced about the value of assessment. What do you do?

The challenge here is to persuade a loyal and hardworking faculty member to accept responsibility for a new task that he believes is superfluous to program quality and student success. Dr. Schmidt does not recognize that assessment data are now the gold standard for institutions wishing to demonstrate program quality. Moreover, he does not understand how assessment outcomes of student learning can aid the institution in student recruitment and retention, accreditation review, and securing external funding.

These relationships are difficult for Dr. Schmidt to understand because he does not recognize the connection, for example, between an effective assessment program that evidences student learning and success to the institutional mission. You need to take some action because Dr. Schmidt has avoided assessment as long as the institution has dared to permit with the regional accreditation review just two years away. What would happen if you issued a firm directive to Dr. Schmidt that included a timeline for implementing an assessment plan? Would it help to link this request to Dr. Schmidt's merit pay review? These strategies would only work if you were certain that procrastination was the only reason he had not yet developed an assessment plan. The program is important to the institution so it is not an option to permit Dr. Schmidt to persist in ignoring program expectations that could jeopardize institutional accreditation.

Because he is hardworking and loyal to the institution, it is more likely that he does not recognize the value of assessment to the institution. Should you issue an ultimatum? If not, how might you engage Dr. Schmidt in a discussion that would permit him to understand that assessment has become crucial for demonstrating program quality and student academic achievement, both of which are essential to fulfilling the institutional mission?

Knowing the context for a task and understanding the value of the work to the institution can transform a bureaucratic task into a noble charge. What factors would influence whether you did an assessment and mission tutorial as a one-on-one meeting with Dr. Schmidt or as part of a group discussion involving other program directors? To determine what the most effective meeting format is, you would want to consider whether Dr. Schmidt's understanding will be enhanced by hearing other program directors talk about how they use assessment to enhance program quality and whether the other program directors also need the information. How would you structure such a conversation or meeting? What other steps might you take to resolve the perceived conflict between Dr. Schmidt's individual perception of the assessment initiative as being unnecessary work and the needs of the institution?

ANALYSIS AND APPLICATIONS

In the rapidly changing landscape of higher education, faculty members are being asked to accept new and varied tasks that impose on their autonomy. When individual tasks can be positioned within the larger context of the institutional mission, there is an opportunity to showcase how those tasks are central to the mission. By creating an operational understanding of the mission, chairs and deans can facilitate success. When faculty and staff are empowered to carry out their responsibilities in ways that advance the mission, the mission is transformed into action and a higher level of personal, professional, and institutional success occurs. Let's review the essential elements of each application:

- Operationalize the institutional mission for faculty and staff.

- Provide the institutional context for individual responsibilities.

- Illustrate the importance of individual work to the institutional mission.

- Create choice for faculty and staff.

◆ Operationalize the institutional mission for faculty and staff.

In their leadership role, chairs and deans need to determine what information will enable faculty to develop an operational understanding of the institutional mission and how to help faculty acknowledge and accept the mission as a goal that informs decision-making. While the specific approach can vary with the department and the campus, any approach will require chairs and deans to consider the perceptions held by faculty and staff.

It is not enough to provide faculty and staff with a copy of the institutional mission. Nor is it sufficient to discuss the institutional mission in general or abstract terms. Instead, chairs and deans must facilitate specific discussions about the institutional mission as it relates to and directs specific activities. This way faculty and staff can develop an operational understanding of the mission. Only when individual faculty and staff possess a working definition of the institutional mission will they be able to think independently about what they can do to advance the mission.

The objective is to have the mission so clear and present in the minds of faculty and staff that they are empowered to know what actions will help achieve the mission without daily or constant supervision and direction. In the example of the institution that revised its mission to encompass global learning, faculty need to understand what is meant by global learning before they can begin to think about how to revise courses and programs to achieve the mission. Similarly, faculty at the research institution that revised its mission to place greater emphasis on undergraduate instruction need help internalizing what this change means for their daily work. As chair or dean, how would you lead a discussion with faculty about these changes in the institutional mission? Can you describe in pragmatic terms the implications of the revised mission for individual faculty work?

Consider the example of Dr. Schmidt, the public relations program director who does not understand how implementing an assessment program advances the institutional mission. How does he think about the institutional mission? Is it likely that as a program director he even thinks about the institutional mission? If not, how might you operationalize the institutional mission for Dr. Schmidt? The best approach will require that you establish in Dr. Schmidt's mind a clear and salient connection between what he strives to achieve and the institutional mission.

Chairs and deans might help someone like Dr. Schmidt obtain an operational understanding of the mission by helping him determine what components of his program align with the goals of the mission. Also, an operational understanding can be reached by pointing out the value of the public relations program to the institution. This provides a context for understanding the specific ways in which the program serves the mission. For example, by noting how the high retention and graduation rates for students majoring in public relations serve the institutional mission, you can help foster pride in the program and reinforce the importance of student retention and timely graduation.

◆ Provide the institutional context for individual responsibilities.

Once faculty have an operational understanding of the mission, it is important to consider what types of data will be perceived as credible and facilitate an understanding of the institution's situation. Chairs and deans can reduce resistance from faculty and staff by linking individual tasks and performance expectations to the larger context of the institutional mission. Without a contextual understanding, the simplest of tasks can appear arbitrary and unnecessary. This leadership communication strategy also helps to defuse potential conflict that might exist when faculty believe that the chair and dean are attempting to control faculty.

In the example where the program director, Dr. Schmidt, perceives the implementation of an assessment program as unnecessary extra work, the perception exists because, in his mind, implementation of an assessment program represents a spurious request. He believes that the request will disrupt the business at hand by adding nonessential work. Yet the program's objective is to educate and prepare students majoring in public relations for work after graduation, and the purpose of assessment of student learning is to document that students have been educated and prepared for work in public relations. So, in Dr. Schmidt's mind where is the disconnect? The perception of assessment as an unnecessary task exists because Dr. Schmidt is intent on meeting the goal without understanding why measuring success in doing so is important to achieving the institutional mission.

As program director, Dr. Schmidt exhibits a strong commitment to the public relations program, but he does not understand how his daily work relates to or advances the institutional mission. How would you help Dr. Schmidt understand the relationship between assessing student learning and achieving the institutional mission? How would you frame the issue? Would you, for example, describe how assessment provides proof that the institution is fulfilling its mission? Or, would you frame the discussion around the public relations program, which is his primary concern as program director? You might review with him the need to demonstrate to accrediting agencies and other external constituencies that the public relations program educates and prepares students for work after graduation and invite Dr. Schmidt to think about what, if anything, is in place to do this. You may learn that he already has some assessment measures in place to inform his decision-making about the program, but that these provisions are not perceived by him as activities that could be part of a more developed program to assess student learning. However, if, as program director, he can understand how the assessment of student learning will document the effectiveness of the public relations program and in turn support the institution's mission, then Dr. Schmidt will be less resistant to the request for assessment activity.

By relating the work of individual faculty and staff to the institutional mission, chairs and deans make clear the institutional value of individual contributions. Faculty and staff are more likely to satisfy performance expectations when they understand the importance of what they do to the overall success of the institution. Also, recognizing the contributions of faculty and staff to achieving the mission can motivate other faculty and staff to make further progress.

You should realize that persuading Dr. Schmidt to see the value and importance of assessing student learning will not likely eliminate all resistance. It should, however, considerably soften the resistance attributed to the perception of assessment as an unnecessary bureaucratic task. But it will not lower resistance that derives from concerns about workload. How might you address this type of resistance? What is the likely outcome if you opt to ignore this resistance? When leading a new initiative like assessment, resistance to change will be more manageable if the initiative being implemented is recognized as essential to achieving the institutional mission. If the request to assess student learning seems unrelated to the intuitional mission, it will at best be viewed as unnecessary work and at worst be viewed as an effort by the administration to monitor faculty. However, if assessment is perceived as being about student learning and therefore essential to the institutional mission that promises to provide students with a high-quality education that will prepare them for life, then the request to assess student learning will be perceived as necessary.

◆ **Illustrate the importance of individual work to the institutional mission.**

Chairs and deans need to consider various leadership communication strategies to develop a larger conversation about program quality and external conditions. A key issue at the heart of this conversation is showing faculty that their work is valued but that the institutional mission is still paramount.

When chairs and deans provide concrete feedback on work done by faculty and staff, they can affirm the importance of the work and can use the feedback as a guide for future work. For example, by relating positive student comments about specific faculty to the individual faculty member, it is possible to affirm valued behaviors such as spending time mentoring students outside of class and to relate that behavior to the institution's mission of preparing students for work after graduation. Such evaluative comments will be more instructive if they consistently reinforce what actions are valued and how certain types of individual work advances the institutional mission. At the research institution that revised its mission to emphasize commitment to undergraduate instruction, chairs and deans can illustrate and reinforce the importance of individual work to advancing the mission by recognizing and rewarding faculty work that supports and enhances undergraduate instruction. For example, a chair might make an effort to pass along positive comments made by undergraduate students, recognize effective teaching at the undergraduate level and work with undergraduate students in merit pay, promotion, and tenure reviews, and celebrate publicly achievements in the area of undergraduate education. However, if chair and dean recognition is not consistent, it will be less effective in illustrating the importance of individual work to the institutional mission.

Further, by focusing on behaviors and not personalities when providing feedback to faculty and staff, it is possible for chairs and deans to reinforce the belief that every individual faculty or staff member can contribute positively to the institutional mission. Consider the difference between a chair who describes certain faculty as being especially effective teaching undergraduate students and a chair who says faculty who utilize interactive pedagogy will likely be more effective with undergraduate students. The first identifies certain faculty as meeting the institution's commitment to undergraduate instruction while freeing others from the task. The second statement describes a specific action that is valued because it facilitates success in undergraduate instruction while implying that all faculty members could (and should) adopt the valued behavior.

◆ Create choice for faculty and staff.

While the mission creates a blueprint for decision-making, chairs and deans still need to develop a framework that builds trust and support for the mission. One way to increase faculty and staff commitment to the institutional mission is to permit them some choice in deciding what and how they contribute. Faculty and staff are generally more responsive in taking action that they recognize is valued by the institution if they have some choice in deciding how they can support the institutional mission rather than being directed to take certain action with little or no choice.

Consider again Dr. Schmidt. As a program director, he will likely be more responsive to the assessment initiative if he is permitted to determine how best to document program quality rather than if he is directed to implement pre- and post-test measures in certain courses. Similarly, faculty at the small liberal arts college seeking to implement global learning will more likely become vested in the new mission if they have some choice in deciding how to modify the curriculum to ensure global learning.

Structuring choice permits faculty and staff to internalize the institutional mission, understand the implications of the mission for daily work, and maximize positive momentum. Because not all faculty and staff have the same capabilities, choice also optimizes the use of human resources. Consider, for example, the research institution that wishes to make undergraduate education a priority. The institution does not need all faculty members to teach undergraduate students, but it does need all faculty members to recognize undergraduate education as a priority.

Some faculty may work with undergraduate students on research, others may advise undergraduate student organizations, and still other faculty might teach courses that serve both graduate and undergraduate students.

SOME FINAL THOUGHTS

Institutions of higher education thrive best when individual faculty and staff are empowered to take action in ways that advance the mission. Progress is inevitably slower when chairs and deans need to direct individuals on how to act rather than when individuals possess an operational definition of the mission. With an operational understanding of the mission, members of the campus community are able to assess the types of actions that are supportive of the mission. When faculty and staff possess an operational understanding of the institutional mission, they are empowered to act in ways that knowingly support the mission.

To direct individual behavior, chairs and deans must persuade faculty and staff to take some specific action, which increases the likelihood of resistance. However, when individuals are in a position to make good decisions without direction, progress is not hindered by resistance to directives. Instead, faculty and staff are empowered. They are able to suggest and implement change in support of the institutional mission.

When individuals are able to discern which actions will be valued and helpful to the institution without direction or prescription, they are more likely to suggest the very changes that they would likely resist had they been directed or prescribed by the chair or dean. If they have an operational understanding of the institutional mission, faculty and staff can own actions that are valued by the institution.

Setting Precedents Carefully

Saying yes to an unreasonable request in order to appease a whiner or calm an angry individual can create a precedent that yields more stress and conflict in the long run. This chapter provides chairs and deans with strategies for assessing the merit of individual requests in relationship to institutional policy and practice. Also included here are specific leadership communication strategies for assessing the implications of setting precedents, reasoning through decisions, and determining courses of action that can enhance chair and dean credibility with the other faculty and staff and avoid setting impractical precedents.

Faculty members have historically enjoyed a high degree of individual influence on curriculum, assessment, and personnel decisions. However, as the social, political, and environmental factors in higher education intensify, the landscape in which institutions operate is undergoing rapid changes. These new external pressures coupled with changing institutional contexts needed for response can inevitably limit faculty understanding of how individual actions can influence others now and in the future. Actions or decisions that favor one may disadvantage another.

Individual faculty members are also accustomed to making personal requests. A faculty member might, for example, request a deadline extension for submitting a report on sabbatical activity, grades, or information requested by the central administration. If the request is denied, the faculty member is likely to conclude that the chair or dean is being unreasonable because the subsequent harm from a delayed submission is not apparent to the individual faculty member. Some chairs and deans reading this text know that the harm or inconvenience of a late submission can be so far removed from the minds of individual faculty members that many do not even see the need for a deadline extension and merely render a late submission. Some faculty can become outraged when the campus registrar "badgers" them to turn in late grade sheets. From the faculty member's perspective, the registrar does not recognize or understand that faculty members are busy and how much time is needed to read and grade final examinations. This condition contributes to the image used by some when they liken leading faculty to the challenge of herding cats or frogs.

Chairs and deans need to recognize that decisions made in response to individual requests can have huge ramifications for the institution and for one's leadership effectiveness. The term *individual request* is misleading in that every decision has the potential for setting precedent and influencing the expectations and perceptions of others. Hence, in granting an individual request, chairs and deans help to create future situations that will demand their time and attention. By making an exception to a policy for one faculty member, chairs and deans open the door to the expectation that they will make the same exception for other faculty. It may be that the exception is appropriate and reasonable in a particular circumstance. If so, then it should be clear to all parties why the exception to policy is warranted, and the exception should become automatic if the particular circumstance reoccurs. If the exception is reasonable, it should be made available to all, and the policy statement linked to the exception may need to be revised accordingly.

On occasion it may seem like the best way to manage conflict is to grant the individual request. After all, people seeking special treatment or exceptions to policy can be pushy and difficult to manage. Chairs and deans may hope that granting a request may help a demanding individual become more reasonable in the future. Sometimes the request appears trivial in comparison with the time and energy required to uphold the policy and deny the request. Faced with the immediacy of an unpleasant encounter that could escalate, chairs and deans may believe it is better to grant the request even when it is not, in their judgment, a reasonable one. There exists the temptation to think others will not learn of the request or that granting it will have no dire consequence. However, informal communication channels like the campus grapevine typically work very well and, despite the autonomy that faculty have long enjoyed, it often seems that nothing remains secret or private for very long. Word of mouth can spread like fire and create rumors, especially when it is something that is close to people's emotions—like workload and pay.

No matter how tempting it is to grant the whining faculty member his or her wish, chairs and deans should only do so if the preferential treatment can be made public and comfortably explained to others. In some instances, chairs and deans can minimize the perception of favoritism or other types of backlash by explaining the conditions that warranted an exception. This strategy preempts the rumor mill and cuts down on misperceptions about the decision or about why an exception to policy is warranted. Also, through public explanation, chairs and deans have now established their willingness to respond in the same way to all individuals who experience the same set of circumstances. Taking this action actually helps to enhance chair and dean credibility because it evidences the intent to be fair and equitable in the application of policy.

There is also a need to assess individual decisions in relation to the institutional context. Some policies regarding such matters as faculty workload or course schedules are, to some extent, specific to an institution's type and size. What is affordable on a large campus could seriously hamper resource flexibility at a small institution. Similarly, what is feasible at a small institution may not be possible on a large campus, and what is possible at a private institution may not be possible at a public institution. Consequently, even requests that appear to be personal have implications for the institution and other individuals. Therefore, chair and dean decisions regarding such requests have implications for their leadership credibility and effectiveness. When responding to an individual request, chairs and deans must consider the ramifications to others and the institution.

EXCEPTIONS FOR SENIORITY

Suppose a faculty member with more than 25 years of service to the institution is under the established teaching load when an upper-level special topics course is canceled because of no enrollment. In such instances, the institutional policy is to bring faculty up to load by assigning another class or other work responsibility. The policy derives from an effort to assure equitable workloads for faculty. On rare occasions, an individual faculty member may prefer a reduction in pay in lieu of adding another course or additional responsibility. The institution has accommodated requests for pay reduction because this alternative maintains workload equity but does so by reducing compensation for the hours worked rather than bringing the number of hours worked up to that which is equivalent to full-time.

The policy has been in place for many years, and the full-time faculty trust that all have equitable workloads.

How you might handle a request from a senior faculty member who, with 25 years of service to the institution, declares that he is not picking up another course on short notice? The faculty member comments, "I was prepared to teach the class that the administration canceled so it is not fair that I now have the additional work of preparing to teach another class." When you, as chair or dean, attempt to explain that the policy is designed to provide faculty with equitable workloads, the faculty member responds, "Teaching is only one part of my job. You and I both know that when it comes to advising students and service to the college, I put in more hours than anyone. When you start making other faculty do a comparable amount of service and advising, I'll be glad to add another class."

What do you do? Assume it is true that the senior faculty member has been a strong contributor in the areas of advising and service. Should this influence your decision? Suppose it is also true that this faculty member is seldom under load. Should this fact influence your decision? While the faculty workload policy requires that all faculty members teach, engage in scholarship, advise students, and serve on committees, only the teaching portion is quantified by policy. Should this influence what you would do? What responsibility do you have to other members of the faculty?

These can be difficult questions to answer, especially if you like the faculty member and value his or her long-term contribution to the institution. How might you demonstrate the value of the work and service contributions of the long-time faculty member without taking an action that could be considered favoritism?

It would be easy and intuitive to grant this request and waive the teaching load requirement for the senior faculty member. Granting the request, however, requires giving permission for one faculty member to be paid for full-time work when the workload is less than that assigned to other full-time faculty. Many chairs and deans faced with this decision might reason that it is a well-deserved exception to policy earned for 25 years of faithful service and may view it as an opportunity to repay a valued, long-term faculty member for years of hard work. Although these perspectives are not wrong, they are also not right. They are not right because they are incomplete.

A decision to grant the request for an exception to the faculty workload policy cannot be right and will be problematic unless the decision is made with full consideration of the larger institutional context. Policy exceptions set precedent because they are not isolated decisions; they signal the revision of campus policy and practice. Whether the policy statement is formally revised and promulgated is irrelevant because a decision to apply the current policy differently under certain circumstances will be perceived as such. A decision to grant the exception communicates a new policy provision that says faculty members with many years of strong service to the institution do not need to accept a new class or other work when the cancellation of a course results in them being under the prescribed teaching load.

It may be that this is a reasonable revision of the faculty workload policy. If so, it would be preferable to revise the policy separate from granting an individual request, and the policy change should be communicated to all faculty members. Sometimes it takes an individual request to recognize that a policy should be revised. In such instances, it is preferable to announce the revised policy to all who are affected by the policy before granting the immediate request. Chairs and deans will be perceived as more fair and unbiased if they take the time to view individual requests in relation to the larger campus context. When chairs and deans treat individual requests as isolated instances, they become vulnerable to charges of favoritism.

MAKING LONG-TERM ASSESSMENTS OF POLICY EXEMPTION REQUESTS

Consider a campus policy that requires all faculty and staff to use in-house services such the campus bookstore or print shop. Typically, such policies are intended to optimize use of institutional resources. For example, if an institution supports a printing service on campus, it does not want campus offices to spend institutional funds on outside printing services for those jobs that can be done in-house. Similarly, a campus bookstore operation likely contributes to the general revenue of the institution, thus it is not prudent to permit offices to purchase books and supplies from outside vendors when the items needed are stocked in the campus bookstore.

While most will understand the logic for policy that protects campus entities and conserves institutional resources, it is easy to lose sight of the premise when faced with a pressing need. Consider a situation in which an institution is launching a satellite campus with the goals of increasing revenue and reaching new student populations. The satellite campus will not be full service in that very few offices will have a presence on the campus. In particular, since there will not be a bookstore at the satellite campus, it is important that students enrolled in classes offered at the satellite campus not be inconvenienced. The leadership of the satellite campus seeks permission to work with a local bookstore in an effort to prevent students from having to travel to the main campus for books and supplies. On the surface, the request seems eminently reasonable. After all, if the objective for opening a satellite campus is to capture a different student market, it does not make sense to require students enrolled at the satellite campus to travel two hours to the main campus for books and other course supplies.

Viewed as an isolated decision, the answer seems obvious because granting the exception to the policy seems to facilitate the primary purpose for launching the satellite campus. However, a decision that seems logical when reviewed as an isolated instance can become illogical when considered within the larger context. To determine if a request merits an exception to policy, one must consider the ramifications to the larger campus community. In this example, the relevant data might include revenue lost to the campus bookstore and the cost involved in providing a bookstore presence on the satellite campus. Such data points are fairly easy to assess, and it is important to consider such factors as the economic cost and benefit of approving a request to contract services off campus. This assessment should also consider other alternatives for accomplishing the same objectives. In this example, one might involve the campus bookstore in discussions of what level of service the satellite campus needs to provide to students because the bookstore director will likely be able to suggest ways in which the campus bookstore might provide the desired student service.

Often, individuals believe they need an exception to policy because they are not able to perceive what might be done within current policy. For example, if the primary concern is to provide students enrolled at the satellite campus with texts and course supplies, it may be feasible for little cost to have staff from the campus bookstore deliver the texts and other course supplies needed to the satellite campus on the first day of class. Part of reviewing an isolated request in the larger context is to consider all the available alternatives for accomplishing the purpose of the specific request for an exception to policy or practice. As important as such economic feasibility assessments are, they will not always address the matter of longer-term ramifications of setting a new precedent by granting the exception to policy.

It is more difficult to assess the ramifications of setting a new precedent. This requires anticipating how similar requests might be handled. For example, if the satellite campus is permitted to bypass the campus bookstore, will it also be permissible for other programs and offices to do so. To assess the ramifications of setting a new precedent, chairs and deans need to carefully consider and articulate the basis for the exception to policy. If the satellite campus is permitted to bypass the campus bookstore because it will be more convenient for the leadership of the satellite campus, then convenience becomes the basis for persuading other exceptions. If, however, the satellite campus is permitted to bypass the campus bookstore because students can be better served, the service to students becomes the basis for persuading additional exceptions from the institutional policy.

Granting one exception will spawn requests for other exceptions to policy. This is not to imply that exceptions to policy are never a good idea. Sometimes exceptions to policy are necessary and the right thing to do. If the basis for the exception to policy is clear and well articulated within the campus community, further requests will more likely be consistent with the conditions established in granting the first exception. If, however, news of permission being given to bypass current policy is communicated formally or informally without a clear understanding of the basis for the approval, the one exception will likely produce more policy exemption requests that are motivated for a wide variety of reasons. Worse yet, when the same logic is applied to new requests and approval is not granted, it is likely that those whose requests were denied will perceive the decision as unfair. Without a publicly shared logic for an exception to policy, decisions to waive policy appear arbitrary because the community only knows who was granted permission and who was denied permission.

FACULTY RECIPROCITY

Sometimes informed leadership requires chairs and deans to make decisions or take actions that may appear mean or stingy to those who are less informed of the larger campus context. Many elements of faculty work cannot be postponed when there is extended illness. So when a faculty member becomes ill or, for any reason, must miss several weeks of class during the semester, responsibility for covering the class typically falls to someone else. The work can be burdensome because it is typically short notice and performed on top of one's own assigned classes and other responsibilities, and it should be compensated in some way.

Often faculty within a department or division will work out some form of reciprocity with the realization that at some point, everyone needs a colleague who will step in and teach their classes. The practice of collegial reciprocity works well so long as the process is not abused. It also works because the practice acknowledges that institutions cannot pay two different faculty members to teach the same course. Instead, if a faculty member needs to miss class on an extended basis, the absence is covered through leave policies managed by the human resources office. Should a faculty member go on disability, the institution is able to contract with someone else to be the instructor of record for courses initially assigned to the faculty member on disability.

Suppose Dr. Peterson, a department chair, is aware that one faculty member is covering classes for a colleague who is busy caring for a terminally ill family member. When the number of classes missed increases to 30% of the term, the chair concludes that the amount of work being done by the helpful colleague is excessive and should be compensated. Motivated to express gratitude for the extra work, the chair informs the helpful faculty member that she will be paid for the extra classes taught. The helpful faculty member is surprised but pleased to learn she will receive additional or overload pay for covering her colleague's classes.

Dr. Peterson then submits a statement to the dean summarizing how many classes were covered and asking that a specific amount of compensation be paid to the helpful faculty member. The request comes as a surprise because the dean knew nothing of the arrangement. In reviewing the details, the dean determines that the absent faculty member could have applied for available leave policies to manage his need to be away from campus, which would have enabled the institution to contract the services of another faculty member to cover the missed classes. After the fact, however, the dean is not sure what can be done. What types of follow-up might be implemented to clarify the elements of this situation?

If you were the dean in this instance, you would likely call Dr. Peterson and explain the dilemma. You might ask why you were not notified sooner. Dr. Peterson explains that it was to be a temporary arrangement, but that it became an extended chore, and now it would be unconscionable to have the helpful faculty member do so much work without compensation. What do you do? Would you talk with the absent faculty member? Would you talk with the helpful faculty member? Would you appeal to the administration to make an exception and pay overload to the helpful faculty member?

Before talking with anyone, it is prudent to review the relevant policy. Even when one believes that he or she has an understanding of the policy, it is helpful to review the actual policy statement when deciding how to approach a particular instance. Suppose in this case, however, you review the policy and it affirms that a faculty member who needs to miss class for this amount of time should work with the human resources office to apply for family leave, but this was not done. You also affirm that campus policy precludes assigning more than one person to any faculty position, so there is no easy way to compensate the helpful faculty member. What do you do?

As chair, Dr. Peterson insists to you that it is "only right" that the helpful faculty member be paid. Further, Dr. Peterson is not sure when the absent faculty member will be able to return to work and expresses concern for how to cover the classes if the helpful faculty member stops teaching them. What would you do? In such instances it can be helpful to collect more perceptions of the situation. You might talk with both the absent and the helpful faculty members to learn their perceptions of the arrangement and their expectations for compensation. So, you decide to talk with the absent faculty member, and he is outraged to learn that his chair, Dr. Peterson, has requested pay for his colleague. The absent faculty member describes the long-held practice of collegial reciprocity and cites a few instances in the previous year when he helped to cover classes that his colleague needed to miss for illness and the birth of a child. The faculty member is so upset by the news that he wants to know if his colleague instigated the request and why his chair is "out to get him."

Then, in talking with the helpful faculty member, you learn that she never held any expectation to be paid. In fact, she quickly volunteers that within the program, faculty members have always helped each other out in this way and cites the same examples you heard earlier as she was once helped by the faculty member who now is absent. The helpful faculty member says she was surprised but pleased when her chair "promised" to pay her for the work being done. Now that you have collected all the perspectives, what would you do? Is this an instance that warrants setting a new precedent?

To determine if this instance warrants setting new precedent, you need to consider the larger campus context. If you pay additional compensation to this helpful faculty member, you should rightly and fairly pay every other faculty member who covers a class for a colleague. You might consider setting a guideline for when a helpful faculty member would qualify for additional or overload pay by stipulating, for example, that a helpful faculty member must teach a minimum percentage of a single colleague's class sessions in a term in order to receive compensation for the teaching. Even so, it would be difficult to budget for such expense and setting any limit will likely offend faculty. Some faculty might be offended because the idea of compensation would be perceived as cheapening collegiality. Others might be offended because they covered classes, but not enough to receive compensation. Still other faculty might view the provision for receiving compensation as a way to increase accountability when subbing for a colleague and ask how the work would be counted in promotion and tenure review or merit pay consideration.

This instance developed without your knowledge so it is possible that you would not know how many faculty members might qualify for this type of additional pay in a given year. Should you decide to pay the helpful faculty, the action would likely be perceived as preferential treatment unless a concerted effort was made to identify and pay all other faculty who helped to cover classes for a colleague. Can you anticipate what might happen if you announced a change in policy and declared that faculty who helped colleagues by covering classes in times of personal need would be compensated? What would be the reaction of faculty at your institution? How would the decision be perceived by the central administration? Changing the policy to permit compensation would require other decisions. You would, for example, need to budget for the new precedent and manage other implementation aspects, including the development of a system for keeping track of the classes covered—by whom and for whom. There is also the potential need for establishing guidelines to determine when a faculty absence is acceptable and what, if any, documentation would be requested for an absence.

These issues help to discern the ramifications for setting precedent. Let's work from these hypothetical examples to deduce some general guidelines for systematically assessing the positive and negative ramifications of setting precedent.

ANALYSIS AND APPLICATIONS

Decisions cannot be made in a vacuum—in fact, across campus any one decision has the potential to serve as a compelling rationale and argument for future direction. Chairs and deans need to recognize that decisions made in response to individual requests can have far-reaching implications. When assessing individual requests, it is important to review the requests to determine if they are consistent with the institutional mission and goals and how granting the requests may be perceived. Whether or not an individual request can be granted, it is often helpful to "worry in groups" to examine specific policy changes and needs so that those involved are solicited for potential solutions in light of the institutional mission. Let's review the essential elements of each application:

- Consider the larger campus context.

- Anticipate the ramifications of setting a precedent.

- Consider whether the policy needs to be revised.

- Brainstorm alternatives for managing the immediate situation.

◆ Consider the larger campus context.

Chairs and deans need to discern what types of questions or issues are most important to their institution and the salience of specific issues can help frame the discussion to bring all relevant perspectives together. Chairs and deans can avoid opening a Pandora's box by carefully considering the larger context before making a decision or taking action. The larger context must take into account the institutional mission, policy, key constituencies, and resources. In other words, use the larger context to help reason through potential problems, potential needs, and potential opportunities. Institutional and individual integrity demand that individual decisions support the mission, be compliant with policy, treat all constituents fairly and equitably, and use resources effectively in an effort to advance the institution. Let's revisit the example of the faculty member who believes his years of service should exempt him from teaching a full load when the administration canceled one of his classes for no enrollment. To view this decision as an opportunity to reward a long-term faculty member would ignore the larger campus context because the decision does not take into account campus policy or other faculty.

When chairs and deans make decisions without considering the larger campus context, they are vulnerable to the charge of favoritism. In this example, faculty who teach the full load will likely perceive the exception as unfair. Unless it is absolutely clear to everyone that this one long-term faculty member has a record of institutional service that far exceeds the contributions of any other faculty member, the campus community will perceive a decision to exempt him from the full teaching load as preferential treatment. Extending the exemption to all faculty members might make the isolated instance more equitable, but the decision would have a significant impact on resources.

Failure to consider the larger campus context can confuse faculty and staff. Exceptions to policy and practice signal others that the policy is fluid and open to interpretation and individual application. Especially when the reasons for an exception to policy are not clear or known, chairs and deans can find that granting one request without consideration for the larger campus context will spawn more requests. For example, if one office or program is known to bypass the campus bookstore or printing service and contract services off campus, it will become something others expect to be able to do.

◆ Anticipate the ramifications of setting a precedent.

When determining a course of action or considering a potential precedent-setting decision, it is helpful to determine if the decisions will evidence respect for all your colleagues. One place chairs and deans might start is reviewing the points of agreement or disagreement that exist and from there consider how changes might be perceived.

Taking the time to anticipate ramifications of granting an individual request can serve to validate the wisdom or illustrate the problems associated with the decision to be made. Chairs and deans can anticipate the ramifications for any decision by systematically considering the probable reaction from every constituency that would be affected by the decision. For example, in considering the request to approve additional or overload pay for the helpful faculty member, the dean should consider the probable reaction of several constituencies including faculty, department chairs, the central administration, and staff. Faculty reaction would be the easiest to anticipate, although the faculty response could range from the desire to secure the privilege for all faculty members to questioning the integrity of the chair and dean for favoring one individual faculty member. Chairs in other departments may view the action as rewarding chairs who were less effective in building course schedules in response to student need. The administration will want to know the long-term cost implications for such action. Staff will likely see this instance as more evidence that faculty members are treated preferentially.

By anticipating the reaction of the constituencies that will be affected by the decision, it is possible to process and announce actions in ways that contribute to greater understanding and more constructive perspectives. Processing decisions can also help to reinforce the logic for policy and evidence institutional and individual integrity. Especially when a request to exempt policy would likely be perceived as preferential treatment, processing the request can help to clarify the boundaries for policy exceptions and impress all of the importance of equitable treatment. Best yet, it helps to stifle other requests that are motivated by self-interest.

Chairs and deans also need to consider the ramifications to human and fiscal resources. This is more than calculating the cost of making an isolated decision and must also include an estimate of the cost associated with implementing the one instance campus wide. For example, if one faculty member is permitted to receive full pay without teaching a full load because his class was canceled for underenrollment, the institutional cost of this decision is more than the three or four credits involved in the isolated instance. The cost of this decision is determined by considering the application of the new precedent campus wide.

◆ Consider whether the policy needs to be revised.

When making a change, it may be helpful to consider how the old and new policy fits within the institutional mission and current institutional conditions.

Since policy does not live forever, revisions may need to be made as internal and external conditions constantly change. When chairs and deans find that there is a legitimate basis for granting an exception to policy, it may be time to consider a policy revision. For example, suppose the campus printing service has not kept pace with technology, and it is actually less expensive to have certain printing jobs done off campus. Unless the campus plans to upgrade the campus printing services, it makes sense to revise the policy. While chairs and deans are not likely to have the final say on this policy revision, they can clarify the need for it.

Generally, it is preferable to revise policy when needed than to continually grant exceptions to outdated policy. First, revision saves time at several levels in that faculty and staff do not need to submit requests that chairs and deans will grant automatically. Second, the need to contend with one "dumb" policy can damage the credibility of other policies when the administration fails to appropriately revise policy. To be effective, policy must be clear and support the mission and operation of the institution. Confusing or outdated policies contribute to inefficient campus operation and undermine the credibility of those who must apply them. Thus, a revised policy that assures consistency, relevance, and clarity can eliminate the causes of misunderstanding and misinterpretation.

◆ Brainstorm alternatives for managing the immediate situation.

As chairs and deans, it is important to determine what types of information will create an open atmosphere and enable faculty to have a greater understanding of the mission and improved communication between members of the department.

It can be difficult to deny an individual request even when consideration of the larger campus context makes it the right thing to do. For example, it can be hard to tell a faculty member who has taught 30% of an absent colleague's classes that she will not receive additional or overload pay, especially after her chair told her that she would. Similarly, it can be hard to tell the leadership of a new satellite campus that they must use the campus bookstore located two hours away. Effective leadership will brainstorm other alternatives for managing the situation that produced the request for an exception to policy or practice.

Brainstorming other alternatives is most effective when chairs and deans involve others, especially those seeking the exception to policy. How might you structure a meeting to be sure that the right people are involved in the discussion? In the example of the satellite campus, a discussion between the leadership of the satellite campus and the bookstore director could be framed to permit all to learn more precisely the services needed at the satellite campus, enabling the bookstore director to consider how the unique needs of the satellite campus might be accommodated.

Similarly, including the long-term faculty member in a discussion about the reasons for coming up to load enables the faculty member to present his perspective and the chair to learn more about that faculty member's perceptions. Armed with this information, it is easier to generate alternatives that might be more palatable to the faculty member. For example, if the conversation makes it clear that the request is prompted by some projects that have made this semester particular heavy and challenging for the faculty member, it might be possible for the faculty member to make up his load during an intercession or the summer. Or, you might discover that the faculty member would prefer to work at reduced pay rather than picking up another class, but he was not aware that this was an option. Brainstorming that brings together all the parties creates a joint effort and the solutions become a part of everyone's thinking.

SOME FINAL THOUGHTS

Virtually every request for an exception to policy or practice holds the potential for setting precedent. While there is nothing inherently harmful in setting precedent, chairs and deans must take care to be informed and intentional when charting new guidelines and policy revisions. The only way to protect institutional and individual integrity is to recognize that individual requests are not isolated decisions, but decisions that will be viewed by others in relation to personal and institutional considerations.

You may have heard the saying, "No good deed goes unpunished." Chairs and deans who treat individual requests as isolated decisions will find this saying to be true. The quickest way to feel punished for doing something nice is to approve an individual request, especially when the approval comes without consideration for the larger context. The good feeling one gets, for example, from rewarding the long-term faculty member by waiving the workload policy will be short lived when other faculty complain about favoritism. The good feeling one gets by permitting a program to bypass the campus bookstore or printing service will be short lived when others assume they can do the same thing or when the campus bookstore and printing service explain how they might have accommodated the special need at a savings to the institution. The good feeling one gets from paying additional compensation to a faculty member who covered classes for an absent colleague will be short lived when other faculty submit requests for such payment and you do not have sufficient budget to cover the requests.

The only way to ensure that the precedent being set will be positive is to consider the isolated decisions within the larger campus context and anticipate the ramifications of granting the request. This includes specific consideration of the need to revise the policy for everyone and the availability of other alternatives for managing the need that prompted the specific request. Chairs and deans need to determine if the outcome being sought can be accomplished in some other way. Chairs and deans also need to help the central administration recognize when policies need revision to remain current and to be effective with changing conditions.

Even when it is the right thing to do, it can be hard to deny an individual request because the person making the request is likely to feel dismissed or disregarded. Chairs and deans can ease the tension and ill will that can accompany the denial of a request by processing the request with others and involving the person making the request in those conversations. This strategy will help the person seeking special permission to understand both the larger context and the ramifications of the decision. Often when individuals seeking permission realize the larger context, they will withdraw or modify their request. However, without such processing, they are likely to have an unfavorable reaction to the denial of their request. The best way to convince those seeking special favor that a negative response does not mean that the chair or dean doesn't care or understand their plight is to permit that person to view the decision as the chair and dean must view it. Granted, this strategy will not absolve all anger and disappointment, but it will go a long way toward appeasing individuals who are able to understand the larger context and who are not motivated solely by personal gain.

It can be intuitive to view individual requests as isolated instances and act in a way that seems helpful. However, this approach will likely create more conflict and animosity for chairs and deans to manage. This anguish can be spared when chairs and deans understand that individual requests are not isolated instances but represent decisions that can have far-reaching ramifications for the campus and their leadership credibility.

Sharing Decision-Making
Criteria to Inform Requests

Most chairs and deans would acknowledge that it is impossible to please everyone all the time, but denying individual requests can be uncomfortable because it is often difficult to separate the request from the person. There are communication strategies for saying no that not only depersonalize both the issue and the decision but also demonstrate that the chair or dean is being responsible and not just arbitrary in saying no. This chapter provides chairs and deans with leadership communication strategies for depersonalizing the evaluation of individual requests in ways that do not invite a grievance or fuel hard feelings but which can instead enhance chair and dean credibility and minimize conflict.

Most faculty and staff recognize that institutional resources will not permit chairs or deans to grant all individual requests. This, however, does not diminish the indignation and anger that can result when an individual request is denied. Faculty and staff make requests in order to obtain support for something they deem important to their professional development or their work at the institution. When chairs and deans deny a request, the decision can be interpreted as a lack of support for that which the applicant believes is important or, in some cases, as an action against the person making the request. It is this sense of individual professional need that tends to make the request very personal.

The denial of an individual's request will likely be interpreted as a lack of support for his or her professional development or work at the institution. Because each request represents a self-assessed need, it is easy for faculty and staff to personalize a response to their requests. Thus, a seemingly simple request for travel funds to support attendance at a conference may be impossible because available resources will not cover the cost or it might not be the most pressing priority for using available resources. Yet to the person making the request, the travel is important and having the request denied can feel very personal and unfair. Similarly, a request for an exception to a personnel policy is often motivated by personal need. A faculty member who battles an extended illness, for example, may request an off-campus assignment in lieu of the typical teaching load to avoid being placed on short-term disability, which carries a reduction in pay. Even though the request may be judged as inappropriate and unfeasible to the chair and dean, denial of the request will likely be perceived as a personal affront to the individual faculty member seeking the policy exception. The denial of even extraordinary requests can be interpreted very personally with the requester concluding such things as, "They know I'm ill, but won't help me," or "This is the thanks I get for being a faithful and hardworking faculty member all these years."

Few situations are more stressful for chairs and deans than coping with the ramifications that occur when faculty and staff perceive that they are not supported by the academic leadership. Such perceptions can have an adverse affect on morale and productivity and make it more difficult for chairs or deans to obtain cooperation and will ensure that they experience greater resistance to virtually everything. Because most chairs and deans have an appreciation for the negative ramifications that result when individuals believe the denial of a request signals a lack of support for their work or a disregard for a personal situation, it may seem better to grant an inappropriate request than deny it.

In order to spare the disappointment that would otherwise result, chairs or deans may be prompted to grant individual requests, even when logic and salience are missing. It can be especially uncomfortable to deny a request when the individual making the request interprets the denial in a personal way. For example, when considering the probable negative ramifications of denying a late-year request for travel funds, it seems better to grant the request than to face the negative reaction that will follow if the request is denied. In this instance, a chair might reason that the account balance covers the cost of the travel so why not fund the request? The response seems reasonable, even though the proposed travel is not typically covered by the institution at any other time of the year, and similar requests submitted by other faculty earlier in the year were denied. In this instance, a chair might reason that it would be better to spend remaining funds rather than have the funds lapse. Why deny a request that is, at the moment, affordable? Where's the harm in granting the request?

The harm in granting the request can be significant on many levels. First, in granting the request, the chair or dean damages his or her credibility with other faculty because the action represents an inconsistent application of policy and practice. Given that similar requests were denied earlier, this action challenges the chair's or dean's credibility in treating all faculty members fairly. Second, it makes the chair or dean vulnerable to charges of favoritism—which can chip away at departmental morale. Third, it makes future decisions more difficult because all requests become more personal. No longer will policy be accepted as a credible basis for reviewing and granting or denying requests. After all, if the chair or dean can make an exception to the policy for one professor, why can't the chair or dean make a similar exception for others? Thus, taking an action that seems to be the most expedient to keep from disappointing one professor can cost a chair or dean more time in restoring his or her credibility and rebuilding morale.

There is tremendous advantage to using policy to inform decision-making. When consistently applied, policy can help individual faculty and staff understand that the denial of a request is not personal. Instead, the denial of their request indicates that their desire fell outside the boundaries established by policy or other institutional parameters. Further, denial is easier to accept if individual faculty and staff can be confident that any person submitting the same proposal would get the same response. Then the negative decision is not personal. Finally, when chairs and deans are consistent in acting on individual requests, individual faculty and staff will be better able to assess the merit of a request before making it. If, for example, all faculty members understand which travel will not receive financial support and are confident that the same rule applies to all, they will be less likely to spend time drafting a request that is outside the funding parameters. Hence, chairs and deans will find that upholding policy can protect their credibility and their time. By finding comfort in equity, chairs and deans make it possible for individuals to view specific requests in relation to the larger context that inevitably governs decision-making.

SHARING INFORMATION TO CONTROL PERCEPTIONS OF UNFAIRNESS

Consider the responsibility chairs or deans have for assigning faculty to classes and class times and allocating departmental resources (fiscal and physical) to individual faculty. While most chairs and deans understand that the appearance of favoring some will both damage their credibility and have an adverse affect on the department climate and faculty morale, they may not realize how little it takes to create the appearance of favoritism. Most chairs and deans intend to be fair and equitable in carrying out their responsibilities. However, the best intentions do not guarantee that chairs and deans will be perceived as making fair and equitable decisions.

Imagine what you would do as chair of a department that is striving to become more visible at national and international levels. Should this goal inform your decisions regarding the allocation of travel funds to individual faculty? Would you, for example, factor the cost of the trip into the allocation rather than giving all faculty members the same sum regardless of whether their travel destination was regional, national, or international? Can you anticipate the reaction of individual faculty who receive different travel allocations? Would the reaction of individual faculty be better if you opted to allocate the same dollars to every faculty member regardless of the travel destination? It is likely that either decision would cause some faculty to view the allocation as unfair. Faculty who incur greater travel expense because of the location of a conference would consider it unfair if the funds available for travel were divided equally among the faculty without regard for the cost of the trip, while faculty with plans for regional travel would consider it unfair if colleagues with international travel plans received more support. How might you structure the situation to alter faculty perception and reaction and evidence that your decision-making process is fair? Would it help to share the relevant information used in making the travel allocations? If so, specifically what information would you share and how would you make the information available to faculty? Would you, for example, send a memo or engage faculty in a discussion? How might you evidence that you are consistent in applying decision-making criteria so that you dispel unfair and negative perceptions for your treating some faculty preferentially?

Similarly, consider the situation in which faculty have traditionally been asked which classes they wish to teach and when, but declining enrollments and other fiscal constraints now demand a more streamlined curriculum and class schedule to permit students to complete programs in a timely and efficient way. The need to build an efficient class schedule is made more important because the campus is implementing a new general education course required of all students. In this situation, how would you respond to the faculty member who is angry for having been assigned to teach at 8:00 a.m.? Remember, when faculty are unaware of the larger context and decision-making criteria, they are more likely to view chair and dean decisions from a personal perspective and, when they do, there is a greater likelihood that even good and fair decisions will be viewed as unfair or inequitable. Would it be sufficient to tell the upset faculty member that the class needed to be scheduled for 8:00 a.m. so it did not conflict with the new general education course? To answer this question, you need to consider if the explanation has meaning for the faculty member. In other words, is the information provided in the explanation sufficient to be credible? One way to answer this question is to consider how the individual faculty member will reply to the explanation. While this is difficult to do when considering a hypothetical example in a text, it is relatively easy to do on your own campus with individuals whom you know. Try this experiment. Consider an announcement you might make to the faculty with whom you work that would come as a surprise to them. You might tell them, for example, that the teaching loads would be increased or that there is no longer any funding support for professional development. Can you anticipate the specific reaction you would get from each faculty member? You may find that you already anticipate the reaction of many faculty members—complete with the precise wording and emphasis. This technique can help you assess whether an explanation will be perceived as credible by an individual. Only if an explanation is perceived as credible can it help to sustain perceptions of chair and dean credibility.

Stress and the potential for conflict can also cause well-intentioned chairs to make expedient decisions that seem harmless in the short term but create inequities and greater conflict in the future. For example, what would you do with a late-year travel request to attend a regional conference when no funds were given for attendance at a regional conference during the routine allocation cycle? The request is for $50 and because of a canceled trip you have $400 remaining in this budget line. You might reason that the allocation can be made because it is late in the year and it makes sense to spend the balance of remaining funds. If so, would you communicate this change in practice to others in the department? Would you involve others in the department in making the decision?

This decision might create an inequity that would likely contribute to future conflict. The decision, for example, might invite others to expect support for travel to regional conferences and devalue the importance of travel that nets national and international visibility for the program. Would faculty be more likely to view the decision to fund the late request as a prudent use of available resources or as evidence of preferential treatment? How might you navigate this decision in a way that enhances your credibility? The immediate request is not an isolated decision. Are there other possible uses for the budget surplus that would support the objectives inherent in the existing allocation criteria? For example, is it possible to increase previous allocations or approve reimbursement in amounts larger than those initially allocated, but in a way that preserves the rationale for making allocations that are consistent with departmental goals and the institutional mission? Asking such questions will help place the immediate decision in a larger context and identify alternatives.

FAIRNESS AND THE SABBATICAL

Consider a situation in which a faculty member is displeased with the application of institutional policy that prescribes how to calculate the teaching load credit to be awarded for sabbatical leave. The policy recognizes that faculty teaching loads can vary each year, as individuals are awarded release time to do research or perform specific administrative duties, and it calls for the sabbatical leave calculation to be based on a three-year average of credits taught by the faculty member. The calculation is used to determine the credit assigned for the sabbatical leave with the understanding that this number is subtracted from the full-time teaching load to determine the number of credit hours to be taught by the faculty member in the other semester during the year in which the sabbatical is taken. The full-time teaching load on campus is 21 hours, and if a faculty member has taught 21 hours each year for the past three years, the sabbatical leave would be worth half that, or 10.5 hours, and thus the faculty member would be expected to teach 10.5 credit hours in the other semester.

Suppose Dr. Harris, a full-time faculty member in your area of responsibility, has carried teaching loads of 21, 18, and 6 hours for the past three years for a per-year average teaching load of 15 hours, making the sabbatical leave worth half that, or 7.5 credit hours. According to institutional policy, Dr. Harris would then need to teach 13.5 hours in the other semester during the sabbatical leave year. Precedent on campus permits the rounding of credits in a manor that advantages the faculty member so you can round the credit hours awarded for the sabbatical leave from 7.5 to 8 hours, leaving the faculty member to teach 13 credit hours in the other semester.

Dr. Harris is upset and approaches you for an exception to the policy. How do you proceed to fairly consider the request? Do you involve others in making this decision, and if so, who? To answer this question, you need to consider if the decision is yours to make or whether granting the request would require approval from others. You also need to consider who else might be affected by the decision. Would granting the exception, for example, establish a condition upon which other faculty could seek exceptions to the policy? If so, granting the exception would serve to revise the current policy. If you decide the exception is warranted, would it be preferable to revise the policy at the same time the exception is granted? Before deciding to revise the policy, you would want to consider the ramifications of the change on such things as the cost of sabbatical leaves and faculty workloads.

Dr. Harris then points out that although the institutional focus is on teaching, faculty are also expected to engage in scholarship, and the year in which the teaching load was 18 credit hours he was awarded release time for research. He argues that he is being penalized for doing research. Does his argument have merit? Dr. Harris also contends that it is unfair to count the year in which he only taught 6 credit hours because he was ill that year and to do so is to punish him for being ill. Does this argument have merit? Would your view be altered if you knew that during the yearlong illness the faculty member was given special non-teaching assignments to permit him to fulfill his full-time load from home to prevent him from going on short-term disability at reduced pay? Would it alter your thinking to know that two years earlier another faculty member who had been similarly supported through a yearlong illness canceled her request for sabbatical leave in acknowledgement of the institution's generous support during her illness? Should these additional pieces of information influence your decision to support this particular request? Why or why not?

Again, to answer these questions, you need to consider the scope of the policy and the ramifications of making an exception to the policy. This requires looking forward as well as backward. Assume you grant Dr. Harris's request and next year a faculty member argues an exception to the policy because her reductions in teaching load were taken to engage in political service off campus. Her request for an exception to policy is based on the fact that a similar request was granted by you last year. You might contend that the situations are different, but the faculty member counters by pointing out that another responsibility of faculty is to engage in service, so how could her request be different from the one that sought consideration for release time to do research? Or, a faculty member who elected to use the parental leave policy now requests an exception to the sabbatical leave policy, saying that his case is no different than the instance when a yearlong illness was forgiven in calculation of the load credit for a sabbatical leave. How would you respond to that request? When and where might it end?

FAIRNESS AND THE NEW HIRE

Consider a situation in which to hire a strong candidate, the chair agrees that the new faculty hire will be able to honor extensive travel and consulting commitments made before accepting the position. Everyone who participated in the search agrees that this one candidate is exceptionally qualified for the position and that the other candidates rank far below the first choice. Everyone also recognizes that there is much at stake as the new hire fills a critical need in the department. In making the formal offer to the preferred candidate, you as chair learn that the candidate has commitments for consulting work that will require travel during 14 of the first 15 weeks of the semester. What do you do? Do you move on to another candidate in the applicant pool? Do you reopen the search? Do you accommodate the preferred candidate's need to be gone for most of the first semester? What other options might you have? To make this decision, you need to consider many other factors. For example, how would the work assigned to the new hire be managed during the first semester if you approve the absence? How will granting the privilege be perceived by other faculty? What would be the impact on the program and the faculty if the preferred candidate is not hired?

Once you gather this information, you need to consider if others should be involved in the decision. You may wish to involve others even though you have the authority to make the decision because permitting others to wrestle with the dilemma will offer insight into their reaction to the available options. If, for example, you brief other faculty in the department about the dilemma and they start thinking through how to manage duties that would normally be assigned to the new hire during the first semester, you might get a sense that making a special arrangement would be palatable for other faculty. If, however, they respond with "Who does she think she is?" or "We're back to square one," you'll know that making the special arrangement would not play well with current faculty. You may wish to float the same balloon with the dean, the human resources director, and anyone else who is in a position to judge the merit of your decision.

Assume that the preferred candidate offers to accept the position but without pay until spring semester, when all of the consulting commitments have been concluded. Would this influence your decision? If so, would you be prepared to grant a similar absence to other full-time faculty who wish to be away to consult? If so, what notice would you require and how would you assess the merit of the consulting activity? Would such a program of active consulting have an adverse affect on the academic program? Or, in others words, can the academic program sustain a practice of active consulting should more faculty seek the same arrangement? If you believe that other faculty should not be entitled to a similar arrangement, on what basis might you make that distinction and how would you communicate it to faculty?

Decision-making is fraught with land mines that can hurt chair and dean credibility, lower faculty and staff morale, and decrease departmental productivity. Some of the essential tools that chairs and deans must use to make credible and effective decisions consistent with institutional policy and practice include knowing relevant policy and practice, sharing relevant data, determining the fairness standard, and subjecting decisions to a litmus test. By considering these tools, chairs and deans can find comfort because the consideration of equity requires individuals to know and understand the context within which specific requests are assessed. Chairs and deans can pave the way by keeping faculty and staff informed about the larger context that governs decision-making. Good decision-making does not happen in a vacuum. Instead, good decision-making takes into account such context issues as available resources and spending priorities. Responsible department chairs and deans strive to match finite resources with spending priorities in ways that best advance the institution's mission yet remain fair to all concerned. When faculty and staff understand the larger institutional context, they are empowered to interpret the response to individual requests less personally. Individuals are more likely to recognize and understand that the denial of their request for travel funds does not imply a lack of regard for their professional development or work, but instead signals the unavailability of resources to support all worthwhile requests.

ANALYSIS AND APPLICATIONS

Higher education's segmented and autonomous nature mean that many faculty members still work in relative isolation—adding to the perception of individualism. Thus, when making a request, a faculty member may not be aware of the larger institutional context and the denial of that request may be seen as personal. When chairs and deans base the criteria for decision-making on policy, sharing the decision and answering other special requests becomes easier and more consistent. As important, when the decision-making criteria are known, faculty and staff are able to predict the decision, which removes the perception of bias or favoritism and enhances credibility. Let's review the essential elements of each application:

- Know relevant policy.

- Share relevant data.

- Determine the fairness standard.

- Subject decisions to a litmus test.

◆ Know relevant policy.

Because of their role, chairs and deans need to be aware of how policies are implemented and communicated and how their leadership and stewardship of the policies determine if campus practices are consistent or perceived as consistent with the policy. Thus, how chairs and deans structure the discussion of policy in the examples presented has an impact on whether faculty perceive the conversation as focused on the policy and not the individual and his or her situation.

Chairs and deans quickly get into trouble when they make a decision without considering relevant policy. The simplest matter can create conflict if a request is granted or denied in a way that contradicts printed policy. In the example of the new hire who wishes to negotiate as part of his contract permission to be absent 14 of the 15 weeks in his first semester of employment, it is important to know if institutional policy would afford current faculty the same privilege. Most campuses have provisions for how much time can be spent away from campus to do consulting work and for how to seek permission in advance. If policy forbids current faculty from doing this, there is less justification for making an exception for a new faculty hire.

As important, policy can help to shape a response that otherwise would be uncomfortable. Referencing policy when granting or denying an individual request will help to depersonalize the request, which is especially important when one needs to deny a request. Let's return to the same example and consider how comfortable you would be explaining that institutional policy does not permit any faculty member to spend so much time on consulting. In contrast, would it be more or less comfortable to simply deny the request? With the response, the chair explains why his or her hands are tied in considering the request, whereas in the second reply, the chair appears to be making an arbitrary decision. No matter how reasoned or appropriate the response, the new hire could view it as a lack of support.

Involving faculty in the development of a policy that will govern decision-making will help individual faculty know which requests are appropriate and likely to be supported. For example, if you involve faculty in deciding the criteria for allocating limited travel funds, they will have a context and frame of reference for understanding allocations. One faculty member may not like that she received less funding to travel to a regional conference than did another faculty member who sought support to travel to an international conference. When faculty members understand policy or the rationale used to inform decisions, they are able to predict what the chair or dean will decide and are much less likely to take any outcome personally.

Chairs and deans also need to be aware of relevant precedent. It is possible that precedent deviates from printed policy, and if so, campus perception will more likely mirror precedent than the written policy. For example, if it is common knowledge that most faculty members can stipulate the time they teach, they are likely to resist the chair or dean who assigns class times with the explanation that it is essential to preventing conflicts. After all, how essential can scheduling be since most faculty are permitted to set the times of their classes?

It is also important to realize that any single decision can set a precedent. Individual decisions are seldom isolated events, and chairs and deans can expect faculty and staff to know of and use previous decisions to shape future requests. Further, whether individual decisions are made public, the informal communication network on campus will carry news of what requests are approved or denied. Consequently, all decisions have the potential of setting precedent. This is illustrated in the example of the faculty member who seeks an exception to the institutional policy for calculating the load credit for a sabbatical leave.

◆ Share relevant data.

In framing any discussion, chairs and deans need to consider the salient points and determine how much information can be shared with others. It can be counterintuitive to share information for several reasons. Chairs and deans may believe, for example, that sharing information would take too much time and is unnecessary because the decision only affects one or just a few individuals. Chairs and deans might believe that sharing information would confuse matters or raise red flags that should remain furled. However, sharing information helps to evidence the logic for the decision and therefore helps to defuse conflict that might develop because a decision seems arbitrary, illogical, or preferential.

Decisions cannot be made in a vacuum. All decisions have a context that governs the outcome. Effective chairs and deans use data and other information to determine whether a request is affordable, feasible, and desirable. By sharing relevant data, chairs and deans enable faculty to assess the merit of a request even before making it.

When data are shared in advance of making specific decisions, the data are more credible and can help shape individual requests that are more reasonable in light of current resources and other constraints. Sharing data can help to inform individual requests and defuse the potential for conflict when requests are denied. Let's return to the example of allocating resources and assigning classes and class times. Such decisions are more likely to be viewed personally by individual faculty. Faculty members assess the decisions from very personal perspectives based on what they wish to receive. Unless faculty members understand the context and you as chair or dean share the relevant information, faculty have no choice but to evaluate the merit of such decisions from their personal perspectives.

It is easy to note when faculty do not understand the larger context or do not possess the relevant information because they make evaluative comments about decisions that reflect personal bias. For example, if, when allocating travel funds, you hear the following statements, then you know that faculty members do not understand the larger context or the relevant information, "You don't value my professional travel." "You clearly have favorites in the department and I am not one of them." "What do I have to do to get a travel allocation like the others get?" These statements imply favoritism in decision-making, which indicates that the faculty member believes the decisions are arbitrary and do not reflect any predetermined logic. Sharing relevant data can help faculty understand the logic for decisions even when they do not like them.

If sharing relevant data helps to inform faculty and staff of the logic supporting the decision, then sharing decision-making criteria will permit faculty and staff to know what is required to obtain a favorable decision. Chairs and deans strain their relationship with faculty and jeopardize their credibility when they appear to make arbitrary decisions. Only when faculty and staff understand the criteria for important decisions, such as when a new faculty line will be added, will individual decisions more likely be perceived as fair even when the request is denied. If the criteria for allocating travel funds is to spend available resources in ways that obtain the greatest visibility at national and international levels, then faculty are less likely to make a late request for funding to support regional travel. Similarly, if it is clear that there can be no exceptions to the policy for calculating sabbatical leave load credit because teaching is the primary mission of the institution, faculty will be less likely to seek exceptions. However, if you grant an exception to policy, you communicate to faculty that the policy is subject to exception and revision. In other words, you communicate the absence of clear criteria and open the door to consideration of exceptions.

The same is true for preserving chair and dean credibility with the central administration. In either direction, chairs and deans can enhance their credibility by making public the decision-making criteria. Doing so establishes that the chair or dean exercises sound judgment and that decisions are not arbitrary. Consider the example of the new hire who seeks permission to be absent the first semester in order to honor consulting commitments. Consider the dean's reaction if you as chair propose granting the request because the new hire fills a critical need in the department. How critical can the need be if the department can have the new hire be absent for the entire first semester? Hence, in pitching the request, you would be undermining the criteria established for making the hire.

◆ Determine the fairness standard.

An institutional understanding of the campus mission and priorities may play a role in the decision process. And, based on that understanding, any exception could have multiple interpretations.

The standard for what is recognized as fair is cultural and can vary from one department to another and from one campus to another. The standard of fairness encompasses process as well as outcome in that *how* chairs and deans share information and communicate decisions must also meet the cultural standard of fairness. Faculty and staff expect equitable treatment with regard to process as well as with decision-making, and even a negative decision is easier to accept if one believes that he or she was treated fairly. If you find yourself making an exception to policy with the hope that it will not be discovered by others or become widely known, you are probably violating the fairness standard for your culture.

In the example of the faculty member seeking an exception to the policy for calculating load credit for sabbatical leave, assume that this faculty member is one who is known to whine and persist until the desired outcome is secured. Suppose you as chair or dean opt to grant the exception on the basis that it will save a lot time and frustration. While there is a logic underlying your decision, it is not one that would meet the fairness standard. Indeed, it is a logic that you would be loath to share with anyone because it communicates that whining and persistent behavior is what secures approval from you. To meet the fairness standard, the logic that underlies a decision must communicate equitable treatment for all within your area of responsibility. This does not mean that you should never make an exception to policy, but rather you should only make exceptions or set precedent when the conditions for doing so could be easily and comfortable extended to others.

Chairs and deans must apply policy and decision-making criteria evenly across individual requests or they quickly lose their credibility. Over time, consistency can help faculty and staff assess the merit of a specific request before making it. At a minimum, chairs and deans should understand and be able to explain the basis for granting or denying a request and the factors that make one request different or similar to another so that decision-making evidences an equitable and consistent application of policy. Consider again the need to allocate limited resources for faculty travel. It is likely that even the faculty member receiving the largest allocation will believe that he or she should have received more. The task of allocating travel funds produces a no-win situation for chairs and deans unless steps are taken to depersonalize the allocation process in ways that make clear that all faculty are being treated equitably and that you are consistent in allocating travel funds. If you can make the basis for allocating travel funds clear and there is no appearance of favoritism in applying the criteria to each request, you will be perceived as consistent and fair, which in turn will enhance your credibility with the faculty.

There is tremendous advantage in being predictable. When faculty and staff can predict what decision a chair or dean will make, it permits them to know what initiatives and requests are worth their time and reduces the number of requests that do not fit expectations. For example, if the process of assigning class times is clear, faculty will be able to predict when a class they are to teach will likely be scheduled for 8:00 a.m. By making the logic for decision-making public, you become predictable. While a faculty member may not like teaching at 8:00 a.m., he or she will more likely understand that the decision was not personal but necessary, given the departmental or institutional goals and objectives. However, if you make decisions out of context or if faculty and staff do not know the context for your decisions, you will appear more arbitrary and inevitably less consistent in applying the same rules and logic to every instance. It is important to remember that faculty and staff will evaluate the fairness of your decisions and assess your credibility as chair or dean based on whether you appear to be consistent in your decision-making.

◆ Subject decisions to a litmus test.

Chairs and deans can prepare faculty and staff in advance of decisions. For example, it is an appropriate strategy to assess the decision through the lens of departmental goals. When a decision is consistent with known goals and fits within the context of the institutional mission, it can be easier to predict how the decision will be received.

Thus, chairs and deans can test the validity of each decision by anticipating the reaction and revising their response to specific challenges. When chairs and deans have a reasoned reply to what might be said by the toughest critic, they have a decision that passes the litmus test. This will be easier to do than one might think. Typically, chairs and deans can not only predict what individual faculty and staff might say, but they can also actually hear them uttering the words under their breath. Earlier in this chapter you were asked to predict how each faculty member in your area of responsibility would react to a surprising announcement. If you tackled that exercise seriously, you will need little more to convince you of your ability to predict what others might say. If you use this information to inform how you present information and communicate decisions, you have an effective litmus test from which to assess the merit of your decision.

Another aspect of the litmus test is the chair or dean comfort with the decision. If you would be comfortable explaining your decision to any person or group, your decision passes the litmus test. For example, how easy would it be for you to explain granting a new hire the right to be absent his first semester on the job to other faculty or to the central administration or to the human resources director? If you find yourself about to make a decision that you hope you never need to explain, it might be a good idea to reconsider the decision.

SOME FINAL THOUGHTS

There is no way to please everyone, but the best hope for getting those who might be displeased to recognize a decision as fair is to inform faculty and staff of the larger context that governs decision-making. Understanding the larger context, possessing relevant information, and knowing relevant policy and precedents can defuse the anger and frustration that results when a request is denied because with these elements there is a rationale for the decision that moves beyond a personal assessment of the individual seeking support.

Decisions always have a context. When chairs and deans view individual requests in isolation, they permit the decision to remain more personal and fail to let the context inform the decision. Decisions that are perceived to be personal are more likely to produce stressful conflict. By placing individual requests in proper context and permitting the relevant policy and precedent to inform the decision, chairs and deans help to depersonalize the decision and establish themselves as administrative leaders who treat individuals equitably. Following the practical tips presented in this chapter can help reduce stressful conflict and enhance chair or dean credibility.

Establishing Your Leadership Credibility

Credibility is essential to effective leadership. Simply possessing an administrative title will not net respect or followers. Chairs and deans quickly lose credibility when they take action that appears to favor particular individuals or when their actions over time appear inconsistent. No matter how tedious, fair and consistent application of policy across situations is important. This chapter equips chairs and deans with leadership communication strategies that will enable them to proactively establish and maintain leadership credibility.

Position titles only beget compliance when a dictatorship or autocratic rule exists. A concept like academic freedom, unique to institutions of higher education, suggests that an individual's voice and perspective are to be heard and protected. Thus, democracy is valued on a campus. Faculty members do not always think alike, and independent thought is tolerated if not encouraged. This means that chairs and deans must have credible voices if faculty and staff are to support their leadership.

Credibility is a construct that has received much attention in the literature. In our discipline of communication, source or speaker credibility has been the subject of more than three decades of research. This research suggests that there are three primary components of credibility: 1) the perception of one's knowledge or ability to do the job; 2) the perception of one's character and intentions or whether one means well; and 3) the perception of one's trustworthiness or honesty and reliability. To build credibility, it is important to understand that credibility is an assigned attribute. In other words, a person who is extremely knowledgeable, has the very best intentions, and is completely trustworthy will only have credibility if others perceive that the person possesses these attributes.

Another sobering fact about credibility is that it is easier to lose than to build and maintain. If this is difficult to internalize, reflect on how we typically respond when we witness a long-time acquaintance behaving uncharacteristically in a selfish or temperamental manner. We may think to ourselves, "I didn't know he has such a temper," or "I never would have guessed that she could be so selfish and demanding." These thoughts suggest that we are quick to assess the atypical or uncharacteristic behavior as part of the person's true personality. We interpret the atypical behavior as a clue to the "real" person and tend not to dismiss it a fluke. Hence, any misstep can cost a chair or dean credibility with faculty and staff.

Credibility is essential to effective leadership. People will not heed or follow leaders who lack credibility. Hence, chairs and deans cannot be effective unless they are perceived by faculty and staff as credible. This isn't easy because faculty and staff do not have common expectations for chair and dean leadership. Therefore, actions that enhance credibility with some individuals might also tarnish one's credibility with others. Similarly, faculty and staff tend to assess chair and dean leadership from a very personal perspective. They assess the effectiveness of the leadership by reflecting on what the particular chair and dean has successfully obtained for them personally, for their department, and for their favorite initiatives or programs. Seldom do individual faculty and staff assess chair and dean effectiveness from a broader, institutional context. Faculty and staff are not able to do so because typically they lack understanding of the institutional context.

Chairs and deans serve many constituencies simultaneously. At a minimum, they need to be effective in working with faculty, staff, students, alumni, parents, and the central administration. In addition, most chairs and deans need to work effectively with external publics including prospective students, area businesses, granting agencies, accrediting boards, and prospective employers. This means that the task of establishing credibility must be accomplished with each constituency. This can be challenging because each constituency can possess different performance expectations for the chair or dean. Consequently, actions that enhance chair and dean credibility with students might diminish credibility with the faculty. These multiple perspectives could have some believing that chairs and deans need to be chameleons that can change with and for each group. However, there is a risk in being one way with one constituency and another way with a second constituency as it can cause a chair or dean to appear fickle or disingenuous. Consistency is essential to building credibility.

Again, we must stress that it is the perception of consistency that is important in building credibility with others. It is possible that chairs and deans may be consistent in their actions, but unless their actions are perceived as such, they will not be perceived as highly credible. The potential for varied perceptions is great because faculty members tend to operate from their personal perspective. In the same way that there can be six different eyewitness accounts of the same automobile accident, there can be multiple perceptions of each chair or dean decision and action. Yet for chairs and deans to remain credible, others who view decision and actions from their own perspective must perceive them as credible.

The likelihood that chairs and deans will be perceived as inconsistent increases when policy is not applied uniformly to all faculty and staff. As discussed in the preceding chapters, chairs and deans may set themselves up as being inconsistent when they respond to individual requests in a vacuum and fail to consider the implications for the larger context or the ramifications of setting a new precedent by making an exception to policy. Inconsistency fuels perceptions of favoritism, and those who are perceived as treating faculty and staff differentially will not be highly credible with those they lead. This is significant because one's credibility often determines one's ability to lead change or motivate others to take action that improves quality.

The objective is to keep the values and message the same across constituencies, even though the phrasing of the message will inevitably vary for the particular audience. It is even likely that a chair and dean will discuss different issues with each constituency, but the discussion of one issue with the first constituency should not contradict, or appear to contradict, the discussion of a different issue with another constituency. The best way to ensure this level of consistency is to be very clear about one's own values and goals. Chairs or deans who understand that the leadership positions they hold are designed to serve others will likely have an easier time articulating their leadership goals because they will have thought about what they might contribute to the institution, department, or program while holding the position. If the leadership objective is clear in the mind of the chair or dean, it is eminently easier to be consistent than if the primary objective is to simply possess the title of chair or dean. However, when the top priority is keeping the job and title, chairs and deans may be motivated to the keep peace or smooth ruffled feathers. These goals will inevitably lead chairs and deans to take action that eventually gives the appearance of being inconsistent.

The Challenge of Introducing Post-Tenure Review

Consider the example of the department chair who recognizes the need for a system of post-tenure review but also knows that any plan to implement this change will be resisted by the faculty. The chair's conclusion about the need for review is motivated by campus-wide activity to prepare for regional institutional accreditation. Meetings held to review changes in the accreditation criteria make clear the need to evidence that tenured as well as untenured faculty are effective in carrying out their assigned responsibilities of teaching, scholarship, and service. The campus boasts an assessment program that measures student learning, but it does not require tenured faculty to regularly solicit student evaluations of teaching or to use the campus-approved teaching evaluation form that is used by untenured faculty to gather student comments on teaching. Tenured faculty members are not required to obtain peer or other reviews of their work in teaching, scholarship, or service. The chair believes having a program of post-tenure review would be to the department's advantage because the documentation would enhance everything from grant applications to the program's preparation for institutional accreditation. The chair also recognizes that tenured faculty will perceive any system of post-tenure review as intrusive, unnecessary, and time-consuming work.

If you were the chair in this situation, how would you introduce and gain favor for a new initiative that will likely be resisted by the faculty? The situation calls for both strategic and credible chair leadership. Leadership can be strategic without being credible in that a chair or dean may be leading the faculty in the best possible (or strategic) direction and still meet tremendous resistance. The willingness of individuals to consider change and the implementation of needed initiatives (even ones recognized as important) requires a certain faith and confidence in the leadership. Hence, in deciding how you might introduce and gain favor for the new initiative, you would need to assess your level of credibility with those from whom you seek support.

As important, you need to think about how to introduce the idea so that you enhance rather than detract from your credibility. How would you introduce an idea that you know will be resisted? Would you, for example, claim the idea to consider post-tenure review as your own and explain why it is important? Or would you explain that post-tenure review is necessary to satisfy the new criteria for institutional accreditation and, therefore, the department has no choice but to implement such an initiative? Would you imply that the central administration expects all departments to have a program of post-tenure review? Would you lobby the central administration to mandate the change so you would be empowered to lead the faculty in designing a program of post-tenure review? Can you list the pros and cons of each alternative? For example, if you attribute the change to the central administration, would it make conveying the need for post-tenure review more comfortable? What is the advantage of having post-tenure review mandated by the central administration? Is there a disadvantage to having the central administration issue a mandate?

In weighing the pros and cons to determine the best alternative, it is important to think about long-term as well as short-term implications. Why does it matter to whom you attribute the change? Would attribution matter less if the change itself was popular with the faculty? It may be that in the short term, having an unpopular mandate attributed to someone else makes the message easier to deliver to resistant faculty. Over the long term, what impact might this alternative have on your leadership credibility with the faculty? It is possible, for example, that faculty might perceive you as an agent of the central administration or as a chair who cannot convey their perspective to the administration. Before taking the approach that seems more immediately comfortable, you need to anticipate the long-term ramifications of the action.

Chairs and deans may find it more comfortable to attribute an unpopular idea to someone else. This spare-the-messenger approach to leading change, however, can have an adverse effect on your credibility with faculty and staff. In the situation described earlier, what would you communicate to the faculty if you introduce the need for post-tenure review by saying that the central administration was demanding the change? It is possible that faculty would see you as ineffective in protecting the department from unwarranted change and senseless additional work. When and how might your credibility be enhanced by attributing the change to some external force? Similarly, what would you communicate to the central administration if you lobbied them to issue a mandate to all departments? The central administration might doubt your commitment to the institution or your ability to lead the faculty. It is possible that by taking the action that provides the most immediate comfort, you create a situation that is counterproductive to building and maintaining your own credibility.

Sometimes when chairs and deans seek to escape an anticipated negative reaction from faculty and staff to a new initiative, they unintentionally lower their credibility with the very individuals they strive to lead. Although this strategy may increase your initial comfort when leading change, it more often damages chair or dean credibility. Ducking attribution does not free the chair or dean from being responsible for implementing the new initiative, and that implementation will require faculty and staff be informed and acquire a basic understanding of the circumstances that warrant the change. When the change starts to make sense to faculty and staff and implementation becomes more manageable, they will have no reason to credit the chair or dean with ineffective leadership. Hence, taking the more comfortable action might not be the best leadership communication strategy.

MANAGING INTRADEPARTMENTAL CONFLICT

Tensions must be managed when conflict exists among faculty within a department. When faculty members are unable to manage conflict with colleagues, typically they expect the chair or dean to intervene in a way that resolves the conflict. While it is reasonable to expect the chair or dean to manage a conflict, this is not an easy undertaking because each party typically believes the only fair solution to an existing conflict is to have the chair or dean impose an outcome that is consistent with their individual perspective of the disagreement.

What would you do as department chair to manage an escalating conflict between one faculty member, Dr. Allston, and the rest of the department? Dr. Allston seems to be persistently at odds with everyone else in the department, so would you focus your efforts on getting her as the odd person out to fit in better with the others? Let's assume that the disagreements are about everything from who deserves to be department chair to when department meetings are called and how they are conducted to who teaches which courses. The conflict has been festering for a few years, and you notice that a majority of the faculty have adopted a-path-of-least-resistance approach in that they agree to or vote in favor of Dr. Allston, even though she is in conflict with the others, but do so in order to keep the peace or perform the human equivalent of throwing a bone to an angry dog. Nothing seems to work in that, no matter what concessions are made, Dr. Allston perceives herself a victim of mistreatment. Recently, when the department voted to support her request to teach a course outside the specialization for which she was hired, Dr. Allston complained to any who would listen about how long the department took to grant permission and how they really didn't want her to teach it, but the dean made them accept her proposal.

How would you as chair manage this conflict? Would you talk to Dr. Allston, who professes to be the lone victim, and if so, what would you say? Would you encourage the other faculty members to behave differently toward a consistently upset Dr. Allston? If so, how? Are there others whom you would consult, and if so, whom would you consult and why? You might, for example consult the dean, the human resources director, and/or the campus ombudsman. Consider the role that each might play in helping to manage the existing tension. For example, the ombudsman typically serves as a neutral observer in conflict situations with the purpose of improving communication between and among individuals. Would the presence of a neutral observer be helpful in managing this conflict?

It can be helpful to enlist the assistance of others on campus to manage a conflict, but only if the conflict itself can be helped by the responsibility entrusted to the outside person. It would not make sense, for example, to use the ombudsman if those engaged in the conflict cannot be helped by the presence of a neutral observer.

Suppose Dr. Allston is known to have terrific connections with faculty and administrative leaders outside the department because she serves on the faculty senate, teaches in the honors program, and participates in numerous cocurricular institutional programs. Would this information alter your approach? Suppose you also know that no one else in the department is as well known across campus as Dr. Allston. Would this alter your approach? If so, can you say why and how you would handle the conflict? To answer these questions, you need to consider who might be helpful to you in managing the conflict. For example, if someone outside the department is a credible source for all within the department then that person may be helpful in mediating the tension.

Suppose Dr. Allston looks to you as the department chair to stop what she labels instances of injustice. The other faculty members in the department look to you to put an end to what they might label as bullying behavior that is motivated by self-interest. How might you manage the conflict without losing credibility? Is it possible to manage a disagreement without having one side view you as unfair or biased? Because leadership credibility is based in large part on the perception of one's honesty and equitable treatment of others, then the goal is to have both sides recognize your approach and any outcome or resolution as fair.

It is easy to look the other way and hope that individuals will iron out their differences. Some chairs and deans may even rationalize that it is not their place to intervene in a personal conflict. If the dispute is about the placement of a fence between the yards of two colleagues who also happen to live on adjacent properties, then it would be proper to conclude that the conflict is not the responsibility of the chair or dean to manage. However, when a conflict affects the work for which the chair and dean have leadership responsibility, ignoring the conflict would be irresponsible leadership. Furthermore, because it has festered and escalated through several years, it is unlikely that the conflict will ease without constructive intervention. In fact, the longer the conflict persists, the more difficult it will be for either party to view any outcome other than their own desire as fair.

Suppose the newest volley in the escalating conflict of the upset Dr. Allston against the rest of the department involves who will succeed the current chair who is planning to retire at the close of the academic year. Now assume the position of dean and consider how you would manage the tension that exists within the department. Dr. Allston believes she should be chair. Indeed, she has told everyone she knows across campus that the position is "rightfully" hers. She reasons that she is next in line because of her tenure and seniority in the department and cites as evidence one meeting five years earlier in which all agreed that the work as chair should be rotated among the department members. She further believes that based on the five-year-old discussion, the chair title should be handed to her without department election. Her expectation is that you, as dean, will make this happen.

Others in the department remember the conversation of five years ago differently. They recall reaching consensus that no one member of the department should be saddled with the reasonability of serving as department chair indefinitely, and the conclusion was that all should be willing to take on the chair role from time to time. They deny that the conclusion was to rotate the chair without holding an election. The others in the department live in fear that Dr. Allston might become department chair. They expect you, as dean, to protect them from a colleague who they perceive as unreasonably demanding and motivated by self-interest. What would you do? Where would you start? Is it possible to manage this conflict without losing credibility with either party? Dr. Allston informed you of the need to name her department chair two weeks ago. Because you have not yet acted on her counsel, she is now telling anyone who will listen that you have your head in the sand.

If as dean you render a decision, it is likely that at least one party will view the decision as unfair. If you decide to name Dr. Allston chair, the others in the department will likely view the action as preferential treatment for a difficult colleague. If, however, you choose not to name Dr. Allston, she will likely conclude that you do not understand how unfair her department colleagues have been and/or conclude that you too are treating her unfairly. To persuade all parties that your decision is fair, it will be necessary to reveal the logic imposed in making the decision. You might, for example, reference policy on chair selection and review with all concerned how you interpret the evidence that helped you reach a particular conclusion. Faculty and staff will not perceive chairs and deans as fair in making decisions unless they believe that all perspectives were heard and considered, that relevant policy was applied equitably, and that the decision was the only one that could be reached given the circumstance and governing policy.

ANALYSIS AND APPLICATIONS

Credibility and trust are earned from interactions with others. Unfortunately, it is easier to loose both than to earn them. This means that listening to and understanding others, providing critical feedback, and consistent, honest communication create a foundation that over time can lead to trust. Chairs and deans need to make an effort to create a strong foundation and solid framework for operation. They can improve their credibility by not only clarifying their roles and responsibilities but also by demonstrating predictable and consistent decisions tied to the mission. Let's review the essential elements of each application:

- Work from facts and reason.

- Gather relevant perspectives.

- Be honest.

- Live in the sunshine.

◆ Work from facts and reason.

This leadership communication strategy will help make the task of managing conflict more comfortable. When a chair or dean articulates the rationale used to reach a decision, he or she also demonstrates his or her grasp of the issue. It is important that you reason out loud so others recognize that important decisions are based on logic and not personal whim. By starting with institutional policy and by reviewing relevant facts, it is possible to demonstrate that the decision is reasoned, even when it is not popular.

A review of the facts can help all parties obtain perspective on a conflict that may have become personal. Take, for example, a situation in which a faculty member is upset because she believes she has not been treated fairly by her colleagues. A review of the facts that evidence specific instances of favorable action taken by department colleagues might help temper the faculty member's perspective, especially when the actions reviewed challenge the belief that colleagues are out to get her or intend to do her harm. By reviewing the facts that lead to the dreaded or unwanted conclusion, chairs and deans can change the discussion from *should* we change or do something differently to *how* should we change to manage the factual information presented.

Similarly, the department chair seeking to implement a program of post-tenure review might begin by reviewing changes in the accreditation criteria. By first presenting faculty and staff with the facts rather than your conclusion, it is possible to empower them to take ownership for solving the same issue or problem. Nothing other than time is lost to this process, and the results can be very constructive. It is possible, for example, that the faculty and staff will offer other solutions to the set of problematic facts presented. They may even reach the same conclusion you did, which effectively eliminates the anticipated struggle to persuade them of the need to take a certain action.

If the chair, for example, describes the new accreditation criteria and asks for ideas on how to demonstrate that all faculty (tenured and untenured, full-time and part-time) are teaching effectively, faculty will likely begin by reviewing the measures in place to evidence teaching effectiveness. This discussion in turn will likely reveal that the department has data in the form of student and peer evaluations on all faculty members except tenured professors. At this moment, the chair can ask for suggestions on how to document the quality work being done by tenured professors and the issue has changed from *will* we engage in post-tenure review to *how* will we engage in post-tenure review.

◆ **Gather relevant perspectives.**

In their role, chairs and deans need to determine if there is a perception that they are moving too fast. One way to ensure that the decisions are not perceived as being made on the fly is to gather all relevant perspectives.

When a chair or dean is willing to discuss the pros and cons of a particular issue with others who might criticize the decision, he or she demonstrates a desire to hear diverse views and to inform decision-making. Even when individuals are not pleased with the outcome, it is important that they know their voice was heard. Consider the example of Dr. Allston, the upset faculty member who believes she is entitled to be the department chair. While others may see her position as unreasonable and motivated by self-interest, she is convinced that the only fair outcome would be for the dean to name her as chair. By hearing her recount why she believes the only right and fair thing to do is to name her the department chair, you give her the satisfaction of being heard and obtain an opportunity to ask questions or seek clarification that might help her reassess her position.

Assume, for example, that Dr. Allston relates to you that the primary reason she deserves to be chair is that it is "her turn." You might ask how she knows it is her turn and together review the campus policy for chair selection, which requires a vote of the department faculty. Listening to Dr. Allston's perspective offers insight into what factual information is missing from her reasoning. If you fail to first hear her perspective, anything you say will more likely be perceived as taking the side of those she already believes to be unfair.

◆ **Be honest.**

One aspect of honesty is to ensure that everyone has the same information. This will help faculty and staff view the information as credible and can facilitate an environment of honest, open communication.

Honesty is essential to building and maintaining one's credibility. More important than having all the answers is being honest about what you know and what you don't know. Leaders lose credibility when others believe they cannot be trusted. Trust, like credibility, is a perceived attribute, so it is important to consider what behaviors evidence trustworthiness. To demonstrate trustworthiness, it is imperative that your behavior makes clear that you treat all equitably and that policy is applied consistently to all faculty and staff. The quickest way to plant the seed of distrust is to evidence favoritism or deal-making. In the example of the upset faculty member, the dean can lose credibility with other faculty if the action taken suggests that the upset faculty member is being treated preferentially.

Being honest about the facts, even when they are tough to hear, can enhance credibility. Consider the example of the chair faced with the need to present and lead a change that will likely be met with resistance. If as chair you start by reviewing the facts that warrant a change, it is possible to demonstrate your grasp of the issues facing higher education, your understanding of the new accreditation criteria, and your vision for how to strengthen the program in the face of new challenges. These are attributes that can enhance your leadership credibility even though the change may be met with resistance. Furthermore, as noted earlier, by informing faculty and staff of the facts that make change desirable, one can lower resistance to new ideas and initiatives.

◆ Live in the sunshine.

The communication practices you use can enhance or inhibit your credibility. There is a saying that sunshine kills fungus. If you consider the fungus to be misperceptions and misunderstandings that fester and grow rapidly into cancers that threaten the health of the institution, you will quickly grasp the advantage of living in the sunshine to kill fungus. Living in the sunshine means keeping everyone informed about the larger context and the facts that guide individual actions and decisions. Fungus grows when faculty and staff who lack an understanding of the larger context are permitted to attribute motives for actions and decisions that may or may not be true. The rumor mill is alive and well at most institutions and unless individuals can check the validity of rumors against information presented openly and honestly, fungus will thrive.

Consider the instance of the upset faculty member who is quick to assert that the dean is on her side when doing battle with department colleagues. Unless the faculty can trust that the upset faculty member is not being treated preferentially by the dean, this name-dropping tactic might prompt other faculty to surrender or go along with an action that is against their better judgment. Further, if the other faculty members believe that the dean is truly on the side of the upset faculty member, the name dropping will likely have a negative impact on the dean's credibility with the other faculty.

Unfortunately, it is frequently impossible for chairs and deans to know when individuals are taking liberties that decrease their credibility with other faculty and staff. The best defense is a good offense in that chairs and deans should make a practice of living in the sunshine so that faculty and staff learn to count on their openness and honesty. With this leadership communication strategy as the ongoing practice, it becomes easier for faculty to challenge individuals who may be misstating the chair's or dean's position. This is especially important for chairs and deans who accept positions at new institutions because the process of building one's credibility with others starts anew.

SOME FINAL THOUGHTS

Leadership credibility is absolutely essential to chair and dean success. Without credibility, it is impossible to lead change or be a respected voice in managing daily work or guiding future direction. Much of the work to be done by chairs and deans involves motivating others to take strategic action. This will not happen unless those needed to do the work have trust and confidence in the leadership, which is the true essence of credibility. Summarily, chairs and deans will not be entrusted with leadership by the central administration unless they are perceived as credible.

Credibility is an attribute that most individuals want to possess. It is doubtful that any of us know even a single person who aspires to lack credibility with others. However, wanting leadership credibility and possessing leadership credibility are two different things because credibility is an assigned attribute. In other words, we only possess credibility if others perceive us as being credible. Becoming credible then means understanding that how others interpret and assess our decisions and actions will influence their assessment of our credibility. More specifically, if others who observe you making decisions and taking action perceive you as knowledgeable, honest, and trustworthy, they are more likely to find you credible. Because credibility is an attribute assigned by others, an individual's credibility is inevitably linked to how we interact with others.

The quest for credibility is never-ending, and sadly it is easier to lose credibility that it is to acquire it. Chairs and deans who are perceived as highly credible will discover that making one significant decision or taking one significant action that appears to others to be uninformed, dishonest, or motivated by self-interest can hurt one's credibility. Chairs and deans must always be about the business of preserving and enhancing their leadership credibility because possessing leadership credibility is essential to being and effective and successful chair and dean.

Building Relationships

Building relationships that support and empower effective leadership requires more than social rapport or the usual collegiality. Chairs and deans need to build professional relationships that are based on mutual respect and trust for honest communication, even when the news may not be well received or when individuals must work through disagreements. This chapter provides chairs and deans with leadership communication strategies for building professional relationships that will serve as a foundation for collaboration with faculty and staff on the complex challenges facing higher education.

Too often social relationships are viewed as similar to professional relationships. While a chair or dean may enjoy strong social relationships with individuals with whom they also have a professional relationship, the two types of relationships are very different. Further, the existence of one does not ensure the presence of the other. In fact, the existence of a strong social relationship can work against the formation of the type of constructive professional relationship that enhances chair and dean leadership. It can be, for example, more difficult to counsel needed improvements in the work performance of a faculty member who is also a close personal friend. Sometimes a strong social relationship can license a chair or dean to be more direct with an individual, but at other times a strong social relationship can inhibit the chair or dean from being direct. Consequently, it would be a mistake to assume that social and professional relationships are necessarily the same or that the presence of one type of relationship enhances the other. Further, it would be a mistake to assume that professional relationships must be built on social relationships.

Social relationships typically develop around some common interest, experience, or passion. The common ground that binds individuals in a social relationship is personal and need not have any bearing on or connection to one's profession or work. In contrast, professional relationships are prescribed by the position one holds at work. The organizational chart at the institution dictates formal work relationships by noting reporting lines and prescribing the way in which work is to flow on the campus. Professional relationships are comprised of those individuals with whom one must work to achieve assigned job responsibilities. Hence, professional relationships can vary from one institution to another. Take, for example, a career services office, which on some campuses may report to the vice president for student affairs and at others to the vice president for academic affairs. The particular placement of career services in the organizational chart will shape the professional relationships held by staff in career services. On campuses where a career services office is housed in an academic area, more formal professional relationships with faculty might be facilitated.

Each staff member, faculty member, chair, and dean has specific job responsibilities. It is essential to the institution that each person recognizes the responsibility that comes with the role. When prescribed working relationships are ineffective or dysfunctional, work outcomes are jeopardized. Civil and collegial communication is important to building constructive professional relationships, but it is not necessary for chairs and deans to form more personal social relationships with faculty and staff. Some may confuse friendship with civility and collegiality, but it is possible to not only work together but to work together well without being good friends or having personal and social relationships with colleagues. While friendship may or may not coincide with a prescribed working relationship, friendship is not essential to building or sustaining an effective working relationship.

An effective working relationship is characterized by a mutual understanding of each other's role and job responsibilities, a mutual respect for the job done by each, honest and clear communication, and a shared understanding of the institutional mission. Chairs and deans can empower effective working relationships by promoting common understanding of the mission, the interdependence of assigned roles, and how individual responsibilities support the work of others. When the institutional agenda serves as the guideline for decisions, chairs and deans empower working relationships in a way that will enhance department or program productivity. Even when these constructive connections are intuitive, the pressure of deadlines and volume of work can prompt well-intentioned chairs and deans to take shortcuts in building a context that would empower effective professional relationships. A chair or dean, for example, may focus on what task needs to be completed by a prescribed deadline without informing those working on the task about the larger context or how the immediate task advances the institutional mission. Such shortcuts can devalue the work to be done because the task remains unrelated to the institutional mission or a larger context and denies individuals the opportunity to understand and appreciate how their individual assignment supports the larger purpose. Ironically, without an understanding of how individual efforts support and help to advance the institutional mission, any shortcut seldom saves time or enhances the work outcome or effective working relationships.

Chairs and deans can promote a mutual understanding among faculty and staff regarding individual roles and responsibilities and a respect for the job done by each member of a department or academic team. Teamwork is essential to institutional success because no one person can unilaterally ensure the success of a program or department. Yet even hardworking and well-intentioned faculty and staff can fail to comprehend the interdependent nature of roles and responsibilities on campus. Chairs and deans can help to promote effective working relationships by helping individuals connect—in a meaningful way—with work being done by others in support of the institutional mission. When individuals are permitted to work in isolation of colleagues or engage in silo thinking, there can be little understanding of how one individual's success is, in part, dependent on work done by others at the institution. When faculty and staff understand how their individual work efforts contribute to the team effort, it can help to promote pride in one's individual work and motivate each to complete work in a timely way and do it well.

Just as important as developing a mutual understanding of different roles, chairs and deans must also establish the expectation for honest and clear communication among faculty and staff. Working relationships will not be effective if ill will and distrust exist between and among faculty and staff and if communication regarding work and the interdependence of the various roles and job responsibilities is confused or ambiguous. It is not enough simply to clarify role responsibilities. Chairs and deans must establish and sustain a clear expectation of honest and clear communication between and among faculty and staff. Communication clarity is a skill that requires experience and a desire to improve one's proficiency. Chairs and deans can help to reinforce the expectation for communication clarity and underscore each individual's responsibility to strive for communication clarity by encouraging all faculty and staff to engage in active listening and to assume ownership for initiating messages that keep others informed.

This is not as easy as one might presume because it requires faculty and staff to be other-centered in their communication around work. For example, faculty and staff need to think about what information would be helpful to others and then construct messages and frame information in a way that is meaningful to others. Similarly, faculty and staff must listen actively, which means hearing another person's words as they are intended, and that can be different from the literal meaning of a message and even more different from the meaning conveyed if one listens from a personal, biased perspective. Chairs and deans can promote clear communication by explaining what it is, why it's necessary, and modeling it in their own behavior.

Honest communication is fundamental to communicating clearly, and it evidences one's professional intent to work with integrity for the good of the institution. It is possible for a statement to be literally true and dishonest at the same time. Consider the following statements made by a faculty member in reviewing a colleague's classroom teaching:

> Statement A: Professor Kane exhibits tremendous authority and command of the subject matter.

> Statement B: While Professor Kane knows his subject well, he might be encouraged to use a variety of instructional approaches to improve students' understanding of the subject.

The first statement may be both literally correct yet dishonest if it notes a level of effective teaching that does not exist. The second statement acknowledges that Professor Kane knows the subject, but more honestly discusses this attribute in relation to student learning. Communication is honest when accurate and contextual meaning is conveyed, which requires more than literal precision in using words. Chairs and deans can encourage honest communication by modeling how it is possible to be honest without appearing mean and by demonstrating how honest communication is more constructive to working well with others.

A Reaccreditation Dilemma

At a university preparing for reaccreditation, the chair and dean realize that one program offered within the College of Education does not meet national accreditation standards. The process of preparing for the accreditation site visit permitted the chair and dean to engage in conversations with state and national leaders in education about the one program that cannot demonstrate it meets accreditation criteria. State leadership suggests that the institution suspend admissions to the deficient program so it is not part of the upcoming accreditation review. The chair and dean recognize that this action will be offensive to the faculty who teach in the program but also recognize that it would be suicidal for the College of Education to proclaim the program as being in compliance with accreditation criteria. In fact, to stubbornly persist in championing a program that is obviously out of compliance with the accreditation criteria would likely jeopardize the Board of Examiners' review of the other programs offered through the College of Education. The chair and dean are convinced that the best course of action is to heed the advice offered by state and national experts and suspend admission to the program that can only be found to be out of compliance with the new accreditation criteria. The chair and dean reason that doing so could enhance their credibility in a way that would help secure a positive review outcome for the other programs offered through the College of Education.

Assume the perspective of the chair and think how you would present this issue to the faculty. Would you, for example, talk first or exclusively with the faculty who teach in the deficient program? How would you frame the issue? Would you present it as an issue to decide or would you present it as something the dean has already decided? Would you present it as something you and the dean agree on and seek faculty support for the action or would you present it as a view held by you and the dean and seek faculty views on what to do? Would you send out any information in advance of a meeting or present all the information during a meeting with the faculty? Clearly, this situation can create considerable discomfort for the chair.

How you frame the issue is important. If you frame it in a way that suggests the faculty members are part of the decision, then you must accept their input in reaching a final decision. What would be the reaction of faculty, for example, if you frame the issue as still undecided when in fact the dean believes that you have agreed to suspend admission to the deficient program effective immediately? It may be more comfortable to involve the faculty in making a decision, but there is a risk in taking this approach. What would you do, for example, if the faculty vehemently opposed suspending admission to the deficient program or if the faculty wanted to take a month or more to study the matter? How would you reconcile the difference between what the dean believes is already decided and the faculty position and belief that the decision is not yet made? This dilemma could hurt your credibility with the dean and/or with the faculty if not carefully managed.

The chair's existing relationship with the dean and the faculty will influence the alternatives available to the chair and the chair's comfort with each alternative. For example, if the chair has a good working relationship with the dean, the chair may be more comfortable asking the dean to hold a decision until the faculty have an opportunity to hear all the relevant information and be party to making the decision. Similarly, if the chair has a good working relationship with the faculty, the chair may be more comfortable updating the faculty on the events that led to an unavoidable decision to suspend admission to a program that was obviously out of compliance with the new accreditation criteria. Effective working relationships permit chairs and deans more comfort in managing difficult situations for which they are accountable to faculty, staff, students, or other constituencies.

Effective working relationships are one of the essential foundation blocks for leadership in that chair and dean leadership is enhanced when the chair or dean enjoys effective working relationships with others. At the same time, it is difficult to build effective working relationships when one's credibility is low. The good news, however, is that the same leadership communication strategies that cultivate good working relationships also enhance chair and dean credibility. In the example given, the program chair's comfort and freedom to be honest and direct with the faculty about the need to suspend admission to the deficient program would be greater if the chair was confident of his or her credibility with the faculty.

THE DILEMMA OF THE FRIENDLY DEAN

Consider the dean who is extremely gregarious and charming with everyone on campus. The dean is adored and perceived as someone who is 150% supportive of every individual program or initiative. The dean has the rare ability to recall specific details about every faculty member's individual effort at the institution, so casual meetings become opportunities to inquire about a project or activity. Consequently, each and every faculty member perceives that he or she has the full support of the dean. From the dean's perspective, his conversations with faculty members about their projects and interests are one important personal way that he can demonstrate his interest and appreciation for the individual work being done by all the faculty members.

The dynamic between the dean and faculty poses a problem for department chairs responsible for prioritizing initiatives and allocating department resources. The same dean who is personally interested in individual faculty projects and activities holds the chairs accountable for investing finite resources in programs that best serve the institutional mission and/or help grow student enrollment. Fiscal constraints make it impossible for department chairs to provide all the funding support requested by individual faculty, and prioritizing requests has produced some significant animosity between the chair and several of the faculty members in each department.

The growing tension between the chair and the faculty is inevitable and has no easy remedy because the chair and the faculty hold very different perceptions of the situation. The chair's view is that a prioritization of activities for resource allocation is not only expected by the dean, it is also the only logical course of action since the budget will not support all projects. The faculty not receiving the level of support requested believe the chair is out of the loop in terms of what is important and worthy of funding because they believe the dean values their particular program activity and would want them to receive the funding requested.

Assuming that budget remains finite, the situation will likely deteriorate for the department chair without some constructive intervention, and a solution can only be effective if the analysis of the situation is accurate. Can you analyze the dynamic in terms of what you know about professional and social relationships? For example, would you define the dean's relationship with individual faculty as professional or social or both? How might the dean perceive his relationship with individual faculty? You might consider if faculty members perceive their relationship with the dean the same way. Assume for the moment that the dean believes his interactions with individual faculty are primarily social and that he references their work on campus as a way of demonstrating his appreciation for their good work. Do you believe, however, that faculty members are confusing a social relationship for a professional one? How might the chair clarify the confusion?

Assume the faculty perceive their informal chats with the dean as evidence of the priority the dean places on their work relative to other work underway in the department and at the institution. Because these conversations tend to be one-on-one interactions, there is no way for individual faculty to relate or interpret comments made by the dean about their work in a larger context. Assume the role of department chair in this situation and think how you would manage the escalating conflict. Would you discuss the problem with the dean and ask him to alter his interactions with faculty? If so, how would you frame the issue? Would you work with the faculty to help them more accurately interpret their interactions with the dean? If so, how would you frame the issue? What other options do you have for managing the tension? If a series of one-on-one conversations contributes to the conflict, the chair needs some mechanism for building a context from which the faculty can more accurately and realistically assess the dean's comments.

Let's assume that as chair you gently broach the topic with the dean and find significant resistance to your suggestion that his conversations with individual faculty could possibly contribute to the escalating tension that you experience with some of the faculty. The dean insists that such conversation is integral to the campus culture and his personal leadership style, which is based on relationships. The dean suggests that if tension exists between you and some of the faculty, it may be because you have not built effective relationships with the faculty. You leave the conversation thinking it is time to move to Plan B, but what is Plan B? How realistic is the dean's suggestion that you ease the conflict by improving your relationship with the faculty? How might you do this and how might it help the existing tension? If it will not resolve the existing tension, what else might you do? Depending on the degree of tension you experience with the faculty and the intensity of the dean's resistance to your suggestion that he contributes to the escalating tension, you might conclude that the best possible Plan B is to update your curriculum vitae and seek other employment. However, for the purposes of gaining the most from this chapter, please persist in finding alternatives for managing the situation in your present position.

ANALYSIS AND APPLICATIONS

Professional relationships differ from social relationships. Just because you respect someone doesn't mean that you like them, and vice versa. A strong social life with colleagues doesn't ensure a successful working relationship. In fact, a strong social connection can often create challenges when making decisions and implementing change because the social relationship can create a perception of inside knowledge or preferential treatment. If decisions are to be credible, they must be made around identified key, shared values, not interpersonal connections, and the decision-making process should serve as a road map for creating trust, upholding individual responsibility, and serving the common good. Let's review the essential elements of each application:

- Be honest and open in sharing information.

- Be predictable.

- Recognize position responsibility.

- Make the institutional agenda your agenda.

- Treat all equitably, not equally.

◆ Be honest and open in sharing information.

By openly sharing the information used to inform decisions it is possible to help others understand the basis for a given decision. When faculty and staff understand the underlying logic, they are less likely to second guess the outcome, misattribute motive, or take the decision personally. When the information that informed a particular decision is not shared openly, even the most reasonable decision can appear arbitrary or motivated by self-interest. However, when the underlying rationale for a decision is not known or understood, individuals are forced to evaluate the merit of the outcome from personal perspectives, which means they are focused on how the decision affects them and not on whether it was a good decision for the institution. The more sensitive the issue, the more helpful it will be to build a context for understanding a specific decision or outcome that may fall short of an individually desired expectation.

Return to the situation in which the education chair must talk with the faculty about suspending admission to the program that is out of compliance with accreditation criteria. At a minimum, the chair should expect resistance from the faculty who identify with the program. So, if the decision to suspend admission is presented without sharing the information that informs that decision, the faculty will be more likely to view the action as a personal affront to their work at the institution. If, however, enough of the relevant information can be shared that faculty reach the same conclusion, resistance to suspending admission to the program will likely dissipate. The leadership communication strategy of sharing information helps to build an informed context that in turn shapes how others view a particular decision or action.

Next, consider the situation in which the dean's informal chats with individual faculty might be contributing to the escalating tension between the department chair and the faculty. If, in approaching the dean about the problem, the chair begins by sharing his conclusion that the dean's friendly chats are contributing to the tension, one might predict a defensive response from the dean. What would happen if instead the chair begins by describing the worsening dynamic with individual faculty members and offers some factual information that demonstrates the growing animosity derives from the perception that individual faculty work carries a high priority for the institution, which results in irritation when the chair doesn't confirm the high priority status in allocating resources? Is it more likely that the dean will realize the possible link between his informal chats with individual faculty and their increasing animosity with the chair who is held accountable for prioritizing individual activities when allocating resources? Inevitably, it is generally easier to have others understand the merit of a particular decision if they are permitted to reason from the same information used to reach the decision.

◆ Be predictable.

It is important to think and reason out loud. Ideally, decision-making should be so clearly linked to the mission that faculty and staff who understand the mission can predict what decision will be made even when it is not the outcome they prefer. Achieving a level of transparency in decision-making has several advantages. First, it encourages faculty and staff to possess an operational understanding of the institutional mission because this knowledge will enable them to predict decisions and outcomes. Second, it discourages faculty and staff from spending time developing requests they know will not likely be approved. Third, it helps to direct faculty and staff efforts in ways that support the mission. Fourth, it establishes clearly what activities will be supported and which cannot be supported, sparing the chair and dean the onerous task of denying individual requests.

Return to the example of the education chair who now must persuade faculty of the benefit to suspending admission in a program with which they identify. Would that task be easier if all faculty members had a clear understanding of the need to demonstrate that every program is in compliance with the accreditation criteria? How might the scenario change had the chair and dean promoted the importance of accreditation to the institution as a common goal in serving the institutional mission in advance of and as part of preparing for the accreditation review? How might the situation change had the chair and dean involved faculty in assessing the degree to which each program satisfies accreditation criteria? If faculty had been more involved in making the case that demonstrates how each program is in compliance with accreditation criteria, they would possess information that enables them to predict the outcome, which would likely lead them to a conclusion that they might otherwise resist.

Similarly, if the chair facing increased animosity from the faculty had established with the dean a constructive working relationship that permitted the dean to have full confidence that the chair was supportive of the dean's leadership and wanted the best for the institution, the existing working relationship would inform how the dean interprets the chair's concerns about the dean's informal chats with faculty. Working relationships serve as a foundation for interpreting a colleague's motives and predicting a colleague's actions. Ironically, one can help build and sustain an effective working relationship with colleagues by being transparent and predictable. Emphasizing this leadership communication strategy helps to build one's trust with others.

◆ Recognize position responsibility.

Each role carries a defined set of position responsibilities. Chairs and deans, for example, both have positions of leadership, but each has a distinct set of position responsibilities. Assigned role responsibilities help to shape the leader's perspective regarding the issues and decisions. To effectively build and sustain constructive working relationships, chairs and deans need to take into account the position and role responsibilities held by others.

A person's position at the institution can help to explain and predict decision-making. Chairs, for example, have assigned responsibility for departmental leadership. Therefore, deans and others should expect chairs to take positions that advantage or champion the needs of the department. Deans have assigned responsibilities that assume a more macro perspective, and therefore deans are expected to be impartial and not favor a particular department or program. While these role differences are predictable given assigned responsibilities, they create a disparity in chair and dean perspectives that inevitably creates some tension between chairs and deans. The chair facing increased animosity from department faculty is responsible for tasks that render the chair's working relationship with the faculty critical to his leadership success. The dean's leadership success, on the other hand, is less contingent on effective working relationships with the faculty and more closely linked to working relationships with department chairs. Understanding such role differences can enhance one's ability to predict perspectives and decision-making. If you were the chair in this situation, how would you frame a conversation with the dean about the escalating animosity from faculty? Consider the dean's position and assigned role responsibilities and determine how the escalating animosity threatens the dean's leadership success. This analysis will help inform how to frame the concern in a way that makes it salient for the dean. For example, the dean's leadership success depends on the chair's ability to lead the faculty, so the dean should understand the importance of sustaining effective working relationships between the chair and the faculty. Therefore, the chair might describe the escalating animosity from the faculty as jeopardizing the chair's ability to implement change directed by the dean.

◆ Make the institutional agenda your agenda.

When chairs and deans are clearly and unquestionably carrying out their assigned role responsibilities in a manner that best serves and advances the institutional mission, they can substantially reduce resistance to their leadership or criticism of their decision-making. However, when chairs and deans give the appearance of pursuing a personal agenda, they will find it difficult to sustain effective working relationships. Informed faculty and staff will more likely respect and trust chairs and deans who demonstrate their commitment to the health and welfare of the institution. When faculty and staff are confident that the chair and dean can be counted on to make decisions based on their commitment to the institutional mission, they will be less resistant to chair and dean leadership and more likely to accept and support decisions, even when the outcome is not what they hoped it might be.

Return to the situation in which the education chair seeks to persuade faculty that the best course of action is to suspend admission to a program that is out of compliance with accreditation criteria. If the faculty members have full confidence that the chair is committed to the institutional mission and to the program's welfare, they will be less resistant to the suggestion that admission to the program be suspended because they trust the chair's perspective and recommendation. How might a chair or a dean demonstrate his or her commitment to the institution? Is it enough to remind faculty and staff that you are committed to the institution? If not, what actions would be credible and how might you sustain this attribute of an effective working relationship? As chair or dean, how might you reinforce your commitment to the institution?

Now consider the situation in which the chair believes that he is disadvantaged by the dean's informal communication with individual faculty members. Would the dean's assessment of the chair's commitment to the institution influence how the dean interprets the chair's concern? If so, how might the chair use this to help manage the escalating conflict? How might the dean respond if, for example, the chair discusses his concern that he will no longer be an effective change agent with the faculty? Will this matter to the dean, and if so, why? Evidence of a selfless commitment to the institution can fuel and sustain an effective working relationship.

◆ Treat all equitably, not equally.

Treating all equitably is not the same as treating all equally. In fact, chairs and deans can sometimes create inequities by treating all equally. What would happen if, for example, the education chair took the position that no program should be singled out for different treatment and that the College of Education with all its programs would stand united through accreditation? Some might argue that this posture would be fair because all programs (and faculty teaching in each program) would be treated as equally important to the college, but would it be equitable? One could make a case that it would not be equitable because it treated all programs equally even though all programs were not equal in their compliance with accreditation criteria. In persuading faculty of the need to suspend admission to the one program that is out of compliance, the chair must make clear how treating all programs equally would not be equitable because the action might be costly to the programs that were in compliance with accreditation criteria. If you were the education chair, how would you frame this discussion? How important would your social relationship with faculty be in managing this situation?

SOME FINAL THOUGHTS

There is a significant difference between a social relationship and a working relationship. While it is possible to enjoy both types of relationships with a colleague, the working relationship is more essential to leadership success. Working relationships are built slowly over time, and even the most effective working relationships require continuous maintenance. Every decision and action that chairs and deans make will help to shape their working relationship with faculty and staff and each other. Among the behaviors that are most helpful to building effective working relationships are honest and open communication and demonstrating one's commitment to the institution. These attributes permit chairs and deans to be predictable, which connotes a trusting leadership.

The working relationship between the chair and dean is paramount, even though each possesses different role and leadership responsibilities. An effective working relationship between the chair and dean must take into account the role differences. If either the chair or dean expects the other to think in a similar way, much will be lost. While there is an inevitable tension because the chair and dean hold different role responsibilities, their different perspectives are both essential to effective and successful campus leadership. The leadership communication strategy of sharing relevant information will help to transcend tension that is attributable to role differences.

YOUR FOUNDATION FOR EFFECTIVE LEADERSHIP COMMUNICATION

The leadership communication strategies presented in this section of the text can help you build a foundation of basic skills and avoid taking the path of least resistance, which can produce more stress and conflict. As you move through your daily activities and face the challenges of managing difficult issues, situations, and people, we hope the analysis and applications provided in this section offered you a glimpse of how an operational understanding of the mission and relevant information can guide conversations by creating a context for decisions and add to transparency in decision-making—essential elements of leadership communication strategies.

As you move to Part II of this book, which continues to develop fair and effective leadership communication, it may be helpful to remind yourself of the following:

- Effective working relationships are impossible to build and sustain when leadership credibility is low.

- Every decision and action has a ripple effect, so effective leadership always considers the context.

- Brainstorming, sharing the criteria or data for decisions, and understanding the institutional perspective all contribute to your ability to be predictable and to be recognized as honest and fair—key aspects of credibility.

Imagine yourself charged with implementing an unpopular mandate. In particular, you recognize the need to streamline the curriculum. You understand that a tighter, more structured program would yield some concrete advantages for the department. For example, a more structured program would make it easier to assess student learning and would likely contribute to improvement in student learning assessment scores. More structure in the curriculum would also help reduce faculty workload in that there would be fewer classes to teach, and this would remove the expectation that faculty would teach substantial overloads each semester. Moreover, a streamlined curriculum would make the department appear more viable to the central administration because with fewer courses offered, enrollment in each class would be optimal, whereas currently the enrollment in department courses hovers around a 55% fill rate. You understand why the central administration is requesting that departments revise and streamline the curriculum.

At the same time, however, you recognize that the department faculty will be resistant to any suggestion that the curriculum be streamlined. For starters, faculty believe they have full autonomy over all curricular matters. Further, individual faculty members have personal interest in certain courses, so the elimination of any particular course would likely be met with resistance. Also, the department faculty do not perceive a problem with the size or scope of the current curriculum. In fact, some believe that without the same degree of choice in courses, the department enrollment would decline.

How would you set about to lead the department through a review and eventual streamlining of the curriculum? If you attribute the need to take action to a mandate imposed by the central administration, you risk your credibility with the faculty who expect you to represent the perspective of the department with the administration. On the other hand, you jeopardize your credibility with the central administration if you argue against taking action that you realize would accrue several advantages for the department and the institution. At the same time, if you champion the requested change with the department faculty, you might be perceived as having sold out and taken sides with the administration. This too could lower your credibility with the department faculty, and it is virtually impossible to succeed as a leader without credibility. The task of implementing an unpopular mandate can be stressful for the chair (or dean) and, unless managed effectively, will likely escalate conflict and threaten chair (or dean) credibility. The objective is to carry out your responsibility and implement the revision in a way that enhances your credibility with both the department faculty and the central administration.

This objective will seem impossible to achieve unless you frame the issue in a way that does not center on the us-versus-them view currently held by the faculty. In particular, as chair, you might want to use the institutional mission to frame the immediate task. If you lead the department in a review of whether the current curriculum satisfies the institutional mission, the discussion will shift from one that focuses on faculty autonomy versus administrative control to one that considers whether the current curriculum is the best that it can be to effectively serve the institutional mission. It will not be sufficient to assert the relationship between the department curriculum and the institutional mission, but rather you will need to demonstrate the connection. For example, if the mission is to prepare students for life and work in a global society, then faculty will need to consider how well the current curriculum satisfies this mission and whether curricular revision might improve the department's ability to achieve the institutional mission. A streamlined curriculum will be more effective in that it controls the instructional path a student takes to degree completion, whereas a loosely structured curriculum with vast course choice leaves the instructional path to the student's discretion. In any event, by linking the issue to be addressed to the institutional mission, you can frame the discussion in a way that depersonalizes the mandate and, consequently, reduces the conflict that might otherwise surface.

This approach will also enhance credibility if you use honest communication in framing the issue and demonstrating your understanding of the issue and its impact on the department. This requires sharing all relevant information with the department faculty so they can understand the situation for themselves and realize the advantages of streamlining the curriculum. By not taking shortcuts, you permit the faculty to perceive the mandate and the issues as you do. This does not mean that all will agree on how to streamline the curriculum, but it will at least build consensus about the need to revise the curriculum.

As you move to Part II of this text, please keep in mind these leadership communication strategies essential to establishing a foundation for effective leadership communication. The next section builds on these foundational elements to examine leadership communication strategies relevant to specific administrative processes, including managing interpersonal conflict, the search process, performance counseling, faculty morale and supervision, and external constituencies.

Part II

DEVELOPING A FAIR AND EFFECTIVE LEADERSHIP COMMUNICATION STYLE

This section offers leadership communication strategies for working effectively with faculty and staff, with attention to both one-on-one communication and communicating with groups. The chapters address specific tasks such as managing the search process and conducting performance counseling. These tasks, more than many others, contribute to the development or destruction of chair and dean credibility with faculty and staff. Other chapters in this section address various genres of leadership communication that are important to chair and dean success. To be effective and comfortable leaders, chairs and deans need to be skilled in communication strategies that enable them to manage disappointment, avoid double standards, preserve faculty morale, use data to inform faculty decision-making, and optimize the allocation of scarce resources. These ends require that chairs and deans be proficient in using leadership communication strategies in the conflict situations detailed here.

Managing Interpersonal Conflict

Chairs and deans will inevitably spend time mediating conflict between and among faculty, staff, and students. On occasion, chairs and deans must also manage conflict between themselves and others. As institutions realize diversity goals, chairs and deans need to be proficient in keeping differences fueled by gender, race, age, and other defining descriptors constructive. There are several communication strategies that can help make this task more manageable but which may not be intuitive. This chapter will offer specific leadership communication strategies for how chairs and deans can manage interpersonal conflict more effectively.

Conflict is a natural outcome of human interaction, so it is inevitable that chairs and deans will need to manage conflict. Conflict exists when individuals working together hold different attitudes, beliefs, or expectations. Conflict develops when individuals who work together have different perceptions about what has happened and possess different expectations on what needs to be done. Consequently, interpersonal conflict exists when individuals working together do not think alike. This is not inherently harmful, but is rather a core benefit of diversity because good decision-making and effective problem-solving require the consideration of multiple perspectives. It is virtually impossible to weigh the relative merit of any decision or course of action if those contributing to its selection think alike. The presence of conflict, therefore, can be advantageous if it is managed to yield constructive outcomes. Interpersonal conflict, however, can be destructive if it is permitted to lower morale, increase defensiveness, create divisiveness, and threaten effective problem-solving and decision-making.

The management of interpersonal conflict is both a science and an art that requires an understanding of human nature and skilled communication. Efforts to manage this conflict will inevitably fail unless chairs and deans accurately assess the source and nature of the conflict and have a clear understanding of individual perspectives, expectations, and fears. This is the science of conflict management. On the other hand, the art of conflict management resides in the communication skill employed by chairs and deans to promote constructive conflict—benefiting the department and the institution while eliminating destructive conflict that can have devastating effects on faculty morale and productivity. This includes, for example, a communication facility for helping the unreasoned and unreasonable hear and respond positively to a logic or perspective that transcends their personal agenda. It also requires the ability to persuade very confident and all-knowing individuals to hear ideas presented by others and, simultaneously, it requires the ability to encourage the more passive souls to contribute to group decision-making and problem-solving.

Conflict management is different from conflict resolution. The goal of conflict resolution is to eliminate (or resolve) the disagreement, thus ending the conflict. The goal of conflict management, however, is not to eliminate the conflict but rather to help individuals air their differences in a manner that enhances decision-making and problem-solving. With effective conflict management, decisions evidence consideration of multiple perspectives and represent much more than the will of the majority or the will of the strongest personality. Chairs and deans need to employ effective leadership communication to permit and encourage thoughtful and constructive consideration of all perspectives. By doing so, chairs and deans can transform an ugly conflict fraught with winners and losers into a situation in which all perspectives are valued and contribute to reaching a decision or solution that best serves the common good. In effective conflict management, everyone wins—there are no losers.

Effective conflict management requires chairs and deans to be proactive by anticipating potential issues and intervening on likely disagreements before they develop into personal and potentially destructive conflicts. Chairs and deans can enhance their efforts by establishing the expectation that all perspectives are valued and that disagreements will be aired in a professional manner. When conflict is viewed as a natural outcome of human interaction, faculty and staff are less likely to consider a difference of opinion as an attack on their thinking or as someone's personal agenda. By establishing a climate in which faculty and staff can air different and individual perspectives without fear of retaliation or humiliation, chairs and deans make it possible to build meaningful consensus and improve problem-solving. This is not accomplished overnight but requires chairs and deans to model and reward the valued behavior over time. Chairs and deans can model that all perspectives are valued, for example, by ensuring that the more silent or passive individuals are encouraged to share their views. Chairs and deans can model and illustrate the benefit of diversity by showing how a perspective they had not previously considered alters their view of an issue or situation. Similarly, they can praise others who hear and incorporate different perspectives into their own thinking.

When interpersonal conflict or any type of conflict is not managed effectively, differences can be destructive. Faculty and staff will more likely champion their own perspective without consideration of other views. Thus, decisions often become contentious votes and informed decision-making is replaced by politicking and lobbying for votes. Effective problem-solving, the kind that is evidenced by collective wisdom, is replaced by something that suggests that there is a winning perspective. Those that are then identified with the losing perspective are likely to feel demoralized and bitter about the outcome. Instead of feeling satisfaction that their ideas were heard and contributed to the final decision, those on the "losing side" of destructive conflict will more likely feel dismissed and devalued. Worse yet, destructive conflict with an outcome that clearly labels some winners and some losers will help to shape the votes in the next contentious issue or conflict. Even when no one remembers the crux or main issues of the previous discussion, they remember the coalitions formed and who "won" or "lost." These unhealthy alliances can also shape department communication on other less contentious issues and ultimately have an adverse affect on faculty morale and productivity.

Because chairs and deans are responsible for leading discussions of issues pertaining to the department or the campus, faculty and staff expect chairs and deans to manage conflict. But conflict is not limited to the discussion of relevant issues. At times, chairs and deans are responsible for decisions that can place them at odds with some faculty and staff including, for example, instances when a chair or dean might recommend against tenure or promotion, reallocate space, or deny a request for new resources. At other times, faculty and staff may turn to the chair or dean for help with other, more personal conflict. Faculty may seek the chair's assistance in mediating a disagreement with a student or colleague. This practice places chairs and deans in the role of mediator—a role that can be more intense than the role taken in facilitating the discussion of an issue on which faculty hold different perspectives. While managing conflict is essential to effective leadership, chairs and deans find that their role can vary from that of mediator to participant to the source for the conflict.

Regardless of the role that chairs and deans have in a particular conflict, their response to the situation will impact the conflict. If, for example, a chair nods in agreement when listening to a faculty member's account of a colleague's action, the chair will likely be perceived as supportive of the faculty member's perspective. While there is a natural tendency to be supportive when listening to someone who is upset, some supportive behaviors (verbal and nonverbal) may give the appearance of taking sides or playing favorites when it is important that chairs and deans remain neutral and reinforce principle or policy. The simple gesture of nodding affirmatively can cause a disgruntled faculty member to become empowered by a belief that the chair or dean is in complete agreement with the perspective being expressed. When the chair's or dean's nonverbal behavior gives the impression of taking sides, it will be more difficult for that chair or dean to demonstrate the objective perspective that is essential to managing the conflict.

Nonverbal communication such as a person's vocal intonation or volume, facial expressions, and hand gestures impact the conflict because these nonverbal cues influence how others perceive the communication. When nonverbal actions contradict the words being spoken, most people will believe the nonverbal communication. Consider the simple statement, "It's been a great day." If this statement is accompanied by a sarcastic tone and exaggerated shoulder shrugging, most people hearing the statement would conclude that the person making the statement is being facetious and that the person's day has been anything but great. Nonverbal cues help us assign meaning to the words being used. Even silence impacts conflict. The chair who intentionally ignores a conflict between two faculty members that are heard arguing near students may unintentionally license the disagreement and the behavior. While the chair may hope that the faculty members will realize it is inappropriate to wage an argument within earshot of students, the faculty may conclude that the chair would say something if he or she perceived their actions as inappropriate.

Chairs and deans hold positions of leadership that make them responsible for managing conflict. Because chairs and deans work directly with faculty and staff, their leadership role provides them with an opportunity to facilitate decision-making and problem-solving discussions in ways that permit the constructive airing of different perspectives. If managed effectively, chairs and deans can stifle the potential destructive practice of politicking for votes to support a particular personal view. Faculty and staff are more prone to discuss department or campus issues in subgroups when there is not a forum in which to air and hear individual perspectives. By creating the opportunity to hear perspectives and weigh the pros and cons of various alternatives, chairs and deans reduce the need for faculty to pursue discussions to persuade others to particular outcomes privately. Similarly, when chairs and deans find that they are participants in a destructive conflict, they have the best vantage point for clarifying misunderstandings that may have contributed to the conflict. Decisions and announcements can cause individual faculty and staff to make attributions about the views held by the chair or dean that then places the chair or dean on one side of a conflict. Even when chairs and deans must make a decision that will not please everyone, they can minimize this type of destructive conflict by sharing the basis for the decision and illustrating that the decision represents a fair and unbiased application of institutional policy. Chairs and deans, however, find that effective conflict management requires proactive intervention.

DENYING A NEW FACULTY LINE REQUEST

Consider the example of a department in which the faculty members believe the dean is unsupportive because he or she denied the request to add a new faculty line. The faculty members perceive the denial of their request as evidence that the dean does not appreciate the department or understand how hard the faculty work. After all, why else would the dean deny a request that would permit the department to expand their offerings to encompass new courses that would be attractive to current and prospective students? The dean, however, finds it incredulous that the department would request a new faculty position when the department's enrollment has been steadily declining for the past six years. In fact, the department's enrollment does not even support the current number of faculty positions let alone the addition of a new position.

A conflict exists because the dean perceives the request as unreasonable, whereas the department faculty members believe that the new faculty position is essential to growing department enrollment. The conflict derives from different perceptions of both the problem and the desired remedy. The department chair may feel caught in the middle of the conflict because while understanding the dean's perspective, there may also be a feeling of being obliged to champion the department's request since the faculty members are united in their view that a new position would enable them to grow the department enrollment.

Assume the position of dean and think about how you would help the department faculty understand that the request for a new faculty position is ill-timed, if not unfounded. Would you talk with the entire department or communicate only with the department chair? A number of factors should be considered in answering this question, including, for example, your confidence in the chair's ability to accurately present your view to the faculty. You would also want to consider the department faculty members' perception of a meeting with the dean. Would they appreciate that you took the time to discuss the request with them or would the meeting be viewed as a waste of time since the request has been denied? If you decide that it is preferable to meet with the department faculty, would you inform them of your decision to deny the request in advance or inform them at the meeting? Your decision will depend in part on your credibility with the department faculty and how salient the issue is to them.

Let's assume that a meeting has been set for you as dean to talk with the department faculty about your decision to deny the request. How would you prepare for the meeting? Would you bring data or other evidence to present in support of your decision? If so, what documentation would you assemble for the meeting? Would you, for example, present data that permitted the department faculty to understand their request relative to requests made by other departments in which enrollment is growing and new faculty are needed to staff additional classes? Or, would you present data that evidences the limits of what is affordable and explain why it is not prudent to invest in a new faculty position without the assurance of enrollment growth? What other approaches might be considered? To answer these questions, you must give consideration to how the department's faculty members perceive the issue. If, for example, the faculty believe the request for a new faculty position should be granted because the department lost a position 15 years earlier, then it will likely be helpful to offer some contextual data that permit the department's faculty to come to view the request differently.

As dean, you can help shape the conversation and the department faculty's conclusions through the framing of the discussion. If, for example, you elect to explain the decision to deny the request because the anticipated enrollment growth is not certain, the discussion might discourage further entrepreneurial thinking within the department. This is not to suggest that this approach is inherently wrong, but it demonstrates the need to think through how the department faculty will internalize the presentation of information and any explanation offered. In this scenario, as dean you would likely want the department faculty to be innovative in keeping the curriculum current and attractive to students.

Revising and updating the department's curriculum, however, should not be contingent on adding new faculty—especially when the new faculty position was requested in order to add new courses to the existing curriculum rather than considering the need to revise outdated courses to make room for courses that would reflect more current thinking within the discipline and be attractive to students. How might you frame the discussion to encourage curricular innovation while helping the department faculty understand how that might be done without (or before) the addition of a new faculty position? Would it help, for example, to point out that their plan places the future of the department in the hands of the newest faculty member? You might ask what a new faculty member would bring that they believe the department is currently lacking.

Their responses might suggest an alternative approach. For example, if you learn that the department faculty believe a new faculty member is essential to growth because they would intentionally hire a colleague with training in new areas of the discipline, you might engage them in considering other ways to acquire the coveted discipline expertise. Perhaps a current member of the department could invest a sabbatical leave in learning the new area or perhaps the department might explore a partnership with a department at another institution that would permit students to take coursework in the new area of the discipline. As dean, you will want to frame the discussion to help the department faculty understand the basis for your decision and also to gather information that will help you lead them in a constructive direction that you can support. How you frame the discussion will affect both their understanding of the current conflict and their future action.

If as dean you choose to present data that demonstrate why the department's request for a new faculty position was assessed to be a lower priority than the new position request received from another department, the discussion could fuel a competition between departments that might not serve the institution. Especially if both departments are in the same broad discipline such as the social sciences or the humanities, the comparison might deter future collaborations between the departments. Tall walls between departments are costly, so the price associated with unintentionally inviting competition between two departments that might otherwise collaborate on any number of initiatives is high. When resources are limited, institutions generally benefit when faculty collaborate across departmental boundaries on such initiatives as teaching cross-disciplinary research methods, developing assessment measures, or pooling student internship opportunities. The information presented in discussing one conflict will likely influence future thinking, so with each conflict management opportunity, chairs and deans need to consider how their approach will likely influence future conflicts.

DELIVERING BAD NEWS

Consider the department chair who makes a practice of blaming the dean for any unwelcome news. As front-line managers, chairs are sometimes in the position of explaining new initiatives or information to faculty. When the matter being presented will not be received as good news, the chair is in an uncomfortable position because simply sharing the information can create conflict. To reduce personal discomfort and disassociate themselves with the information being presented, some chairs are quick to give attribution or place blame with the dean or the central administration. While this may have the immediate effect of making the situation more comfortable for the chair because the tactic permits the chair to side with the faculty in opposition to the dean or the central administration, the practice will fuel conflict and over time will destroy the chair's credibility with both the faculty and the dean. Typically, chairs who engage in this practice employ the same strategy when communicating with the dean about faculty resistance and departmental progress. Chairs who find it more comfortable to align themselves with the faculty when discussing the dean's request will also find it more comfortable to align themselves with the central administration when discussing the shortcomings of the faculty. Though perhaps more immediately comfortable, the chair's credibility is destroyed because the practice demonstrates to both faculty and the administration that the chair is unable to exercise effective leadership when working with the other constituency. In particular, faculty tend to doubt the chair's ability to explain or champion their perspective to the dean and the dean learns to doubt the chair's ability to lead the faculty in ways that advance the institutional mission. Such efforts to bypass the discomfort associated with managing conflict can be suicidal for chairs and deans.

Effective conflict management does not rely on placing blame, but instead focuses on helping individuals understand the various perspectives and constructively consider the available alternatives. In the situation described, the chair will be more effective in managing conflict if the unwelcome information is presented without placing blame on the dean or the central administration. In fact, the issue can and should be presented without making a negative attribution. To illustrate why it is preferable for the chair to resist placing blame as a strategy for making conflict management more comfortable, consider this. In preparation for the upcoming institutional accreditation review, all department chairs are expected to lead faculty through discussions to determine if departmental activity meets the new accreditation criteria and standards. As chair, you worry about adding to faculty workloads. In the past three or so years, faculty have become increasingly intolerant of committee work, which takes enormous time and energy. You fear that faculty will resist adding discussions about accreditation to their workload and anticipate that the task will anger some and frustrate most of the faculty. How do you present the assignment to the faculty?

If you have experienced the task of presenting faculty with an unpopular assignment, you can probably understand the desire to preempt or minimize the anticipated hostile or negative reaction. How might you do this? Would you explain that the dean has made the same request of all departments? If you believe this approach would minimize the negative reaction, you are assuming that faculty will be consoled by learning that all faculty and areas have the same task. If the misery-loves-company approach is not likely to offer much consolation, then it will do little to minimize the anticipated negative reaction. Or, would you present the issue as one on which the department has no choice, so losing time to complaining only increases the time the faculty will have to spend on the task? This approach assumes that the faculty objection to the discussions will derive from time spent on something perceived to be unnecessary. Again, this approach will only be effective if your assessment of the basis for the negative faculty reaction is accurate. Would you consider framing the task as an opportunity? You might, for example, point out that all have a vested interest in the institution's accreditation and express appreciation that the department is being trusted to shape how its discipline is presented to the accrediting body. In what circumstances would this approach help to minimize the negative response? For this approach to have the desired affect, the claim made needs to be believable, and it will be more likely to be beneficial if you, as chair, are a credible leader for the faculty.

For every conflict, there is a range of alternative approaches. The best approach is the one that responds to an accurate assessment of existing attitudes and perceptions. In other words, a solution will only be successful if the problem has been accurately assessed and it responds to the core issue at the root of the conflict. Beyond this, conflict management is helped if chairs and deans are perceived as credible leaders and there exists a mutual respect between and among the individuals who are in conflict.

OFFICE SPACE

Consider the conflict that can develop between staff in an office. Even though all staff members occupy space owned by the institution and work to serve the same office, they can become possessive about equipment they do not own and territorial about the responsibilities assigned to them. To illustrate the conflict that can develop when there is no basis for disagreement, consider a dispute among three assistants in the same office over the placement of a common printer. To save resources and provide the office with a high-quality printer, the technical support team opted to purchase one large printer for the office staff instead of three small desktop printers for each assistant, which was the original request. The assistants were thrilled with the suggestion to purchase one top-quality printer because its features will make several tedious jobs easier. When the assistants were consulted individually about revising their original request for new desktop printers, they enthusiastically expressed their support for the idea of one large printer.

Attitudes remained positive until the new printer was delivered and the technician asked where the printer should be set up. Almost in unison, the three assistants answered with three different locations. Each strongly believed that the printer should be nearby, and each had several compelling reasons in support of their individual preference. This is clearly a situation in which the final decision cannot possibly please everyone. Worse yet, because the printer is viewed by each assistant as absolutely essential to his or her work, each is likely to view a decision other than the one individually requested as a value judgment about his or her contribution to the office.

Assume the position of chair (or dean) and consider how you would navigate the conflict as the supervisor of all three assistants. Would you talk to each individually to hear his or her reasons for a particular printer location? Or, would you assemble the three to air their differences in a group meeting? While meeting with each individually may evidence your willingness to hear each point of view, the process will inevitably leave you with three different preferences and a tough decision to make. However, by meeting as a group, you can help to ensure that each assistant hears the perspectives held by the others. You can also make certain that office and work priorities are considered. This approach holds some possibility that the reasons presented will help each of the three assistants to consider other views and perhaps be persuaded toward some compromise.

As you prepare for the meeting with the three assistants, consider how you would frame the discussion. Does it matter who talks first? Should the three assistants be given an agenda (and possibly an assignment) in advance of the meeting? You might, for example, tell them that the purpose for the meeting is to review all the possible printer locations to find the best one and suggest that they note the work issues they believe should be considered. You might ask them to bring copies for everyone attending the meeting. Especially when individuals are emotionally invested in an issue or decision, having them write out their thoughts or justification can help to depersonalize the conversation. It also keeps the conversation on issues and not personal preference. There is a significant difference, for example, between deciding who should get to have the printer nearby and which office projects require the most printing. The former issue would frame the discussion as a personal matter whereas the latter helps to set a work-related basis for deciding the best location for the printer.

If this scenario occurred in your office, you would have the advantage of knowing the individuals involved. This information should be used to prepare for the meeting. For example, if you know that one of the assistants is prone to interrupting others mid-sentence, you would want to give some thought to how you would manage that behavior. If not managed constructively, such behavior could serve to escalate the conflict. In short, it is helpful to use all the information at your disposable to prepare for and conduct the meeting with the three assistants. Further, if the printer placement decision is, for any reason, an intense issue for even one of the three assistants, you may not be able to reach closure in one meeting. In fact, you may wish to terminate discussion before reaching a decision in the first meting to permit the three staff members to think about the options. It may be especially advantageous to interrupt the conversation if one or more of the assistants seem to be reacting to the fear of "losing" the outcome. By interrupting discussion on heated issues, the individuals involved have time to reflect and rethink their positions.

ANALYSIS AND APPLICATIONS

Managing conflict effectively requires proficient communication skill and experience. While this can take time to develop, most faculty and staff will recognize and value leadership efforts to air differences constructively. Through this process, chairs and deans can demonstrate that they know their job, have the best intentions, and are trustworthy. These attributes translate to leadership credibility which in turn will enhance one's ability to manage conflict effectively. Although the task of managing conflict may be daunting, it is one that can pay huge dividends to the institution and for one's leadership credibility. Let's review the essential elements of each application:

- Establish a climate conducive to airing differences constructively.

- Get everyone on the same page.

- Depersonalize conflict.

- Share decision-making criteria.

◆ Establish a climate conducive to airing differences constructively.

Chairs and deans can enhance their ability to manage conflict by establishing a climate that is conducive to airing differences constructively. A climate conducive to managing conflict exists when individuals exhibit mutual respect through honest and open communication and are willing to hear and consider ideas that are different from their own. When faculty and staff evidence these attributes, the department climate becomes conducive to airing differences constructively as individuals are more inclined to give each other the benefit of the doubt and are less likely to perceive views that differ from their own as threatening. In all the examples described in this chapter, the task of managing conflict will be easier if the climate in the department and/or on the campus is conducive to airing differences constructively. Different perceptions, attitudes, and beliefs are inherent in diversity. The greater the diversity in a campus community, the greater the variation of perspectives and the advantage for good decision-making and problem-solving.

Leadership credibility also contributes to a climate conducive to airing differences constructively. Remember that leadership credibility is comprised of three components: a person's knowledge, good intentions, and trustworthiness. Chairs and deans will find it easier to manage conflict if faculty and staff perceive them as credible. At the same time, it is important to keep in mind that credibility is an assigned attribute. When chairs or deans take refuge in placing blame with others, they hurt their long-term credibility. Though it may seem counterintuitive to accept ownership for the decision or problem to be solved, doing so can enhance one's leadership credibility.

◆ Get everyone on the same page.

Framing the conflict is the key to managing it. It is important to frame the conflict in neutral terms. This can be done by employing several leadership communication strategies. First, chairs and deans can minimize the influence of personal perceptions by providing all parties with common data and other factual information. As in the example of the denied request for a new faculty position, the dean can dispel the perception that the decision evidences a lack of support for the department by sharing information regarding the criteria used to determine the need for a new position. Second, the issue of conflict should be framed in a way that transcends personal identities or vested interest. For example, rather than discussing the need to update a particular course that is always taught by the same faculty member, it is preferable to discuss the need to keep curriculum current and relevant for today's students. Third, frame the issue of conflict in a professional way. Just as there is little room for name-calling in professional communication, it is unprofessional to fan the flames of conflict by placing blame.

◆ Depersonalize conflict.

Conflict is easier to manage when the disagreement is not taken personally. Chairs and deans can help to depersonalize conflict by addressing specific behavior rather than personality traits. There is a significant difference between telling a faculty member that he or she only cares about his or her discipline and making clear that all are expected to understand and advance institutional priorities. Similarly, in the example of the three assistants who cannot agree over the best placement for an office printer, the chair (or dean) must keep the discussion focused on the best location given the work to be done, as well as other office priorities such as where the consistent noise of a printer might interrupt other work. Efforts to depersonalize the conflict empower decision-making that serves the common good rather than a personal agenda. It also takes the sting out of not getting one's preferred outcome. It will be easier for the assistants to accept a printer location because it is best for the office than it would be to accept that one assistant got his or her way in the location of the printer.

◆ Share decision-making criteria.

Seldom does a decision please everyone. Conflict that might result when faculty or staff are disappointed with a decision or outcome can be managed by sharing the decision-making criteria. If, for example, all faculty understand that new faculty positions are only approved when department enrollment increases to the point of requiring an additional faculty member to staff courses that will fill, then the department faculty will not be surprised when a request that is not built on this criterion is denied. This does not mean that the faculty will like the outcome, but they will at least understand the negative decision and will be less likely to take the denial personally or view it as evidence that the dean does not support the department. By sharing decision-making criteria, chairs and deans make the outcome predictable. When an outcome is consistent with expectations, the potential for outrage or indignation is dramatically decreased.

Chairs and deans can further reduce the likelihood of conflict by sharing decision-making criteria well in advance of the decision. If faculty, for example, know and understand the criteria for receiving a new faculty position, they can make an informed decision as to whether they should spend time drafting a proposal for a new position. Ideally, when faculty and staff can predict the outcome, they are better able to prepare requests that are responsive to both institutional priorities and available resources.

SOME FINAL THOUGHTS

Many chairs and deans report that managing conflict is the toughest responsibility of leadership. Some openly admit to dreading the task and others talk about fearing it. Yet it is imperative that chairs and deans enhance their ability to manage conflict effectively because conflict is inevitable. The most harmonious department will hit a bump in the road or find themselves at odds with the chair or dean. Chairs and deans can count on the fact that conflict will develop, and it is their responsibility to manage it effectively. The good news is that conflict need not be destructive. In fact, conflict can be constructive because airing and considering multiple perspectives enhances decision-making and problem-solving.

The objective is for chairs and deans to manage conflict constructively in order to capitalize on one of the benefits of diversity. This requires chairs and deans to be proactive in managing interpersonal conflict. The wait-and-see approach is not typically helpful, and it is important to remember that when chairs and deans remain silent or avoid managing conflict, their inaction still impacts the conflict. The art and science of managing conflict requires chairs and deans to understand human nature and employ communication skills directed toward building a climate that is conducive to airing differences constructively, getting everyone on the same page, depersonalizing the conflict, and sharing decision-making criteria.

Effective conflict management is an important responsibility that is essential to chair and dean leadership. It is also important to chair and dean leadership success because one's ability to manage conflict effectively has a direct bearing on whether others perceive a chair or dean as possessing leadership credibility. At the same time, often the best approach to managing conflict is not the intuitive response. For example, while it may be more comfortable to place blame somewhere else when presenting unwelcome news to faculty, the don't-kill-the-messenger approach will be short lived because it reveals leadership weakness. Similarly, although a specific conflict may give the impression that the chair or dean needs to make a decision that will favor one person at the expense of another, it is usually possible to frame the discussion in a way that depersonalizes the issue and the decision so the focus is shifted from who wins and who loses to what is best for the department or the institution.

Managing the Search Process

Searching to fill position vacancies can produce conflict unless the chair or dean manages the search process effectively. If the job description is not clearly defined, one invites members of the search committee to screen candidates from a personal perspective, which will likely reflect self-interest and turf concerns rather than seeing candidates in terms of institutional need. This chapter provides chairs and deans with leadership communication strategies for working out differences and building consensus around the position description and duties to be assigned prior to advertising, potentially reducing the conflict associated with reviewing applicants.

Several years ago, *The Chronicle of Higher Education* published a cartoon that pictured a group of faculty looking bruised and battered. One member of the group stood behind a podium in a pose that suggested sheer exhaustion and announced, "I'm pleased to report that the search committee had agreed on a list of finalists." Anyone who has served on a search committee understands the potential for conflict during the search process. Even faculty who share friendships can become combative while searching for the "best" new colleague.

The potential for conflict exists because faculty and staff review candidates' credentials and then assess each candidate's potential fit with both the position and the department from personal perspectives. Even though search committee members have access to the same application materials, they can reach very different conclusions about what each candidate might contribute to the department. This happens because, without intervention, search committee members will inevitably assess candidates from personal perspectives. Personal perspectives are shaped by how individual search committee members envision working with the new hire, previous experiences with colleagues, and the individual viewpoint of what is most needed in the department. One member of the search committee, for example, may want a colleague who holds similar values on certain issues, while another search committee member may place a higher priority on finding a new colleague who would enjoy teaching 100-level courses so that he or she may be spared teaching the freshman-level courses.

When faculty serving on a search committee read and rate applications from a personal perspective, a greater probability for conflict exists when deciding which candidates to interview and then selecting the best candidate for the available position. Typically, when there is not consensus on who should even be interviewed, the selection of the best-fit candidate can be very contentious. In these instances, individual search committee members may lobby other faculty members to vote for a particular candidate, thus preempting an objective interview process. Worse yet, the new hire may start with some animosity from the faculty members who "lost" their pick to another choice. Consequently, it behooves chairs and deans to structure the search process in a way that not only decreases the opportunity for personal perspectives to undermine the integrity of the search process but also limits the creation of unnecessary animosity among faculty and staff who will need to work with that new hire.

Chairs and deans can reduce the potential for conflict by building a shared perception of the departmental mission which in turn helps to establish a common understanding of the qualifications needed in the new hire. Building a common understanding of the needed qualifications is not always easy do, and the task becomes more difficult when chairs and deans have not worked in advance of the search to build consensus and enthusiasm for the department's mission. Ideally, chairs and deans work continuously to establish and reinforce a shared perception of the mission so all group decisions can be made within the larger context of the department's purpose and direction. It is one thing to know the essence of the mission statement, but it is another matter to possess an operational understanding of the mission. It is the operational understanding of the mission that permits faculty to translate more lofty objectives such as "preparing citizens in a global society" from the written statement into concrete decisions and behaviors.

When faculty and staff share an operational understanding of the mission, chairs and deans can build consensus around the available position.

Consensus building can be done by involving faculty and staff in preparing the initial position request for the central administration. To obtain permission to conduct a search, chairs and deans must first assess need and then build a case designed to persuade others about the need for the position. This type of review typically considers such issues as enrollment (institutional and departmental), the department's ability to staff the current curriculum, and how a new position would serve both the departmental and institutional missions. When chairs or deans complete this analysis in isolation, they have denied faculty and staff an opportunity to understand the larger context that would warrant the new position. The same assessment and need for contextual understanding exists when a department seeks permission to fill a vacant position. Fiscal realities at many institutions do not make filling of open positions automatic and, typically, the vacant position needs to be justified by the chair and dean before it can be filled. Without being party to these discussions, it is easy for faculty and staff to possess a sense of entitlement about a vacant position and believe that a replacement will be automatic.

The process of building consensus can also be facilitated by involving department faculty and staff in drafting the advertisement and position description. This process will of course be easier if the faculty understand the basis on which the new position was approved. It is easier to reach agreement on the desirable qualifications before search committee members begin to review applications. It is also important to achieve a common understanding of how the desired attributes might be exhibited in the applicants. For example, if the position description calls for a candidate with a "substantial record of scholarship," the members of the search committee should have a common understanding about what the candidate's experience must minimally entail to meet that stated criterion. Will only candidates with published scholarship be considered as having a "substantial record of scholarship" or will younger candidates who demonstrate the potential for doing significant scholarship be considered qualified? Consensus must be reached in advance because once the applications are available for review, search committee members will evaluate the candidates from their personal perspective and their own definition of the criteria. Permitting the application of personal perceptions can be especially contentious if individuals interpret disagreement with their views as a dismissal of the type of scholarship in which they engage.

In addition to building consensus about desired position qualifications before the search process begins, chairs and deans need to continue to reinforce the desired attributes throughout the process of the application review. Chairs and deans might, for example, engage search committee members in a refresher discussion about the position advertisement and necessary qualifications prior to having committee members read the applications. Or, chairs and deans might prepare a form on which committee members are asked to rate each applicant on meeting the advertised position's qualifications. Also, chairs and deans need to be ready to facilitate a discussion that addresses the contributions each applicant might make to the department and the institution relative to how each person meets those advertised position qualifications.

Many position advertisements distinguish between *required* and *preferred* qualifications. Chairs and deans can reduce the potential for conflict by preserving that distinction. When search committee members blur the line between required and preferred qualifications, it is easy to hear dramatically different assessments of an applicant's fit for the position. Required qualifications should be considered deal breakers in that applicants who fail to meet the required qualifications should not be considered for the position. Unless there is a clear distinction between the required and preferred qualifications, chairs and deans may discover that some search committee members are willing to forgo required qualifications when an applicant has some perceived unique talent or special quality.

ACTING UNILATERALLY VERSUS BUILDING CONSENSUS

Suppose a department has been given permission to conduct a search to fill a vacancy created when a 30-year veteran of the department elected to retire. The soon-to-be emeritus faculty member, Dr. Mueller, is well respected across campus, although some faculty members and administrators recognize that Dr. Mueller's contributions to his department are not current with where the discipline has moved in the past decade, and his work is even further removed from where the discipline seems to be headed with its growing interest in interdisciplinary work. Dr. Mueller teaches courses that he designed shortly after coming to campus three decades earlier. His department colleagues never considered eliminating the dated courses out of respect for their most senior faculty colleague and because "Doc" Mueller's classes were always full. Dr. Mueller is highly engaged with students, serving as faculty adviser to the student government and numerous other student groups. He is well known to students across campus, and often his courses enroll students beyond those who major in the discipline. Dr. Mueller has truly been a significant presence on the campus for a long time. He has held every possible leadership position within the faculty senate and continues to be someone the administration believes has and still can articulate the pulse of both the faculty and the students. Often, the dean and president seek Dr. Mueller's assessment of such climate issues as faculty morale or student engagement.

Assume the role of department chair and think through how you would draft the position advertisement to fill the vacancy created by Dr. Mueller's retirement. Would you conduct the search to identify a new hire who could teach the courses that Dr. Mueller teaches? If not, why not, and how would you decide what the new hire should teach? If, for example, you would seek to hire a faculty member who was more cutting edge in terms of where the discipline seems to be moving, then how would you frame the position announcement so that it complements current departmental offerings and would be embraced by other faculty members in the department? Finding the right applicant to fill a vacant position can feel like finding that perfect jigsaw puzzle piece that completes the picture. The task is more complex than just finding a good person who teaches well and is trained in content deemed valuable and important to the program because, to be effective, the new hire must mesh well with department colleagues and with others at the institution.

What might you, as chair, do to ensure that the new hire is a perfect fit for the department and the campus? Is this a task that is best done alone or in collaboration with others? If you are racing to get an announcement placed quickly, hoping that the department might attract the strongest applicants available, you might consider drafting the advertisement yourself. If you anticipate that the department faculty will not be able to agree on position qualifications, the process of collaborating on the position announcement could take considerable time. You might decide that it is better to place the advertisement, perhaps even a less specific ad, in order to get the position advertised and then begin working with the department faculty on what is needed in the new hire. Every decision accrues advantages and liabilities. Clearly moving ahead unilaterally to prepare the announcement has the advantage of getting the position advertised quickly. This can be a significant advantage especially if, on your campus, faculty salaries are less competitive than salaries offered at comparable institutions. Posting the position announcement quickly is also an advantage if you fear that deteriorating institutional budget conditions might prompt the central administration to abort the search and put a hiring freeze on all unfilled positions.

Particularly if you possess a get-it-done leadership style, you may easily discern the advantages of working unilaterally to prepare the position advertisement, but can you also discern the liabilities of taking this approach? Perhaps the most significant liability is that working unilaterally postpones consensus building about the qualifications needed in the new hire. Inherent in building consensus about the new hire is achieving a common understanding about the shared mission of the department within the context of the institutional mission. If faculty members are not on the same page about the departmental mission, it will be virtually impossible for them to reach agreement on the best candidate to fill the vacancy. Simply put, when faculty lack a shared understanding of the departmental and institutional missions, they will inevitably make decisions and prioritize choices based on personal preferences, and those preferences may have nothing to do with either the departmental or institutional missions.

In some instances, it may seem preferable to draft a more generic position announcement in order to advertise quickly and then circle back to build consensus about the qualifications needed in the new hire. This strategy may work well in some disciplines, but it could be problematic if the discipline is one in which subspecialties exist. In those fields that support advanced degrees in subspecialties of the discipline, it is unlikely that a generic advertisement will attract candidates that are focused in one or two of the discipline's recognized subspecialties. A candidate who has specialized in international studies, for example, is not likely to view an announcement seeking a faculty member in political science with experience in comparative political theory, government, and legal and international studies as a desirable position. An unfocused position advertisement that does not reflect departmental needs could likely yield the wrong pool of applicants.

Chairs and deans who dread managing conflict may be tempted to avoid departmental discussions about the most pressing needs in the position or the most needed attributes in a new hire because they perceive that faculty and staff hold different perceptions and know that there will be disagreement. The intuitive thinking may be to avoid creating conflict by not discussing the issues on which faculty disagree. This strategy is short lived and inevitably counterproductive because it guarantees that differences will eventually surface and need to be addressed at a later time. Worse yet, this strategy ensures that the conflict will be confounded by consideration of the various applicants which will in turn make the disagreement more personal. It is significantly easier to air disagreements and build consensus before faculty meet or become personally and emotionally attached to specific applicants.

DIVIDED OPINIONS ON THE SEARCH COMMITTEE

Suppose you decide to run a more open-ended advertisement for the position and now must work with the search committee to identify the top candidate who will be invited for a campus interview. In an effort to save time and money, the dean has asked that departments interview their top candidate and only move on to interview other candidates in the event that based on the campus interview, there is some reservation about the top choice. The dean reasons that spending time and money to interview a longer list of finalists can result in losing one's first choice who may accept a position at another institution before a department can complete all its interviews with candidates further down the list.

The committee members all believe that one candidate is significantly better than the other applicants, but disagree on who that best candidate is. Some committee members have selected an applicant who earned his degrees many years earlier, but left higher education to assume a position in government service. The committee members supporting this candidate believe that this applicant would offer the smoothest transition because he could teach the courses currently taught by "Doc" Mueller. They are unconcerned that the applicant is not much younger than Dr. Mueller and perceive the applicant's ability to teach Doc's courses and his government experience as a plus. Other members of the search committee identified a different applicant as the top choice. The second top candidate is scheduled to complete her doctorate in the spring as her graduate work was interrupted with significant international experiences, and it is these experiences that some faculty members believe would offer much-needed support to the department's program in international studies. These faculty members further contend that the department should want to expand the international studies program because it fits most closely with the institutional mission that makes specific mention of preparing students for life and work in a global society.

From your perspective as chair, you would select a third applicant as the top candidate. You recognize that the department would accrue significant advantage from the third applicant who is currently serving in a full-time term appointment at another institution. Your pick for top candidate is a seasoned teacher who also has experience with student learning outcomes assessment and online course instruction. To date, you have been managing the department's assessment program because it was easier to do it yourself than to persuade the faculty that assessment activity is worthwhile. Similarly, you see an advantage to having a faculty member with experience in online instruction because the central administration has been talking about the need for online courses to serve students enrolled in its continuing education division and to help the more traditionally aged students take courses during the summer when they are living at home and working. As chair of the department, you are also serving as chair of the search committee.

What do you do? Would you use your leadership role to insist that the department interview your top candidate? Would you approach the dean to gain permission to interview more than one candidate? If so, what would you do if the dean grants permission to interview two candidates? It may not be easier to reach agreement about two candidates. How can you move the search committee members to consensus? Interviewing the two candidates about whom the faculty members' opinions are split will only postpone the need to reach consensus until after the interviews, but it will not eliminate the conflict.

What might you do as chair in this situation should Dr. Mueller offer to help screen applications for his successor? While most people recognize that it is inappropriate for any departing person to have a role in selecting his or her successor, it is conceivable that a well-intentioned faculty member who assumes that the new hire will be expected to fill his shoes in the department will believe it helpful to have his interpretation of the relative fit of each applicant for the teaching and other duties that are being surrendered. How would you respond to such an offer to help? Certainly this is not the time to risk offending a beloved faculty member who is about to retire. At the same time, the hire of a new tenure-track faculty member represents a major long-term investment for the department and institution, and it would not be appropriate for Dr. Mueller to influence the selection.

Out of respect, you might consider permitting Dr. Mueller to offer his assessment with the full realization that he will not make the final decision. If you do this, how would you structure Dr. Mueller's participation? Would you, for example, request that Dr. Mueller read the applications independently and share his thoughts with only you? Or, would you permit Dr. Mueller to join the search committee but make it clear that he would not have a vote? In deciding the best possible approach, you would need to consider whether comments made by Dr. Mueller might influence the thinking of others on the search committee. It may not matter that Dr. Mueller will not cast a vote for the new hire if he is in a position to directly influence how others vote. Even if Dr. Mueller makes a concerted effort not to influence the views of others, it is likely that his faculty colleagues will seek his assessment of the candidates if they know that he has reviewed the applications.

This scenario illustrates the complex dynamics and potential for conflict when conducting a search. Chairs and deans can minimize the potential for destructive or counterproductive conflict by taking specific proactive measures.

ANALYSIS AND APPLICATIONS

The task of managing conflict becomes easier if ground rules are established. When chairs and deans build a context for the search, they have established boundaries for candidate review. Thus, they have not only helped to manage conflict during the search process, they have also helped establish clear expectations for the new hire which in turn can enhance the new hire's success. The context for the search must take into account conditions within and beyond the department that will influence the position duties to be carried out by the new hire. Similarly, chairs and deans can exercise considerable control over how the new hire gets started in the department. The search process is an opportunity to clarify expectations for the new hire and build some consensus about department and campus needs for the new hire. Let's review the essential elements of each application:

- Create a level of shared understanding.

- Build a context for the search.

- Structure the search process.

- Help the new hire get started.

◆ Create a level of shared understanding.

When faculty and staff lack a shared understanding about the needs to be filled by a new hire, they will inevitably assess applicants from a personal perspective. This can create conflict among faculty members that would not exist if they were viewing the applicants from a common perspective. If such conflict is permitted, it can have an adverse affect on the new hire. Imagine the introduction of a new hire offered the position because he or she was identified as the top candidate based on a department vote of six to five. Especially if the discussion and vote was spirited, it is unlikely that the five faculty members who lost the vote will heal and be ready to greet a new colleague with much enthusiasm. A close vote typically indicates that those voting do not share an understanding of the desired position qualifications. When a review of applicants yields such divisiveness, chairs and deans would be well served to interrupt the process of reviewing applicants to discuss the needs for the position.

Although it can be a time-consuming activity, there are other advantages to building a shared understanding among faculty and staff. In general, the potential for interdepartmental conflict is substantially reduced when a shared understanding exists of the institutional and departmental missions, the immediate agenda and resource limitations, and other such essential variables. While it will not eliminate all conflict or tension in a department, it will remove the tension that develops when faculty hold different and often unrealistic perceptions of current conditions and expectations.

Ideally, faculty and staff will possess a shared understanding of several factors including the institutional mission and priorities, the departmental mission and priorities, and their individual contributions to the departmental and institutional missions. It is also important that faculty and staff possess a shared understanding of desired qualifications needed in the new hire and how the new hire will work in collaboration with others to contribute to the department. Creating a shared understanding is multifaceted and will not be accomplished with a single memo or meeting. Ideally, the process of creating a shared understanding among faculty and staff is something that chairs and deans tend to on a regular basis. If the task is not started before the need to search for a new hire, it will be more difficult to establish while conducting a search.

◆ Build a context for the search.

The search process is designed to fill a vacancy in the department, and the new hire will need to work collaboratively with others. Chairs and deans can build a foundation for teamwork that encompasses the new hire by building a context for the search that permits members of the department to recognize and anticipate how they might work with the candidate. Part of identifying the candidate who will be the best fit for the position and for the department is finding a candidate who will integrate and work well with others.

When a new hire must take a position vacated by a long-serving colleague, it is particularly important to help others in the department prepare for the new hire who will bring his or her own expertise to the department and who may behave differently when carrying out assigned responsibilities. Building a context for the search also involves discussing what work outside the department will likely be assigned to the new hire. Chairs and deans can anticipate the contribution that the new hire will be expected to make beyond the immediate needs of the department and begin helping others on campus build a context for the new hire. Should Dr. Mueller's replacement have assigned responsibilities that will limit any opportunity for a significant amount of committee service on campus, it would be helpful to signal that in advance so others on campus do not inappropriately hold expectations that will not be placed on the new hire. If, for example, someone other than Dr. Mueller's replacement assumes a leadership role in shared governance, it would be good to have that person become involved before the new hire joins the institution.

Building a context for the search must account for conditions beyond the campus. The context encompasses those conditions that will likely influence the search. For example, the search will be influenced by the availability of candidates with the desired training and how applicants perceive the advertised position, the program, and the institution. Consideration of these factors helps frame a context so that search committee members have a realistic perspective for the search. The search process is not helped, for example, if search committee members believe that the advertised position will be sought by many professionals when, in truth, there are few candidates available with the required qualifications. Similarly, if the position announcement is written to require a doctorate when a terminal master's degree such as an MBA, MM, or MFA would suffice, the search committee will unnecessarily limit the applicant pool.

◆ Structure the search process.

Even when chairs and deans effectively build consensus before advertising a position, it helps to structure the search process in a way that facilitates a more objective review of qualified applicants. For example, it is a good idea to review and discuss the position advertisement before search committee members actually begin their review of applications. Typically, several weeks have passed between the development of a position announcement and the review of applications, thus a refresher on what is needed in the new hire can help search committee members exercise a common understanding when they read the applications. This will not necessarily cause them to read applications the same way or ensure that they will hold unanimous views of the relative strengths of each applicant, but this practice of review will help to keep the hiring objectives in mind. In particular it is often helpful to clarify the *required* qualifications and to distinguish those from other attributes that were advertised as *preferred* qualifications.

It can also be useful to structure the review of applicants in a prescribed time frame. For example, as chair of the search committee, the chair or dean might manage receipt of all applications, notifying those applicants whose files are deemed incomplete that they cannot be considered for the position unless all of the required information is received by a certain date. Managing the search process in this way ensures that search committee members read only completed files. The first meeting of the search committee can then be dedicated to reviewing the position announcement and refreshing the common understanding of the departmental and institutional need for the new hire.

The process of reviewing applications can be time consuming; therefore, it is less efficient to try to review applications as a group. There is a value to having search committee members review the applications independently and reach individual assessments of each applicant's potential fit for the position, the department, and the institution. At the same time, it is important that the independent review of the applications does not encourage (or license) search committee members to stray from the desired qualifications. Reading an application is how search committee members get to know each applicant. It is predictable that committee members will tune in to experiences summarized in the curricula vitae that resonate with them because each search committee member will be reviewing applications with some consideration for how the applicant would fit as a colleague.

This is where reviewing applications can be similar to witnessing an accident. A person's individual assessment or description of the applicant will be shaped by specific facts or experiences that capture that search committee member's attention. This is normal and can even be helpful in teasing out the subtleties of each applicant. However, imposing personal frames of reference cannot substitute for the agreed-upon required and preferred qualifications. Chairs and deans can help the process by supplying search committee members with a form on which each applicant is rated on each of the desired qualifications. An applicant rating form can be constructed by listing all the required and desirable position qualifications and asking search committee members to rate each candidate's strength on each qualification on a scale of 1 (minimal experience) to 5 (optimal experience). While the form might leave room for other observations, the rating scale will help to ensure that search committee members are assessing the applicants from a standard list of criteria.

The use of a rating form can save time and reduce the potential for conflict if chairs and deans ask search committee members to submit the forms in advance of the next committee meeting. Chairs and deans can review the completed forms to place applicants in one of three groups: semifinalists, possible candidates, and candidates no longer being considered.

In chairing the next meeting, the chair or dean would be able to show the clustering of applications in each of the three categories. This can be an efficient way to narrow the list of applicants under consideration without having time-consuming discussions about the candidates that no longer need to take the search committee's time. For example, the chair or dean might ask the committee to read the list of names in the "no longer in consideration" category and refer to their individual notes to see if anyone on the committee would like to make a persuasive appeal to move one of the applicants from that category to the "possible candidates" clustering. Typically, a few search committee members will make a pitch for applicants that firmly fell into the bottom third. However, if the search committee process invites discussion about all the applications, several search committee members will have a lot to say about each of the bottom-third candidates, even if it is only to rehash what they noted in the application that would give the applicant a bottom-third rating.

Next, the chair or dean might ask the search committee members to follow a similar process in reviewing the applicants on the semifinalist list and ask if anyone on the search committee would like to make a persuasive appeal for moving any candidate from that group to the "possible candidates" or middle grouping of applicants. Finally, the same process would be used to review the applicants on the "possible candidates" list to determine if any applicant from that group should move up to join the semifinalists. If such an appeal is made, the search committee members should also be asked to comment on which candidate currently on the semifinalist list would be moved to the "possible candidates" grouping to make way for the one applicant being promoted. By structuring the conversation in this way, chairs and deans can help search committee members weight the relative merits of each application in relation to the previously agreed-upon qualifications for the position.

Depending on the number of applications received, the list of semifinalists may need to be culled to a shorter list of candidates to be invited for an interview. If so, this is where it will be especially important and helpful to have clarified in advance the distinction between required and preferred qualifications. It is possible that this step will take time, especially if there are a substantial number of candidates in the top third of the applicant pool. But by structuring the search process as described, chairs and deans will spare the search committee's time discussing candidates that are not in the top third of the applicant pool. Further, by structuring the search process around the previously agreed-upon qualifications, chairs and deans can minimize the conflict that inevitably develops when search committee members use personal criteria and frames of reference to assess the applicants.

◆ Help the new hire get started.

An effective search process does not end with the return of a signed contract from the new hire. Chairs and deans have significant influence over how that new hire is welcomed and acculturated into the department. It is important that the new hire meet faculty and staff who will be helpful colleagues and mentors. It is also important that chairs and deans demonstrate their respect for the new hire's contribution by intentionally engaging that person in department work.

When filling a vacancy created by the retirement of a long-term, valued member of the department, it is especially important to intervene in ways that permit the new hire to find and establish his or her own voice. This might mean intentionally assigning the new faculty member to committees that are different from the ones on which a long-term faculty member like Dr. Mueller served. If the new hire is assigned the precise courses and service activities that were managed by Dr. Mueller, the chair and dean will invite colleagues to make comparisons between Dr. Mueller and the new hire. This dynamic could allow other people to assess the new hire's contribution in terms of how closely he or she mirrors what Dr. Mueller would have done rather than on the merits of the new hire's work.

How the chair or dean interacts with the new hire is also important. How the chair or dean assigns the new hire to department committees, solicits the new hire's view during department meetings, and involves the new hire in department business and activities will connote to others an expectation for the potential contribution from the new hire. Such proactive intervention is especially important with the hire of a nontraditional faculty member. A nontraditional faculty member is any hire that does not fit the norm. A nontraditional hire might be the first person of color or the first woman (or man) hired in the department. It might be the first term appointment or the first full-time tenure-track appointment made in the department. Such breaks from tradition can result in stereotyping the new hire in a way that minimizes that person's ability to contribute to the department and the institution. Chair and dean intervention to break such stereotypes and to demonstrate a high regard for the contribution to be made by the new hire will help that person have a good start.

SOME FINAL THOUGHTS

The search process carries high stakes for all parties who will work with the new hire. When search committee members do not possess a shared understanding of the expectations for the available position and the qualifications desired in the new hire, then each member of the search committee will evaluate the applicants from a very personal perspective and frame of reference. This variation increases the potential for conflict when reviewing the relative merits of each applicant for the available position. Worse yet, when faculty members apply their individual perspectives during the search process, the potential for conflict increases.

Chairs and deans quickly discover that the conflict derived from personal and varied views about significant department action such as the hiring of a new colleague is not easily resolved. Once search committee members establish their support for a specific candidate, it is more difficult to alter their assessment and conclusion and the search process can take on all the dynamics of a heated election. Furthermore, a new hire that is offered a position following a close vote has a significant obstacle to overcome to do well in the position. Candidates hired from a contentious search process do not start on neutral ground, but instead find that they start with something to prove to both those who voted in their favor and those who preferred a different candidate. This dynamic does not facilitate collaboration and is likely to extend the conflict experienced during the search process into the new hire's working relationships.

Although chairs and deans may resist taking time to establish a shared understanding among the relevant parties before the position is advertised and before the search committee begins their work, doing so will save time and unnecessary conflict later on in the search process. Time spent building a consensus about what the department and the institution need in the position to be filled and in the new hire will ensure that the qualifications of all applicants are viewed from a common frame of reference. While this will not erase all personal preference from the process, it will help to ensure objective standards on which each applicant can be considered.

Similarly, chairs and deans can reduce the potential for unhealthy conflict by structuring the search process in a way that focuses the search committee members' review of applicants in relation to a clearly established set of required and preferred qualifications. This way, time is not lost to discussing candidates who do not require search committee consideration. This encourages constructive discussion about the fit of each applicant while reinforcing the role to be assumed by the new hire.

8

Managing Performance Counseling

Individuals are less likely to resist performance counseling when they recognize that it will enhance their success. To build a climate that enhances faculty and staff performance and minimizes the potential for the type of conflict that can develop when faculty and staff are not meeting performance expectations, chairs and deans need to illustrate the value of the activity to individual faculty and staff. This chapter offers guidelines for how to structure the activity of performance counseling so it is optimally effective and valued by all parties.

Although the specific job description for chairs and deans can vary from one institution to another, virtually all chairs and deans find themselves responsible for the professional development of faculty and staff—and chairs in particular have this responsibility as they hold positions that permit them to obtain firsthand observations of faculty and staff performance. When faculty and staff do not meet performance expectations, chairs and deans must clarify expectations and provide direction and support to enhance faculty and staff performance. Both chairs and deans typically have a formal role in tenure and promotion review, the allocation of merit pay, and other personnel matters that require formal comment on faculty and staff work performance and achievement. But providing required comment on faculty or staff performance as prescribed by such personnel policies is only one component of chair and dean responsibility in the continuous professional development of faculty and staff.

Chairs, and to a lesser extent deans, are in a position to observe faculty and staff performance on a regular basis. Since chairs and deans are responsible for advancing the institutional mission, they must exercise leadership that helps to ensure that faculty and staff members meet performance expectations. If, for example, the institution's mission requires that faculty understand and then teach to the varied learning needs of students, chairs and deans need to help faculty meet this performance expectation. Thus, by carrying out their role responsibilities, chairs and deans find they must offer constructive comment on faculty and staff performance and effectiveness. Even when an institution does not have a formal policy that requires performance review, chairs and deans will find that engaging in ongoing performance counseling with faculty and staff is essential to fulfilling their leadership responsibility.

The task of offering constructive comment on a faculty or staff member's performance can be uncomfortable for chairs and deans. Especially when the chair or dean was promoted from within the institution to the current leadership position, the responsibility of offering constructive comment on faculty and staff performance can be uncomfortable as they now find themselves cast in the position of being critical of long-time colleagues. Ironically, the greater the need for constructive comment to enhance performance, the more chairs and deans are likely to dread their responsibility to offer comment on the ways in which performance must be improved. This is understandable since individual faculty may become defensive when confronted with the need to improve some aspect of performance. Even the most constructive comments can be received as unwelcome criticism, which can make the situation uncomfortable for both chairs and deans. Uncomfortable or not, chairs and deans cannot be successful if they shirk their responsibility for enhancing faculty and staff performance; thus, success often requires that chairs and deans become more comfortable with the task.

It can help to reconceptualize the task of reviewing faculty and staff performance. We suggest using the term *performance counseling* instead of *performance evaluation* because there is a significant difference in the connotative understandings associated with these two terms. *Evaluation* suggests a critical dimension that places the chair and dean in the role of judge or critic. The word *counseling* implies a broader concept that suggests both assessment and coaching. Typically, chairs and deans are more comfortable in the role of coach than critic. Similarly, faculty and staff prefer to be coached rather than judged. The shift in terminology is more than just semantics; it offers a reconceptualization that helps to transform a difficult task into a more manageable one. It also helps to transition an activity from one that is often resisted into an activity that is valued by faculty and staff.

Transforming resisted (and sometimes resented) performance evaluation into constructive and valued performance counseling requires more than using a new terminology. It also requires a change in how the task is structured and carried out. Traditionally, performance review is conducted in accordance with institutional policy. As such, the implicit objective is meeting policy expectations rather than investing in the professional development of individual faculty and staff. Evaluation meetings are conducted as prescribed by the policy, and often policy prescribes only an annual meeting. This gives the process a very formal feel, and typically chairs and deans only take the action minimally required by the policy. If, for example, the policy prescribes one meeting each year, then that is what is usually scheduled, and neither chair or dean nor faculty or staff member seek more interaction regarding an individual's performance.

Yet as educators we recognize that learning and improvement requires frequent and continuous feedback. This suggests that, to be optimally effective, performance counseling should be year-round and not yearly. Similarly, if the institutional policy prescribes annual performance review only for untenured faculty, chairs and deans may fail to offer the same level of professional development support to tenured faculty. At the same time, when academic programs are assessed for teaching effectiveness, program review considers the performance of all faculty members—not just the untenured ones.

The shift from performance evaluation to performance counseling also requires chairs and deans to provide faculty and staff with different information. In performance evaluation, there is a greater emphasis on summative information including, for example, student evaluations of teaching and the number of articles published. With performance counseling, however, there is a greater emphasis on formative feedback. The difference is significant in that the focus on formative feedback helps individual faculty and staff know what to work on to realize improvement. Student evaluations may be discussed, but chairs and deans go beyond the numeric scores and work with the individual faculty member to consider what the student evaluation scores mean and to brainstorm alternatives for enhancing performance and student learning. With performance counseling, the focus is on the professional development of the individual faculty or staff member, meaning that the chair or the dean works with the individual to generate very specific and concrete ways to improve overall performance.

In addition, the shift from performance evaluation to performance counseling requires a different commitment and involvement from faculty and staff. Specifically, performance counseling requires that faculty and staff be involved in self-assessment and goal setting. Faculty and staff assume an active role in performance counseling, whereas in performance evaluation, faculty and staff typically assume a more passive role as they listen to the chair or dean critique their performance. When faculty and staff are actively engaged in the performance counseling process, they will be less resistant to and resentful of the process and the constructive strategies being considered. These shifts in content and process can reframe the activity from one that is resisted to one that is valued by faculty and staff, which optimizes the benefit for all parties as well as the institution. Nevertheless, creating a climate for constructive performance counseling is not easy, especially when individuals resist any effort to assess performance or discuss ways to enhance performance.

THE UNRULY, UNTENURED FACULTY MEMBER

Consider the example of an untenured faculty member who fails to seek counsel when needed for fear of hurting his or her chances for tenure. It is not uncommon for faculty to put the best possible spin on events during the annual performance sessions required of all untenured faculty members. Though understandable, this practice does not enhance performance and it denies the individual faculty member the professional development support important to continuous improvement. While a faculty member may recognize that there is a problem or an area which needs improvement, an effective performance counseling session will help define the salient issues and provide the faculty member with a blueprint for action designed to help him or her make acceptable progress toward tenure. Further, a faculty member can enhance his or her bid for tenure by demonstrating the ability to welcome and respond constructively to suggestions for improving performance. However, this can only happen if the performance counseling is honest and constructive. Should the chair or dean decide, for whatever reason, to soft pedal evaluative comments, the individual faculty or staff member is denied the full benefit of the chair's or dean's support. However, this does not suggest that chairs or deans make mean or hurtful evaluative comments. But it does obligate chairs and deans to offer constructive and relevant evaluative comments that help the individual faculty or staff member more accurately understand the issue and need for enhancing performance.

Assume the position of department chair and consider how you might manage an annual performance review prescribed by campus policy for an untenured faculty member, Dr. Chessman. Dr. Chessman is not making acceptable progress toward tenure, and in particular, the student evaluations of his teaching are mediocre. In addition, several faculty members have complained about the way in which Dr. Chessman engages in committee service. Students report that Dr. Chessman's class is disorganized, the learning objectives and grading criteria are unclear, and that he becomes unreasonably defensive when asked questions in class. Comments from faculty colleagues suggest that Dr. Chessman is overbearing about getting his way on committees. The comments suggest that he likes to take control by prescribing what should be accomplished and is relentless in pestering other committee members to get the work done by phoning them or visiting their offices in between meetings, just to make sure that they are doing the assigned work and doing it correctly (or as prescribed by Dr. Chessman). Unfortunately, Dr. Chessman is perceived as being controlling and overbearing rather than task oriented and hard working.

How might you present this information to Dr. Chessman? Ideally, you would want to provide information that offers him every opportunity to improve his performance in the classroom and with his faculty colleagues. Unless Dr. Chessman is made aware of how students and faculty colleagues perceive his work, he will likely persist in the unsuccessful behavior that has netted him undesirable assessments from students and colleagues. Because you recognize that Dr. Chessman is quick to become defensive, you realize that merely informing him of student and faculty colleague assessments will not be sufficient to motivate Dr. Chessman to work on improving his performance. You have noticed that he appears nervous and tense with the slightest suggestion that something be done differently. Yet unless Dr. Chessman addresses these issues, he will not have a legitimate opportunity to earn student and faculty colleague evaluations that will build a positive application for tenure.

How might you structure the conversation to get the desired result without making Dr. Chessman so defensive that he is unable to hear the comments on his performance or understand the suggestions for improving his teaching and his working relationships with colleagues? What might you do in advance of the meeting to help him perceive the performance counseling as something beneficial to him? What might you do in advance of the meeting to help Dr. Chessman know that as chair, you are committed to his professional development? The professional rapport and credibility that chairs and deans have with individual faculty and staff members are essential to effective performance counseling. Chairs and deans should take every opportunity to preserve a credible and effective rapport with faculty and staff because it is more difficult to build credibility in situations that carry a high potential for conflict. When chairs and deans must coach a defensive faculty or staff member to improved performance, there is the potential for conflict.

Assume you have an excellent rapport with Dr. Chessman and think how you would structure the conversation(s) in which you coach him to improve his performance. You would want to approach the counseling in a way that permits Dr. Chessman to understand that you share his goal. Both of you seek an outcome that allows for Dr. Chessman to be professionally successful. Both of you want his expertise and teaching to be fully appreciated by students, and both of you want his hard work and leadership to be fully valued by his faculty colleagues. Rather than starting with the evaluative comments that are likely to make Dr. Chessman defensive, you would start with building the framework that empowers him to hear and make constructive use of the evaluative comments.

This example helps to illustrate the advantage of reconceptualizing the task from one of performance evaluation to one of performance counseling. If the overarching objective is to counsel and coach Dr. Chessman to successful tenure application, it places the chair and Dr. Chessman on the same side of the issue. If, however, the chair's role is to evaluate Dr. Chessman's performance, the session places the two parties on opposite sides, with one being the judge and critic and the other being the subject of the criticism. Even when chairs and deans do everything possible to frame performance counseling as a constructive activity, they can encounter faculty and staff who remain difficult to counsel.

Consider how you might manage the session if Dr. Chessman becomes emotional in response to learning the feedback from faculty colleagues. What would you do if his emotional response is to assert how hard he is working and offer details as to why he believes that he works harder than anyone else on the committee, and how the work would not get done if he didn't check on his colleagues? Would you listen quietly? If so, how do you think Dr. Chessman might interpret your silence? He might, for example, view your silence as understanding and support for his view. Or, he might interpret your silence to mean the situation is hopeless. Either way, while it is important to hear Dr. Chessman's view, silence will likely not be sufficient to counsel him about how to improve his performance. Would you console Dr, Chessman, and if so, how would you do that? Would you investigate the disagreement further or in any way assess his charge that other faculty do not work as hard as he does? It is important that you help Dr. Chessman see his performance as others perceive it.

For performance counseling to work, chairs and deans need to stay on the issue. The purpose of the meeting is to review feedback that will permit Dr. Chessman to improve his work performance. If you move to a discussion of how hard he works or how hard other faculty work, you will have permitted Dr. Chessman to alter the agenda for the meeting. This may serve to provide Dr. Chessman with immediate reassurance, but it will not help the initial purpose for the meeting. Further, if reassurance is offered in a way that permits Dr. Chessman to conclude that you, as his chair, understand (and believe) that he works harder than his faculty colleagues, you may unintentionally give him license to continue the same behavior, and this will likely escalate conflict between Dr. Chessman and his colleagues.

This is not to suggest that reassurances should be withheld as there are times when it can be helpful to a person's professional development. But chairs and deans need to be careful when providing reassurances so that they do not cancel or undermine the purpose of the performance counseling. You might, for example, need to reassure Dr. Chessman that the purpose for performance counseling is to fuel his professional development and enhance his success at the institution. This is very different from offering reassurance that permits him to believe you are siding with him on differences he may have with colleagues or students.

Effective performance counseling requires you as chair and dean to be perceived as a credible and supportive ally in the sense that you want those you counsel to be successful. If, however, chairs and deans acquire the requisite credibility by creating the impression of taking sides, the performance counseling will never be effective in the long term because taking sides will condition individual faculty and staff to dismiss coaching when they perceive you as agreeing with evaluative comments they cannot accept. Instead of hearing the coaching, difficult and defensive faculty members will attribute the counsel to the belief that the chair or dean has sided against them.

THE EXPERIENCED PROFESSOR VERSUS NEW STUDENTS

Consider how you might engage in performance counseling with the tenured senior professor who is well regarded across campus. As students change, even faculty who have had long careers of teaching effectiveness need to consider new pedagogies. Especially as colleges recruit students with wide variations in academic preparation and learning styles, it is possible to find that the most revered and experienced professor is the target of student complaints. These cases are often sensitive because the better the faculty member, the more pride that the faculty member will have in his or her work. At the same time, the institution may not have a policy that requires post-tenure review. Nevertheless, chairs and deans cannot ignore the need to support the professional development of tenured faculty, and this support inevitably entails some performance counseling. As chairs and deans are accountable for preserving academic quality, this responsibility in turn demands that chairs and deans work with all faculty members to continuously enhance performance.

How would you manage receiving a series of complaints from students enrolled in a course taught by a tenured full professor? A very experienced and committed senior faculty member agreed to help the department by teaching a 100-level course typically staffed with a graduate assistant. You are confident that the faculty member knows the subject, and you assume all is going well until students start complaining. There are some common themes in the complaints including, for example, the students' perceptions that the faculty member "isn't teaching" and "embarrasses" students in class when they do not know or understand the material. As chair, you find these comments hard to believe given the professor's experience level and passion for teaching. What might you do to gain a better understanding of what is happening in the class? Would you ask to observe the next class? Would you talk with the professor about the complaints? Would you remind the students that this professor is one of the best in the department and perhaps encourage them to try harder? Take a moment to consider the various options.

Each alternative course of action has consequences that must be considered. For example, reporting the complaints to the professor might cause the faculty member to become so defensive that the situation will be more difficult to manage to a satisfactory outcome. At the same time, you might appropriately believe that faculty members have a right to know when a complaint has been made about them or their teaching. Similarly, if you elect to sit in on the next class, your action will communicate something to the professor and to the students. Can you anticipate what each party might infer from your presence in the next class, and is this helpful or hurtful to resolving the conflict? Even when a number of student complaints echo a common theme, they represent only the student perspective. It is helpful to understand all relevant perspectives when managing a conflict. In this instance, it would be helpful to learn the faculty member's perspective.

What you would do if, before talking with the professor about the student complaints, the professor approaches you with complaints about the students? The professor tells you that the first-year students are often late and unprepared for class, many are bold about text messaging friends during class, and they whine when assignments are made. The professor is genuinely worried that students are not learning and finds it necessary to repeat the same material several times because students are not willing to do assigned reading or other homework before coming to class. Would you share the students' complaints with the professor? If so, how would you frame the conversation and present the information?

You might, for example, offer student comments as a way to understand how they perceive their responsibility in the class and as information that might be useful to the professor in strategizing the next step to helping the students learn the material. Picking up on the information reported by the professor, you might say, "I believe you're right. Students are not learning as they should in the course." The professor is likely to ask what you know, and you might continue, "A few of your students were in to talk with me about the course. It seems that they feel put on the spot and embarrassed when it becomes clear that they do not know the material—perhaps because, as you say, they are not staying up with the work." Ideally, this would break the ice and frame a discussion of student learning in the class. As chair, you could then engage the professor in brainstorming various approaches that might be tried to affect a better outcome.

Even a tenured full professor is likely to appreciate the chair's counsel in managing a difficult class. The collaborative, coaching approach makes it easier for the chair to follow up at a later time with the professor to inquire about progress. The exchange also empowers the chair to inform the students that the professor is concerned about them and to raise with the students their responsibility for doing the work. Most individuals are forgiving of situations if they believe that their view has been heard and that other parties are attempting to respond to the concerns raised. Hence, whether complaints are raised by students, faculty, staff, or parents, chairs and deans can manage conflict more comfortably and effectively if they begin by truly hearing and understanding the concerns that have been raised. This is not to suggest that the chair or dean must agree with the concern raised for it to be heard. Rather, the process of hearing a concern involves active listening, which reflects an understanding of the concern from the perspective of the person or persons raising it.

INCORPORATING THE DEAN'S INPUT

Would you change the way you manage the situation if you received a call from the dean informing you that a number of students and a few parents have complained to him about the class? The dean adds that the students are threatening to transfer to another institution, and the parents have requested that a different instructor take over the class by next week. How might your relationship with the dean influence how you respond? Would your response, for example, take into account the fact that your relationship with the dean is characterized by a high degree of mutual respect and trust? How might knowing the dean's assessment of salient issues influence your response? Would your reply, for example, incorporate your knowledge that the dean believes student retention is the overarching top priority of the institution? If so, how would this information help to shape your reply? Similarly, would your perception of the dean's regard for the department or for the senior faculty member influence your response, and if so, how would it alter your reply? Should the dean's view of the department or the faculty member influence your reply?

Managing conflict is not a matter of taking sides or deciding who is right. Managing conflict involves understanding the perspectives of all relevant parties and helping all sides find the common ground or common objective. In this instance, all relevant parties are concerned about student learning. The conflict exists because each party has a different view of how student learning happens. The students believe it happens when the faculty member "teaches" the materials and places less importance on the need to do the assigned work. The professor believes that student learning requires student engagement in the course and that places a premium on doing assigned work. The dean most likely believes that effective faculty will find a way to promote student learning, even when today's students seem preoccupied with text messaging and other matters.

ANALYSIS AND APPLICATIONS

To be effective, performance counseling must be an ongoing activity. Evaluative comments that make job expectations clear and set specific, manageable goals move the needed changes from something personal to specific behaviors and actions that can be modified for improvement. Faculty and staff need to perceive the review process as counseling (coaching), not evaluation (criticism). Chairs and deans can help foster a constructive faculty and staff perception of performance counseling by creating a context of the review that is other-centered, by providing faculty and staff with concrete and specific examples and suggestions, and by recognizing and supporting improvement. These characteristics of performance counseling help to make the process and the evaluator's intent credible and constructive in the minds of faculty and staff. Chairs and deans can further reduce anxiety sometimes associated with performance evaluation by establishing a culture and expectation for continuous performance counseling that encompasses both informal and formal comment. When these leadership communication strategies are employed, chairs and deans can transform an uncomfortable process into one that is both comfortable and effective in enhancing performance and supporting professional development. This transformation effectively reduces the conflict that can accrue for performance evaluation. Let's review the essential elements of each application:

- Reconceptualize the task.
- Create a faculty- or staff-centered context.
- Be concrete and specific.
- Establish expectations for continual performance counseling.
- Recognize and support improvement.

◆ Reconceptualize the task.

By reconceptualizing the task from performance evaluation to performance counseling, chairs and deans transform their role from critic to coach. This single change has the effect of placing chairs and deans in a supportive role which in turn minimizes the potential for conflict. Whether working with an untenured faculty member or a tenured full professor, chairs and deans will find that coaching meets less resistance than criticism. The same complaint or concern can be presented as counsel or as criticism, and while the difference may seem subtle to chairs and deans, the difference can be huge to the subject of the performance review.

In the instance of the tenured full professor, the concern that students believe the faculty member is not teaching is one that would offend most senior faculty. Presented as a fact, it represents a criticism that attacks the integrity and professorial ability of the faculty member. It is easy to see how the tenured full professor might become defensive and even angry that the chair or dean could take such student comments seriously. Yet when the same concern is presented in a counseling framework, the criticism becomes a piece of the puzzle—a clue that helps the faculty member and chair work together to understand today's students. Similarly, in the example of Dr. Chessman, a summative evaluation could result in Dr. Chessman becoming angry with his colleagues. By employing a counseling perspective, the chair can help redirect Dr. Chessman's approach more easily because it is understood that both parties want him to be successful.

◆ Create a faculty- or staff-centered context.

Chairs and deans can enhance performance counseling by framing evaluative comments and suggestions by using the other-centered context. Whether the "other" is a faculty member, student, or staff member, chairs and deans will be more effective in obtaining cooperation if they create a context that permits the other to hear and internalize the evaluative comments. The tenured full professor, for example, will more likely hear and internalize student concerns if he perceives that the chair or dean is not simply placing blame but has an appreciation for the professor's situation.

Similarly, Dr. Chessman will be better able to hear that his faculty colleagues perceive his actions as overbearing if he believes that the chair or dean recognizes that he works hard and that his effort to make certain the work gets done is, in general, a positive and valued attribute. Creating the other-centered context can alter the dynamic from one in which the person receiving the evaluative comments feels criticized to one in which the person feels supported. Effective performance counseling facilitates professional development, and it is virtually impossible to support a person's professional development without working from and within a context that takes into account that person's perspective.

◆ Be concrete and specific.

For counseling to improve performance, chairs and deans need to give concrete examples of problematic behaviors and specific suggestions for improvement. If the faculty or staff member does not understand an evaluative comment, it will be virtually impossible to realize improvement. A concrete example can help bring the needed clarity. It is more powerful, for example, when a chair or dean goes beyond telling a faculty member that students find the grading criteria unclear and instead reviews with the faculty member various ways to clarify grading criteria presented in the syllabus. Similarly, if a faculty or staff member is unable to comprehend how to implement the suggestion for improvement, little will be gained.

Effective performance counseling demands the use of concrete and specific examples at every step of the process. First, concrete and specific examples of the problem behaviors are essential to helping that person understand why certain behaviors are problematic. Dr. Chessman, for example, needs to know precisely what he is doing that causes his colleagues to find him overbearing. The use of specific examples helps to depersonalize performance counseling discussions. In other words, it is not Dr. Chessman who is overbearing, but certain specific behaviors give some the impression that he is overbearing. It is not Dr. Chessman who is overbearing, but when he stops by a colleague's office in between meetings to check on work, he appears to be overbearing.

Second, chairs and deans need to offer concrete and specific suggestions for improvement. It does little good to tell a faculty member to "stop embarrassing students" or to "cease being overbearing with colleagues" because unless the faculty member understands precisely what actions contribute to these outcomes and specifically what actions would alter these outcomes, the faculty member is not fully empowered to improve his or her performance. Suggestions should be very concrete and specific. In working with Dr. Chessman, for example, the chair might suggest that he wait until the next meeting to learn what work had been done by his colleagues and not pester them in between meetings. In working with the tenured full professor, the chair might suggest that student questions be repeated and that the class be invited to help answer them as a way to prevent students from feeling embarrassed by the faculty member when asking a question. The desired change or outcome will be easier to achieve if chairs and deans offer concrete and specific suggestions for enhancing performance.

◆ Establish expectations for continual performance counseling.

Chairs and deans need to be clear and specific about performance counseling itself. It is important that everyone understand that performance counseling is a year-round and not a yearly activity because chair and dean support of professional development needs to be continual. When faculty and staff expect performance counseling to be continual, chairs and deans find it easier to offer both formal and informal evaluative comments about what is going well and what might be tried differently. If evaluative comments are constructive and flow freely, there is less anxiety about performance counseling than if faculty members hear the chair or dean assessment of their performance in an annual meeting.

The timetable for continual performance counseling should be guided by the issue under discussion. For example, in working with Dr. Chessman on the need to make grading criteria clear to students, the chair might suggest that he and Dr. Chessman review the syllabus before each term begins and then review student evaluations following the term to learn if students continue to find the grading criteria to be unclear. In working with the tenured full professor to have students recognize that the instructor is assuming responsibility for teaching the class and why doing the assigned work before each class is important, the chair may wish to meet with the faculty member on a regular basis until the concerns have been addressed.

◆ Recognize and support improvement.

Faculty and staff will be more inclined to continue to work for improvement if their efforts are noted. Chairs and deans can motivate further positive action by commenting specifically on progress made or effort invested. Often such recognition of good effort and progress can be accompanied by specific suggestions for further improvement. For example, once Dr. Chessman becomes convinced that he does not need to check on the work being done by his faculty colleagues in between meetings, the next step might be to encourage him to listen to the suggestions of others during the meeting.

Chairs and deans should not rely on financial recognition to encourage performance improvement. Although it is constructive when progress can be rewarded with merit pay or other tangible rewards, it is a mistake to assume that these are the only forms of recognition available. Especially when chairs and deans employ a performance counseling approach to performance review, their personal acknowledgement that a faculty or staff member has made progress will carry a lot of weight. Often such recognition can be informal and private, but it must be credible to the faculty or staff member. When chairs and deans recognize improvement, they encourage and support further improvement.

SOME FINAL THOUGHTS

The continuous professional development of faculty and staff is essential to the long-term health of the department and the institution. Since performance review is fundamental to professional development, chairs and deans find themselves responsible for performance review. Even when institutional policy does not prescribe performance review, chairs and deans will not realize the professional development needed to staff a quality program if they fail to engage in evaluative reviews of faculty and staff performance.

The responsibility to offer evaluative comments on faculty and staff performance can be uncomfortable for chairs and deans. There is typically a direct correlation between chair and dean discomfort and faculty and staff performance in that the more a faculty or staff member is in need of evaluative comment to improve performance, the more uncomfortable the task becomes for chairs and deans. When faculty and staff performance meets or exceeds expectations, the task of offering evaluative comment is easier and more comfortable. Put more simply, it is easier to give praise than it is to suggest improvement. The discomfort experienced by chairs and deans can be attributed to the potential for conflict. Chairs and deans realize that most faculty and staff prefer to receive praise rather than suggestions for improvement, and when hardworking faculty and staff receive suggestions for improvement, they can become defensive and confrontational. When this happens, chairs and deans find themselves managing conflict.

Chairs and deans can make the process of offering evaluative comments more comfortable for themselves and for faculty and staff by reconceptualizing the task. Instead of framing the task as performance evaluation, which implies a critical dimension, we recommend conceptualizing the task as performance counseling, which places chairs and deans in the role of coach. Performance counseling empowers chairs and deans to frame evaluative comments and suggestions for improvement as advice that is directed toward helping an individual faculty or staff member be more successful.

Managing Faculty Morale, Changing Duties, and Shrinking Resources

Higher education must respond to changing conditions, which inevitably means that the performance expectations and job descriptions of faculty and staff are ever evolving. Such change can take a toll on faculty morale unless chairs and deans can implement change in ways that help faculty become proficient and comfortable in performing new tasks or managing old tasks in new ways. This chapter will offer current illustrations of how chairs and deans can manage faculty morale in the face of changing duties and scare resources.

It is a challenging time in higher education. Institutions must respond to changing expectations and varied learning styles of students; there is greater public skepticism about the quality of higher education, which creates increasing pressure for institutional accountability; competition for students has increased; and institutions face new accreditation criteria that expect all individuals and initiatives to be about the business of advancing the institutional mission and enhancing quality. Moreover, institutions must manage all of this with finite and scare resources. These challenges not only alter performance expectations for faculty and staff, but they also alter leadership expectations for campus administrators—especially chairs and deans. How chairs and deans lead and work with faculty and staff through the current challenges will have a direct influence on morale which in turn influences productivity and institutional success.

To be effective, institutions must engage the diverse talents of all faculty and staff. The once familiar top-down leadership model, in which a strong president and/or chief academic officer made all key decisions and led by directing the individual efforts of various constituencies, is not an effective leadership style today. Because the nature and scope of the challenges facing higher education require more perspective than any one person could possibly possess, the leadership model has evolved. These challenges require the central administration to work with faculty and staff in ways that bring multiple and varied perspectives and expertise together to help solve significant problems. The need for collaborative problem-solving alters the role of every campus constituency because, when done effectively, faculty and staff assume ownership of the challenges facing higher education. The need to recruit and retain students, for example, is no longer only the administration's concern but has also become a priority for faculty and staff.

The changing roles and responsibilities of faculty can be a difficult adjustment for many, especially long-term faculty. These faculty members entered higher education at a time when faculty enjoyed more autonomy and were not directly involved in addressing such pressing institutional matters as marketing the institution or seeking new revenue streams. The challenges facing higher education today rival the once popular stereotypic thinking that placed the faculty and the administration at opposite ends of every continuum and perpetuated animosity between them. The challenges facing higher education today require the administration and the faculty to work collaboratively. Institutions that lack a successful collaboration between the faculty and the central administration will suffer a significant disadvantage in meeting the challenges facing higher education because the best solutions are ones that require the support and cooperation of both the faculty and the administration to implement.

Chairs and deans find that their success depends on being able to bridge that gap between the faculty and the administration as they hold positions of leadership between the faculty and the central administration. Chairs, for example, find themselves agents of change because they must implement new initiatives. Even when everyone recognizes that a particular change is good, the implementation of new policies and practices can be stressful. Chairs must lead faculty and staff through the stress to implement the agreed-upon change. Deans discover that their success depends on the leadership ability of department chairs to implement change. Deans may manage the chair's front-line leadership role, but they are reliant on chairs to achieve the desired outcome.

Change alone can threaten faculty morale, but new responsibilities add to the struggle because new performance expectations require faculty to engage in tasks for which they were not trained and in which they may have little interest. Indeed, some new responsibilities may be so foreign to what faculty members expect to do that their jobs become unrecognizable. Senior tenured faculty find themselves doing work that they did not sign on to do. Depending on the type of institution, faculty may be engaged in very intentional ways to improve student recruitment and retention, assess student learning, or prepare a familiar course for online delivery. Faculty today find themselves reviewing productivity data that offer a glimpse of how attractive their courses are to students. Faculty members work to find and supervise internships and other experiential learning opportunities for students. They work to transform material once presented as a lecture into a class exercise that permits the students to engage with the subject. To some faculty, the job is no longer recognizable. While these changes will exhilarate some, they can also take a toll on faculty morale.

Productive faculty members do not enjoy idyllic lives of leisurely reflection but instead endure very full days. Faculty members quickly become overworked when they attempt to add new performance expectations on top of old responsibilities. Yet it is difficult to surrender the familiar tasks. Resources do not permit institutions to hire more faculty members to handle the new work, so it falls to chairs and deans to persuade the faculty to change what they do or how they work. This can be difficult and painful, especially for faculty who distrust technology and prefer, for example, to keep their own handwritten files on the academic degree progress of the students they advise rather than use the electronic student file, which includes an automated course evaluation that summarizes precisely what students need to take to satisfy degree requirements.

Chairs and deans need to be cognizant of faculty reaction to new performance expectations and adjust the implementation of such change accordingly. Some new tasks will become easier with faculty development while others may require some creative matching of skill and experience to the task. For example, the approval of a new interdisciplinary common course required of all students will need at least some investment in faculty development for those who teach the course. At the same time, it is likely that not all faculty members will be well suited to teach an interdisciplinary common experience course, no matter how much development support is provided.

Some change is designed to enhance faculty productivity and/or effectiveness. For example, the implementation of software designed to enhance faculty communication with students can save faculty time while providing students with easier access to faculty and course materials. Even though such change strategies are designed to alleviate faculty workload, they can hurt morale because faculty can be rather territorial about specific courses they teach and tasks they perform. Faculty can become set in their ways, and the introduction of new software or methods that require some retooling can breed resistance, and at times even resentment, unless faculty recognize the benefits of supporting the change.

Change can be especially difficult for faculty who previously possessed a greater degree of autonomy. New responsibilities require a significant amount of collaboration and teamwork. In contrast to developing a course syllabus and grading papers, new responsibilities such as creating an assessment plan or developing ways to integrate career preparation across the curriculum require group discussion and cooperative action. Collaboration requires faculty and staff to meet with colleagues, and this in turn creates a structure to the day that has the effect of changing the conditions for faculty who at one time were able to set their own hours. This is not to suggest that faculty did not work hard in earlier decades, but the expectation for more extensive collaboration on such major initiatives as assessment of student learning has altered the prerogative that faculty exercised in establishing personal schedules for when and where they worked to prepare lectures or grade papers.

HANDLING PROPOSED BENEFIT CUTS

Think about how faculty typically react when they learn that the institution is unable to fund an annual salary increase. Even faculty who understand the impact of low enrollment on budget will not relish the news of a missed salary increase. It is difficult for individual faculty and staff to adopt an institutional perspective when interpreting actions that have very personal ramifications. This is understandable, but it illustrates the importance of framing decisions and outcomes in a way that minimizes the personal perspective. Without a clear and accurate understanding of the facts and conditions that led to a particular decision, there is an increased likelihood that individuals will interpret decisions and outcomes from a very personal perspective. When this happens, collaborative decision-making and shared governance crumble, and sound decisions can be perceived as having hurtful motives.

Suppose a small private institution is wrestling with increasing health care costs. For decades, the institution took pride in keeping the employee contribution to health care premiums small, but escalating health care costs no longer make this practice feasible. The administration has held a number of open forums to relate the facts to faculty and staff in an effort to explain that the only way the same quality of health care can be provided is to gradually, over a period of some years, increase the employee contribution to the health care premium to 15%. The administration presented regional and national data that demonstrated the typical employee contribution at other institutions is significantly greater than 15%. Yet despite sharing health care costs and budget information, faculty perceive the decision as an unfair reduction in faculty compensation.

Assume the role of chair and consider what you might say should the faculty in your department seek your support of their view that the decision to increase health care premiums is yet another example of how the administration will cut institutional costs at the expense of faculty. Would you agree with them? Would you repeat some of the data presented at the open forums in an effort to explain the decision as a reasonable (and fair) response to some difficult circumstances? What might faculty say that may influence your reply? What would you say, for example, if the faculty contend that the administration could afford salary increases if they wanted to recognize the hard work done by the faculty? Would your response be the same if the faculty threatened to refuse all service assignments in the event they receive no salary increase or that benefit costs increase? Your response is likely to vary with the faculty perspective because the position taken by the faculty indicates the thinking that must be addressed. The first faculty statement makes clear that they do not believe that data demonstrate that the budget will not support a salary increase or that health care costs should rise. Instead, the first statement illustrates faculty believe that it is a willful act on the part of the administration. The second faculty reaction to the change in health care coverage does not comment on the believability of the budget data, but issues a threat that suggests the faculty perceive the administration as exercising unreasonable control over events that affect faculty welfare.

How might your assigned role responsibilities influence your response? As chair, you occupy a position of front-line leadership, which means you are responsible for representing the central administration's view to the faculty and the faculty's view to the administration. How might you reconcile these two seemingly opposite responsibilities? Is it possible to be true to two different constituencies when they do not agree? What might happen if you shared with each constituency the views held by the other? If presented factually and honestly, taking this action might enable the administration to respond constructively to faculty concerns while helping faculty better understand the basis for the unpopular decision.

As chair, your ability to make a positive difference as a front-line leader will correlate directly with the credibility you possess with each constituency. If, for example, the faculty perceive you as having "joined the administration" or "pro-administration" in your perspective, you will be less able to help the faculty understand the basis for the administration's decision. Similarly, if the administration perceives you as "pushing the faculty agenda" without consideration for the larger institutional context, you will be less able to capture the administration's attention. It is your credibility with each constituency that empowers you to both lead and represent the faculty. Your credibility correlates directly with your ability to manage conflict between parties or constituencies. Hence, assessing your leadership credibility with each constituency is an essential element of deciding what action would be most helpful and effective. If, for example, you recognize that the faculty perceive you as championing the wishes of the administration at the expense of the faculty, it will do little good for you to repeat data presented by the administration at the open forums. Instead, you might listen to the faculty concerns so you can learn and then help the administration know why the data presented thus far has been unpersuasive in demonstrating the need to increase the employee contribution to the health care premium.

Now assume the role of dean in this illustration and imagine a meeting with faculty during which you hear their concerns about the increase in employee contribution to the health care premium. They are reasoned in their presentation and exhibit some understanding of the fiscal conditions that fueled the decision. At the same time, they express a serious desire to avoid increasing the employee contribution to the health care premium. The nine faculty members meeting with you sense that a lower employee contribution to the health care premium can only be saved if the sum to be covered by employee contributions is found elsewhere in the budget. One faculty member suggests that the sum might be obtained from changing the institutional policy on tuition remission. Currently, faculty and staff can enroll up to two dependents for a cost of 5% of the full tuition price. The suggestion is to alter the tuition remission policy so that faculty and staff using this benefit pay half the tuition instead of merely 5% of the tuition cost. Another faculty member offers a friendly amendment by suggesting that tuition remission remain at 5%, but that the benefit can be for faculty only. A third faculty member takes the conversation in a very different direction by suggesting that any salary increase be adjusted downward to preserve the lower employee contribution to the health care benefit.

As dean, how would you manage this conversation? What do the specific and varied suggestions tell you about the faculty perception? Health care, tuition remission, and salary increases are all employee benefits. When faculty members disagree on the distribution of such benefits, it typically reveals that they are expressing a preference based on their individual position. For example, faculty who do not benefit from the tuition remission policy are generally more willing to cut it before other benefits that they use. Differences can also develop over the method to be employed in distributing a benefit. For example, long-term faculty earning higher salaries typically prefer a salary increase model that calculates salary increases as a percentage of the faculty member's base pay, whereas newer faculty with lower salaries typically prefer a model that calculates salary increases as a flat dollar amount that is added to everyone's base pay.

As dean, what hope do you have for reaching consensus when this happens? How might the variation in individual faculty preferences enable you to manage the conflict regarding the increase in employee contribution to the health care premium? You might, for example, point out that any action will be unpopular with some and the one targeted for increase affects all faculty and staff equally. What might happen if you asked faculty to discus such alternatives among themselves and bring the matter back when consensus is reached? If you do this, you would need to be ready to discuss any alternative action on which the faculty members agree. This is not a sound approach if a decision has been made and there is no opportunity to reconsider that decision. Generally, chairs and deans will lose credibility with the faculty if they invite them to engage in meaningless or futile exercises. Few things lower faculty morale more quickly than asking faculty to commit time and energy to a project that does not materialize.

SUPPORTING FACULTY INITIATIVES

Consider a situation where the institution is unable to support or fund a faculty-led initiative. Typically, new initiatives are vulnerable to cancellation if they do not take off as anticipated. Consider, for example, faculty-led study tours at a mid-size university. Although the university's mission values experiential learning and faculty are encouraged to use such innovative pedagogies, the practicalities of funding faculty-led travel will override interest and appreciation if the study tour does not enroll the requisite number of students. While this may be understandable as a general operating principle, the cancellation of a faculty-led study tour for low enrollment can feel very personal as the tour is identified with a particular faculty member who has invested enormous time and energy in developing the program of study.

Consider the example of Dr. Tripp, whose passion for Asia propelled her to develop a semester-long study tour that she and one other colleague would lead. As chair, you were aware that Dr. Tripp was working on this program, and the dean made it clear that the tour could not go forward with fewer than 25 students. This enrollment minimum was reached by calculating the cost of the trip. You knew that that it would be difficult to recruit 25 students. You shared your thoughts with Dr. Tripp early in the process in an effort to avoid a situation where she expended a lot of energy on a study tour only to have it canceled for low enrollment. Ever the optimist, Dr. Tripp took up the challenge. At one point, you suggested that she revise the format to offer a two-week intercession tour because you believe that a shorter trip might be more affordable and attractive to the students. However, Dr. Tripp insists that the subject warrants a full semester tour. It seems that nothing you said persuaded Dr. Tripp to make the modifications that you believe would have the study tour fill more easily.

Now, your fear has been realized. Only 14 students have enrolled in the study tour, and the dean tells you that the tour will need to be canceled. You relay the news to Dr. Tripp, who doesn't take it well. How would you answer Dr. Tripp when she professes that the administration does not support her or her work and that you, as chair, have failed to advocate on her behalf? Would you remind Dr. Tripp that you warned her about this possibility and that she failed to heed the suggestions you made to make the study tour available to more students? Would you relay Dr. Tripp's response to the dean to see if there is any possibility the study tour could be reinstated? Would your response be different if Dr. Tripp was one year away from retirement and you knew that this would be her last opportunity to lead the study tour to Asia? Would your response be different if the 14 students enrolled in the study tour were all seniors? Would it make a difference if the 14 students visited you and pleaded for the study tour, saying that the missed opportunity to travel through Asia with Dr. Tripp would be the loss of a once-in-a-lifetime opportunity? What would you say if the students offered to raise funds to cover the deficient funds attributed to the low enrollment?

To illustrate the interdependent nature of such instances, let's assume that you plead Dr. Tripp's case to the dean, who agrees that the study tour can go if the enrollment reaches 18 students. You join Dr. Tripp in canvassing the campus and manage to recruit an additional four students bringing the study tour enrollment to 18. Before you can enjoy the success, another faculty member, Dr. Hawkins, visits your office to remind you that two years earlier, his study tour to South America was canceled with an enrollment of 19 students. He asks why you (and the dean) did not support his efforts as you have supported Dr. Tripp's study tour. How would you respond? While it was never your intent to favor Dr. Tripp, asserting this may not be persuasive. How can you help Dr. Hawkins understand that the assistance you lent Dr. Tripp does not evidence that you favor her over him? What might you say when Dr. Hawkins asserts that Dr. Tripp is the favored faculty member in the department? How can you persuade Dr. Hawkins that Dr. Tripp has not received preferential treatment? Are you certain that Dr. Tripp has not received preferential treatment?

Dr. Hawkins perceives your action to assist Dr. Tripp as evidence of preferential treatment because he views these actions in relation to his own experience. When individuals use their personal perspective as the benchmark for what others get, they will inevitably assess action involving others as illustrative of their standing in the department or with the chair or dean. The only way to dissuade Dr. Hawkins's conclusion is to alter the frame he imposes on the current situation. If the discussion focuses on a comparison of the two faculty, it will invite a summary of preferential treatment. If, however, the discussion disconnects the decisions made with regard to the two study tours and affixes each one to institutional priorities or to the context surrounding it, the chair can more effectively eliminate the tendency to compare faculty.

For the sake of discussion, let's assume that as chair you simply forgot that Dr. Hawkins's study tour to South America was canceled for low enrollment two years ago. Now that he has reminded you of it, you must agree that Dr. Tripp has received preferential treatment, even though that was not your intent, and you are even more certain that it was not the dean's intent because the dean was not an easy sell on reinstating Dr. Tripp's study tour. What would you say to Dr. Hawkins? Is it possible to admit an error in judgment or an oversight without losing credibility? Is it more important that Dr. Hawkins perceive you as honest or be persuaded that Dr. Tripp's situation is different from his? Leadership credibility requires that chairs and deans be perceived as knowledgeable, trustworthy, and possessing good intentions. When a chair or dean offers an explanation or response that undermines these attributes, he or she will not be perceived as credible. To have faculty and staff perceive these attributes, chairs and deans must communicate in ways that evidence they are knowledgeable, trustworthy, and possess good intentions.

ADMINISTRATIVE REQUESTS

Consider the typical reaction when faculty receive a request from the administration to alter (or to consider altering) a practice without full understanding of why the request is being made. Suppose, for example, a department has been asked to reconsider its reliance on adjunct faculty to teach the program's 100-level introductory course. When this or similar requests come from the central administration, faculty are likely to resent the suggestion and resist taking the action or implementing the suggested change. Instead, faculty might react with disbelief or even outrage that the central administration would believe it knows best regarding a decision that rightfully belongs to the department. The faculty resistance and resentment stem from a lack of understanding about the motivation for the recommendation. Specifically, if the suggestion is not related to institutional priorities or anchored in context, it appears arbitrary and intrusive. Such negative perceptions can fuel resistance and lower morale.

Most change follows some review of current practice or policy. It is natural for faculty and staff to become defensive about current practice when the review process leaves them feeling wrong or in some way inadequate. In the example of staffing the introductory 100-level course, the administration implies something is wrong with how the department is staffing the course by asking the faculty to reconsider their use of adjunct faculty in teaching the course. Absent any explanation, faculty and staff are left to interpret the request and infer the motivation for it. The faculty might, for example, view the request as a criticism of current practice. They might infer that the administration is saying that the department is not hiring qualified adjunct faculty or that the full-time faculty should teach the 100-level course. Depending on the faculty's view of the administration and the specific suggestion, it is possible that this simple request will invite resistance and lower faculty morale.

Chairs and deans can manage review and change more effectively by anchoring such suggestions to commonly understood priorities and grounding them in a description of the conditions that prompt the suggestion. In this instance, the administration might anchor the request that the department reconsider the use of adjunct faculty in staffing the 100-level course to the institutional priority to increase retention. If, for example, the chair and dean explain that students who left the institution after one year report dissatisfaction with having classes taught by adjunct faculty, then this brief explanation offers a reason for reviewing the practice and is less likely to offend the full-time faculty. Further, if the chair and dean add that this particular department offers a 100-evel course that enrolls roughly 40% of the entering class, it becomes clearer that the suggestion is being made because the department is perceived as having the potential to contribute positively to a solution. By providing the context for the request, the chair and dean also demonstrate their knowledge and good intentions, which are two important attributes of leadership credibility.

ANALYSIS AND APPLICATIONS

Although conflict is inevitable, when managed effectively, conflict and the existence of differing viewpoints can be beneficial. When discussions are focused on the department or the institution and not the individual, it is often easier for faculty and staff to identify potential strengths, challenges, and the need for change. Chairs and deans can help faculty and staff by framing issues and decisions in ways that minimize the likelihood that faculty and staff will see changes from a personal perspective. When individuals are able to understand the larger institutional context and weigh the merit of decisions in relation to institutional priorities and the future welfare of the institution, they are less likely to assess decisions or actions from a personal perspective. The understanding of the larger context and institutional priorities enables faculty and staff to predict decisions which in turn also make the outcome less personal. When the application of a personal perspective is replaced by the concern for protecting the long-term interests of the institution, faculty and staff will be less defensive and less resistant to decisions and change. Let's review the essential elements of each application:

- Minimize the personal perspective.

- Demonstrate sound, future-oriented leadership.

- Communicate priorities.

- Be an open book.

◆ Minimize the personal perspective.

When faculty and staff are permitted to view decisions and actions from a personal perspective, few will be pleased with the outcome. Good and effective leadership requires action to preserve the whole. In other words, chairs, deans, and the central administration exercise sound leadership when they take action and make decisions that preserve the health of the institution. It is impossible to exercise leadership of a dynamic organization while doing what is best for the personal perspective of every member of the campus community.

The degree to which chairs and deans can help faculty and staff understand the larger institutional context, the easier it will be to have individual faculty and staff resist the temptation to view actions and decisions from a personal perspective. The ability to understand and recognize what is best for the institution takes time to develop. When chairs and deans make a habit of teaching the institutional perspective to faculty and staff, they help to build a foundation that encourages more altruistic behavior and responses from individual faculty and staff. In the example of the department that is asked to reconsider the use of adjunct faculty in 100-level courses, faculty resistance will be minimal if the request is made with faculty possessing a clear understanding of the institutional need to improve retention. When faculty and staff accept that institutional logic must take priority, they will be less prone to viewing actions and decisions from a personal perspective.

◆ **Demonstrate sound, future-oriented leadership.**

Often the conflict that surrounds change grows out of the perception of winners and losers. Chairs and deans can minimize charges of favoritism or taking sides by framing decisions and actions in terms of what best positions the department or college for the future. The decision to cancel study tours that are underenrolled can appear either punitive or responsible. If the decision is framed with the focus on the immediate impact to Dr. Tripp and the 14 students who were looking forward to the travel experience, the decision to cancel the study tour can appear punitive. If, however, the decision is framed with the focus on the long-term health of the institution and the study abroad program, the decision to cancel will more likely appear responsible because individuals understand how and why running study tours that are undersubscribed threatens the program and the institution.

This is particularly important when making decisions that are bound to upset some because the faculty and/or staff are not of one view. The illustration of the faculty who held different views of the most valued benefits represents such a decision, and these are the decisions that may appear to be no-win moments for chairs and deans. By framing the decision in terms of what is best for the institution in the long term, it is possible to escape the perception of favoritism or taking sides. The decision to increase salaries rather than retain a low employee contribution to health care might be best for the institution because an increase in salaries allows the institution to retain its desired standing in the annual American Association of University Professors' survey of faculty salaries, which is essential to recruiting new faculty. At the same time, even an increase to 20% in the employee contribution to health care will still leave the institution's benefit package very competitive with what is offered by other institutions.

◆ **Communicate priorities.**

Faculty and staff are less likely to take exception to a suggestion that reinforces understood and accepted institutional priorities. The suggestion to reconsider using adjunct faculty to teach the 100-level course will be resisted if the basis for the request is not recognized as a priority of the institution. When faculty and staff perceive a request or a decision as making sense given what they know about institutional or departmental priorities, they will be less resistant and resentful. While faculty and staff may not like a change, they will be more accepting of the change if they understand the basis for it.

Chairs and deans can help preserve faculty morale by making priorities clear. If, for example, Dr. Tripp and Dr. Hawkins understand that under-enrolled study tours threaten the future of the study abroad program, they will be less likely to be demoralized by a decision to cancel a study tour that is underenrolled. Similarly, the morale of faculty who are asked to reconsider the use of adjunct faculty in teaching a 100-level course will not be adversely affected if they perceive themselves as being asked to help with an important component of the institution's retention priority.

◆ Be an open book.

Predictability helps to enhance the perception of leadership credibility. Chairs and deans can enhance their leadership credibility by being clear about priorities and the larger institutional context so that faculty and staff can predict an outcome. Even when faculty and staff do not like a particular decision, they are not inclined to resist it or resent it if the decision is predictable. If faculty understand that the institution cannot afford to risk the study abroad program by running study tours that are underenrolled, they will expect tours with fewer than 25 students to be canceled. While they may be disappointed, they are not likely to view the decision as punitive or unfair. Consequently, leadership that enables faculty and staff to predict decisions and outcomes helps to protect faculty morale.

SOME FINAL THOUGHTS

Institutional change and shrinking resources can be hard on faculty morale. Diminishing resources require the prioritizing of current and new activity, which inevitably means that some faculty may lose support for favorite programs. Change is stressful because it upsets personal and departmental equilibrium until new patterns are learned. Even when a change is understood as important and necessary, it can create stress for those affected by it. But when change is not understood, the resistance to the needed change can spawn destructive conflict and lower leadership credibility.

The conditions facing higher education make change inevitable, so to be effective, chairs and deans need to manage change and scarce resources in ways that do not contribute to lowering faculty morale. Chairs and deans can help preserve faculty morale and minimize resistance to change by helping faculty and staff understand the larger institutional context and the priorities that make change necessary. Faculty and staff will evaluate the merit of decisions and actions, and chairs and deans can help manage change by encouraging faculty and staff to view it from a constructive perspective to minimize resistance to it. Chairs and deans possessing leadership credibility will find leading change easier than those who do not enjoy such credibility. For this reason, chairs and deans should always be about the business of enhancing their leadership credibility by engaging in honest communication that is focused on issues and not on personalities or people.

Managing Up and Out

Chairs and deans do not need to be the ranking superior to manage conflict or improve a working relationship. Failure to manage up can impair one's effectiveness at work and contribute to a stressful or demoralizing work environment. Similarly, chairs and deans must effectively manage internal and external constituencies, including faculty, students, parents, alumni, area businesses, donors, and granting agencies. This chapter will offer leadership communication strategies for how to manage up (within the institution) and out (beyond the institution).

Conflict can develop when individuals possess different attitudes and expectations. Conflict can also develop when individuals hold different perceptions about what has happened and/or what should happen. While such differences signal the possibility for conflict, such conflict is not inherently destructive. Different views should be encouraged because airing those views constructively can improve decision-making and problem-solving. However, when different views become competing perspectives or are perceived as competing agendas rather than mutually respected professional differences of opinion, conflict can become destructive.

Chairs and deans have a leadership responsibility to think independently from their supervisors and constituencies or they might fail to provide a perspective that can be important to decision-making and problem-solving. To be more successful in creating an environment where supervisors and the various constituencies understand and respect their leadership perspective, chairs and deans must communicate their views in a way that prevents differences from becoming destructive conflict. Supervisors might interpret a different perspective as lack of support for an institutional priority or as evidence of insubordination, even when chairs and deans intend only to raise a relevant caution or offer a legitimate perspective. Regardless of what chairs or deans intend, the reality they must manage is how their communication is perceived. Generally, it is preferable (and easier) to prevent communication from sending a wrong message than it is to correct a misunderstanding, but prevention requires systematic forethought because many factors influence how different views are heard and interpreted.

Communication variables such as timing, message construction, and message channel all influence how the content of a particular message is heard and perceived. The simple statement, "I'm not sure that is a good idea" will likely evoke different reactions if said by a chair to the dean in a one-on-one meeting or during a group meeting of all chairs or the department faculty. People within earshot of a statement that might appear to challenge a supervisor's view or authority will influence the receiver's interpretation of the message and the sender's intent. If the comment is made in a private setting, for example, the dean will be less likely to view it as an affront to his or her authority or as an effort by the chair to upstage the dean or cause a loss of face or credibility with others.

Metacommunication variables such as the existing working relationship or campus climate and culture will also help to shape how a particular message is heard and interpreted. If, for example, the dean respects the chair that makes the statement, "I'm not sure that is a good idea," the dean will be more likely to give the chair the benefit of the doubt no matter where or when the statement is made. A good working relationship that is characterized by a high degree of mutual respect can alter the dean's reaction from one of viewing the chair as being insubordinate to one of mild annoyance that the statement was not made earlier in private. Similarly, if the campus climate is such that there is growing distrust of the central administration among the faculty, then making the statement in front of faculty will more likely be viewed as an unwelcome and unhelpful attack on the dean's credibility. Chairs and deans will find that their ability to posit a different point of view will be enhanced if they accurately assess and account for the relational and climate issues that influence how statements are heard and perceived.

Managing up and out is important to keeping conflict constructive and working relationships productive. This is not done by surrendering one's perspective or by adopting views held by others for the express purpose of winning favor. Rather, managing up and out requires chairs and deans to help highlight and clarify differences in a professional way that characterizes their understanding of and respect for views that differ from their own. Because it is easier for misunderstandings around disagreements to develop when the opportunity for direct communication is reduced, this can be especially challenging to do when chairs and deans do not have frequent conversations with supervisors or constituencies. Regular communication about issues helps to build and sustain a professional rapport and constructive working relationship which in turn helps inform how messages are heard and perceived. When time pressures and physical space prevent chairs and deans from sustaining regular communication with supervisors and constituencies, chairs and deans find it more difficult to communicate a constructive motive for persuading a different perspective. Such metacommunication variables need to be considered when expressing views that differ from those held by supervisors and other constituencies.

One key to managing up and out is to structure regular communication—that might not otherwise happen—to ensure that differences are aired in a way that demonstrates mutual respect and understanding. Communication that helps others to understand and trust the motives and priorities of a chair or dean will establish a foundation that permits differences to be aired constructively. It is also important for chairs and deans to structure the opportunity for communication with supervisors and constituencies when they recognize the existence of conflict. This can be counterintuitive in that chairs and deans may find greater immediate comfort by avoiding conversation with others about issues of disagreement. A chair, for example, may hope to avoid talking to a dean when the chair senses that the dean is displeased with the chair's performance. Similarly, a dean may prefer to avoid running into a department's faculty after informing the chair that a request for a new position or computer equipment was denied. Although chairs and deans may intuitively seek to avoid conflict by shying away from discussions about disagreements, this intuitive reaction can actually fuel destructive conflict because it permits differences to exist and escalate without understanding the other perspectives.

Daily schedules can also get in the way of managing up or out. The pressure of daily activity can keep chairs and deans so busy that it becomes easier to avoid discussions that are essential to building mutual respect or airing differences constructively. Yet such discussions are essential in preventing disagreements from becoming destructive. When chairs and deans are busy with routine tasks they may forget to give consideration to how their actions will be viewed. The ability to reflect on how others view the words and deeds of chairs and deans becomes more important when chairs and deans hold views that differ from the views of others. It is important to realize that supervisors and constituencies will form perceptions of chairs and deans. Therefore, it behooves chairs and deans to structure communication opportunities that help supervisors and constituencies form positive perceptions of their motives and actions. Without such proactive measures to manage up and out, chairs and deans leave too much to chance when disagreements inevitably develop.

THE CHAIR IN THE MIDDLE

Consider a situation in which a department chair hired from outside the institution reports to a dean who was promoted from within the institution and who enjoys close personal relationships with the department faculty. The chair, Dr. Russo, was hired by the dean, Dean Shearer, and charged with leading some specific changes, including the integration of more experiential learning opportunities for students and the implementation of post-tenure review. Dean Shearer believes that such change is essential to preserving instructional quality and program viability. Dr. Russo was hired as chair primarily because she had made similar changes as the chair of a smaller department at another institution. She accepted the position fully convinced that she was a good fit for the dean's agenda for the department.

Everything was going well until the chair began to work on the change agenda. Faculty seemed unreasonably resistant to discussing the need to review course content, let alone the expectation to consider incorporating experiential learning opportunities for students. In fact, Dr. Russo perceives so much resistance to curricular issues that she has no idea how she might broach the topic of post-tenure review. Since the institution is nearing its accreditation review, she knows it is important for some mechanism of post-tenure evaluation to be in place to demonstrate that the department has a procedure for assessing instructional quality across all courses. Consequently, Dr. Russo believes that she has no choice but to push forward in talking with the faculty about the need to consider these changes. She recognizes that the faculty care about students and hopes that their concern for students will eventually outweigh their apparent resistance to reviewing the curriculum or to having their instruction evaluated.

Dr. Russo is unaware that faculty are talking to Dean Shearer on a regular basis. Specifically, the faculty lament that as the new chair, she does not "understand" the department or the institution. They contend that Dr. Russo fails to grasp how this program is different from the one she left, that she talks more than listens, and that she refuses to recognize their expertise in curricular matters. The most senior faculty member in the department tells the dean that in his 35 years at the institution he has never felt more demoralized than he has since the arrival of the new chair. Dean Shearer is torn and feels responsible for an outcome that has faculty he values upset and demoralized. So, he offers to talk with Dr. Russo about her leadership style. The faculty members feel comforted and protected knowing that the dean understands their concerns and will help the chair learn her proper role.

Dean Shearer schedules a meeting with Dr. Russo during which he expresses his disappointment in how things are going and his concern for the faculty. Dean Shearer explains that the campus "runs on relationships," and he does not wish to be remembered as the dean who permitted faculty to become demoralized. Assume Dr. Russo's role in this scenario and consider how you might respond to the dean. Would you remind Dean Shearer that the change agenda was his idea? Would you describe the faculty resistance to considering any change in the curriculum? Would you take exception to the way you were described by the faculty? Consider each of these options and anticipate how the dean might reply. For example, the fact that the dean has formed conclusions about Dr. Russo's leadership communication style without hearing her view of events is a good indication that not much will be gained by trying to describe faculty resistance to change. What other alternatives are available to you as chair?

Before you can select the best response, you need to give some thought to your objective. If you, as the new chair, were sitting in this meeting with the dean, what would your immediate objective be? At this point, it is important to think both contextually and practically because several of the objectives that may immediately spring to mind and that even seem intuitive could be counterproductive in the long run. For example, you might want to set the record straight and inform the dean that it is the faculty who refuse to listen. Though tempting, this is not likely to be a worthwhile or productive objective because Dean Shearer's comments make clear that he holds the department faculty in high regard and that their feelings and perceptions matter to him. Similarly, reminding him that the change agenda was his idea and was a charge he gave you when you were hired is probably not a wise objective at the moment because Dean Shearer's comments make it clear that he assigns a higher priority to other issues such as faculty morale. Hence, while it may be intuitive to clarify such matters, doing so would likely be counterproductive in the long run.

In selecting the best response, it is important to note that Dean Shearer appears to be rethinking *his* agenda for the department. Perhaps when the dean talked with you about the need for change, he failed to anticipate faculty reaction and now wishes to consider certain parameters for achieving the needed changes. In any event, it is now clear that change will likely take a back seat to faculty morale. This does not mean that Dr. Russo is licensed to ignore the change agenda, but it shapes how she must proceed. The more pressing immediate objective is to reassure the dean that as chair you are very concerned about faculty welfare and willing to be a team player in helping to advance his objectives and the institutional priorities without placing undue stress on the faculty.

Had the chair in this scenario anticipated that the faculty would talk with the dean, she might have preempted their communication and minimized their influence with the dean. Had Dr. Russo, as chair, been the first to tell Dean Shearer that faculty members were apprehensive about making any changes in the curriculum and seemed threatened by the suggestion to consider change, the dean would have had a context for hearing faculty concerns. The faculty claim that the new chair does not understand the department and does not listen is more credible because Dr. Russo had not signaled the existence of a problem to the dean. As far as Dean Shearer knows, the chair does not recognize that faculty members are upset and feeling demoralized. It is understandable that the new chair may not wish to keep the dean informed of unsuccessful efforts to implement change. However, given that Dr. Russo is the newcomer to a campus culture in which her supervisor and faculty enjoy long-term, positive relationships, the chair should anticipate that the faculty will likely take any concern about her leadership directly to Dean Shearer.

As a newcomer to the institution, it is important to assess the culture and climate of the department and campus. One way to do this is to review your plan for leading change with the dean and others to ask their thoughts on how the faculty might react. This strategy has the advantage of providing implicit approval for the approach you take. If it proves to be a poor choice, you are not out on the limb alone. Also, previewing your approach in advance with the dean provides a context for the dean should faculty approach him with complaints. If, for example, Dr. Russo had alerted Dean Shearer to the fact that faculty seemed threatened by the very mention of change and that she was trying to persuade the faculty to take ownership of a review of the curriculum, the dean would be less likely to conclude that the chair was being heavy handed or dictatorial in leading change. Having sufficient background information can empower the dean to help support the chair's efforts. If Dean Shearer is aware of the chair's plan, he can assure the faculty that the chair is counting on them to lead the curricular change and that she has no intention of transforming the department to be more like the program she left. The new chair has little to lose and much to gain by keeping the dean fully informed of her plans and progress.

MANAGING THE POPULAR BUT PROBLEMATIC EMPLOYEE

Consider the example of the dean who inherits a problem employee. It might be that the dean is new or that offices have been reorganized in a way that alters reporting lines. In any event, the dean finds himself responsible for supervising a person who is widely known on campus and in the community. It can be challenging to manage highly visible individuals because they often carry and fuel campus gossip. The situation can be fraught with peril if the individual does not meet performance expectations because the supervisor runs the risk of being perceived as unfair to a well-liked individual. This is the situation in which Dean Knapp finds himself.

Dean Knapp is the new supervisor of Isaac Best, who directs a summer theater program. The summer theater program is wildly popular in the community, but the program operates separately from the productions mounted by the theater department. Mr. Best is an alumnus of the institution who, as a student, performed in the summer theater. Mr. Best likes to tell people that the summer theater program was his fraternity and the only thing that prevented him from transferring to another institution. Mr. Best graduated with a degree in education and spends the academic year teaching history and coaching tennis at the local high school. The institution retained Mr. Best to direct the summer theater following the retirement of the program's founder and long-term director. Although the summer theater has always been a community theater, it enjoys the use of campus facilities, and the institution believes that the money spent on the program is a worthwhile investment in town and gown relationships. Until this year, Mr. Best reported to the vice president for institutional relations. The summer theater's reporting line changed to Dean Knapp, who has oversight for the academic theater program, in hopes that some productive synergies might be gained from structuring a closer relationship between the summer and academic theater programs. It is hoped, for example, that the new reporting line will lead to greater involvement of the theater faculty and new performance opportunities for the students majoring in theater.

Although Dean Knapp did not request the change, he did not resist it and is prepared to pursue the anticipated benefits. While he never worked directly with Mr. Best, he has no reason to believe that working with Mr. Best will be a problem. Dean Knapp appreciates that Mr. Best is experienced in running the summer theater program and anticipates that the new responsibility will not consume a lot of his time. Further, Dean Knapp recognizes that the summer theater program has a very strong and loyal following and hopes that this will be an advantage for the academic theater program. Consequently, Dean Knapp is optimistic about accepting the new reporting line and oversight responsibility for the summer theater program.

A few months later, Dean Knapp realizes that there are several significant problems that warrant his time and careful attention. It seems that Mr. Best is not good with details and counts on a multitude of others to fill in the gaps for him. Unfortunately, most of those who assist Mr. Best are community volunteers who have no training or understanding of institutional policy, so they often skip needed paperwork or complete forms incorrectly. On a regular basis, Dean Knapp receives billing statements from area vendors for which no purchase requisition was processed. Although Mr. Best submitted a budget for each of the four summer productions, the billing statements do not contain information that permits Dean Knapp to assess if each show is remaining within budget. In addition, Dean Knapp receives calls from guest designers and directors who report that they were promised more pay than received. It seems that the visiting artists were asked by Mr. Best to sign blank contracts to expedite payment, but the amount filled in later by Mr. Best disagreed with what they claimed they were told they would be paid.

On countless occasions, Dean Knapp talked directly with Mr. Best about these matters. In each instance, the dean provided Mr. Best with the appropriate policy or forms to be used for making and processing the various expenditures. Mr. Best remains personally charming, but typically of-fers a long list of excuses for each problem and insists that these matters are beyond his control. Mr. Best is quick to remind the dean that his expertise is in running a theater and not in managing the more mundane tasks asso-ciated with "administrative paper shuffling." Perhaps most annoying to Dean Knapp is Mr. Best's insinuations that the dean's office staff should do more to assist the summer theater by managing the paperwork for him in-stead of taking his time to review things he was not hired to do. Dean Knapp now realizes that Mr. Best's understanding of higher education does not extend beyond directing the summer theater program. Assume Dean Knapp's position and consider how you would manage this situation. For instance, would you do more than continue to make performance expecta-tions clear for Mr. Best and discuss each problem with him? If so, what would you do and why?

Another month passes and the situation is getting worse. In addition to persistent errors that require a lot of the dean's time and attention, Dean Knapp has begun to receive calls and comments from prominent (and vocal) individuals in the community suggesting that he needs to be more supportive of the summer theater program. With varying degrees of subtly, the well-meaning community leaders suggest that Dean Knapp do more to assist Mr. Best so the summer theater director can appropriately remain fo-cused on running the summer theater program instead of tending to petty accounting and clerical work. Of course, the callers stress how important the summer theater program is to the community and are quick to refer-ence that the institution possesses a long-standing commitment to running the program. It seems that instead of working to remedy errors made while directing the summer theater program, Mr. Best is busy bemoaning the dean's "overbearing and instructive control" of the summer theater pro-gram to any who will listen.

Assume the position of Dean Knapp and think how you would manage this escalating conflict. Clearly, the community is an important external constituency and how you are perceived in the community will likely affect other issues and initiatives. Would you talk again with Mr. Best? Would you hold a meeting with the community leaders? If so, what would your pur-pose be and how would you structure your message? Would you, for exam-ple, remind the community leaders that you have a responsibility to ensure that institutional policy is followed in spending resources? Or, would you try to explain that Mr. Best has fiscal responsibility for the summer theater program? Can you anticipate the reaction you might receive to each of these approaches? It is important to remember that the community leaders are calling because Mr. Best has persuaded them of his view. Your ability to persuade them to think differently will depend in part on your initial credibility with the community leaders. If your credibility with the community constituency is not equal or superior to the regard they have for Mr. Best, it is unlikely that you will be able to persuade them that Mr. Best is wrong without some external intervention from another highly credible source. For example, the president might be able to persuade them that you are acting appropriately and in the best interest of the institution *if* the president enjoys a strong and favorable rapport with the community leaders.

In working with constituencies, it is helpful to remember that a disgruntled constituency is likely to talk with more than one person. In this instance, it is likely that the community leaders will also talk with the president or other members of the central administration. Since Mr. Best previously reported to someone else at the institution, it is likely that your leadership style is being compared with what was previously done. If all appeared to go smoothly before Dean Knapp assumed supervisory responsibility for Mr. Best and the summer theater program, it is natural that Mr. Best and the community leaders will attribute the current difficulties to Dean's Knapp leadership style and involvement with the program.

Hindsight tends to be 20/20, and chairs and deans are seldom able to anticipate all potential conflict which would permit the opportunity for early intervention. Had Dean Knapp known initially what he now knows, he would have taken different action from the beginning. Assume Dean Knapp's position and consider what might have been done in advance to minimize or possibly prevent the current litany of problems. For example, you might have sought information about Mr. Best and the program from your predecessor. Knowing what you now know, what questions should you have asked of Mr. Best's previous supervisor? You might have asked for a report of the time required to supervise Mr. Best and a list of issues that bear careful scrutiny in order to help Mr. Best do an effective job of directing the summer theater program. It might have been helpful to obtain opinions of Mr. Best from those offices on campus that have reasons to work directly with him. For example, what questions would you have asked of the staff in the business services office? Would it have been helpful to know if the summer theater program typically operated with a profit or a loss? If the program has traditionally operated at a loss, it might be important to have a clear understanding of the program priority for the institution and its mission because this will offer guidance as to what the institution is prepared to invest in the program. In other words, if the institution is accustomed to the summer theater program operating at a loss, is there a limit beyond which the institution would not support the program?

Assume that, as Dean Knapp, you now learn that the summer theater program operates at a significant deficit that has grown each year since Mr. Best was retained. Before Mr. Best was hired, the summer theater program broke even. Ideally, the institution would like to retain the program, but a recent decline in tuition revenue has put the program at risk. You learn further that the president and others were unaware of Mr. Best's shortcomings because the previous supervisor invested an inordinate amount of time to manage the fiscal aspect of running the summer theater program. Your task as dean, therefore, is more complex than containing a budget loss associated with running the summer theater program. It is critical that you manage the situation in a way that permits the president and others at the institution to realize that the source of the problem is not your leadership but Mr. Best's poor fiscal management. What do you do? Where do you start?

When chairs and deans find themselves in such predicaments, the intuitive reaction may be to hope that no one discovers the problem until you figure out how to manage it and to somehow turn things around. Unfortunately, there are problems that cannot be turned around by one person. Since Mr. Best was permitted to run deficits while others handled the paperwork, it is unlikely that he will work to learn these things now that he is reporting to a dean who expects him to be more fiscally compliant and responsible. It is predictable that Mr. Best will instead devote his time and energy to restoring life the way it was before he reported to Dean Knapp. In talking with community leaders and others who are supportive of the summer theater, Mr. Best is working on picking sides for the escalating dispute with Dean Knapp. Dean Knapp can be fairly certain that Mr. Best is not disclosing his errors or contribution to the conflict, but is instead painting a picture of how the conditions he must contend with have changed for the worse now that he reports to Dean Knapp. Consequently, Dean Knapp's best strategy is to share the problem he is having with Mr. Best. Though it may be counterintuitive to report on one's inadequacies, it is the only way in which the dean can provide the president and others with a context and information that will empower them to place comments from Mr. Best and community leaders in an accurate context.

Sharing problems in managing others need not involve a character assassination. In fact, Dean Knapp will be more effective if he resists the temptation to speak ill of Mr. Best. The dean needs only to call attention to the facts. This can often be done by requesting information. The dean might, for example, ask staff in the business services office for recommendations on cleaning up a situation in which a guest designer was asked to sign a blank contract and the amount paid differs from the verbal understanding. The dean might ask the president for some understanding as to how large a deficit the summer theater program can be permitted to run. Discussions about such matters can share a lot of information without waging a personal attack on Mr. Best. For example, the discussion will likely permit the dean an opportunity to share that Mr. Best has never operated the summer theater program without running a deficit and that the size of the deficit has grown each year. As the new supervisor, it is especially important for Dean Knapp to share what he now knows with others.

ANALYSIS AND APPLICATIONS

It is inevitable that chairs and deans will encounter conflict with supervisors and constituencies on and off campus. However, through effective leadership chairs and deans can manage communication in a way that keeps the airing of such disagreements constructive. This objective sometimes requires chairs and deans to resist actions that may seem intuitive, but those apparent intuitive thoughts are really counterproductive in the long run. For example, chairs and deans will generally find it helpful to share with supervisors any management problems that might eventually be reported to their supervisors. Similarly, chairs and deans can prevent any single conflict from defining a relationship through their communication. When chairs and deans execute such communication strategies, they will enhance their overall leadership effectiveness. Let's review the essential elements of each application:

- Help frame issues of disagreement to reinforce common ground.

- Demonstrate respect for professional differences.

- Empower more constructive communication.

- Don't let one disagreement define a relationship.

◆ Help frame issues of disagreement to reinforce common
   ground.

This may appear more difficult than it needs to be. Often common
ground can be reinforced by linking the different perspectives to a mutually accepted goal or priority. Prefacing an objection, for example, with a
simple statement such as, "I know we both want what is best for our students" can help to make a different view appear less confrontational.
Chairs and deans can also help reinforce common ground by framing issues of disagreement or clarifying the agenda in a way that illustrates an
overarching concern for institutional priorities. Prefacing a different viewpoint with a statement that demonstrates one's commitment to a mutually
shared agenda or priority will help to have the opposing view heard and
perceived in a constructive way.

In the example of the new chair, Dr. Russo, and Dean Shearer, whose
conversations with the faculty cause the faculty members to believe that
the dean will protect them from the very changes that the chair is charged
with leading, Dr. Russo needs to be proactive in making sure that the dean
knows and supports the approach being used to carry out the dean's
agenda for the department. Part of this persuasion will necessarily involve
assuring Dean Shearer that faculty members are being heard and that they
have no reason to feel demoralized. Sometimes the common ground needs
to be made explicit. In the example of the summer theater program, Dean
Knapp may need to establish that the common priority is running a viable
program. By establishing this common objective, Dean Knapp clarifies
that the summer theater program is not without accountability.

◆ Demonstrate respect for professional differences.

There are important and valued professional attributes that can only be
demonstrated during instances of disagreement. It is, for example, virtually
impossible to demonstrate respect for diversity when working in a homo-
geneous culture. Only when presented with different views can one
demonstrate respect for different perspectives. Even in dealing with difficult personalities like Mr. Best, it is helpful to demonstrate respect for differences. Dean Knapp, for example, might offer that he too wishes the
institution could continue to run the summer theater program at a deficit
as Mr. Best requests, but the escalating deficit has grown beyond what the
institution can afford.

Dr. Russo, the new department chair, will help to make the consideration of change more palatable for the resistant faculty if she persuades them that she wants to learn their view and respects their professional expertise. She can actually help lead change if she insists on hearing faculty views regarding the current curriculum and suggested alternatives. By listening to faculty views, the new chair forces the faculty to articulate arguments and persuasive appeals regarding the issues that must be considered if change is to occur.

◆ Empower more constructive communication.

The best way to empower constructive communication is to tend to the things that will have others give us every benefit of the doubt when hearing and interpreting our communication. Leadership credibility and effective working relationships are fundamentally important to how one's views are heard and perceived. It is important to know that a negative working relationship need not remain negative. Further, chairs and deans can improve their working relationships with their supervisors or various constituencies by altering their communication. Dr. Russo's fate, for example, need not be sealed by her rocky start as the new chair. She will, however, need to alter her communication with Dean Shearer and with the faculty in order to turn the situation around. In other words, Dr. Russo will need to manage up and out and should not wait for the dean or anyone else to figure out what is happening or intervene on her behalf.

Another way to empower constructive communication is to provide others with the relevant background information that will enable them to more accurately interpret comments and concerns raised by others. In the case of the mismanaged summer theater program, Dean Knapp needs for the president and others to possess a clear understanding of the problems he has encountered in managing Mr. Best. While most would not support Mr. Best's fiscally irresponsible actions such as having guest designers sign a blank contract or spending without regard for budget, they are likely to line up in support of him and a popular summer theater program if they remain unaware of the growing deficit and cavalier practices that contribute to the budget loss. By sharing relevant background information, chairs and deans empower others to use constructive communication.

◆ Don't let one disagreement define a relationship.

It is inevitable that colleagues will encounter issues on which they disagree. Depending on the salience of an issue and the level of personal investment, it is easy to understand how any serious disagreement might adversely affect professional relationships and attitudes toward collegiality. Indeed, you may know of individuals who permitted one issue to taint their long-term view of colleagues, the department, or even the institution. This is a short-sighted and unproductive reaction to conflict and inconsistent with effective leadership. There is no advantage to permitting one disagreement—no matter how salient the issue or how intense the discussion—to define a relationship.

It can feel counterintuitive to reach out to a colleague with whom one has a significant conflict or difference of opinion. Deans, for example, may prefer to avoid the person who submitted the request that could not be supported. However, doing exactly the opposite is important to preventing any single issue from defining the relationship. It is preferable for chairs and deans to initiate conversation with the person who is likely disappointed by their decisions. In doing so, chairs and deans have an opportunity to explain the decision and to reinforce that this one disappointment does not devalue the work being done by that person or the chair's and dean's regard for the person.

SOME FINAL THOUGHTS

Managing up and out is essential to effective leadership. Chairs and deans do not lead in a vacuum, and therefore it is imperative that supervisors and other constituencies on and off campus have an understanding that will empower them to give the chair or dean the benefit of the doubt and to employ constructive communication with others that helps rather than hinders chair and dean leadership. Chairs and deans can help empower more constructive communication by keeping supervisors and constituencies informed. Armed with relevant information, supervisors and constituencies are more likely to perceive the merit of decisions and actions taken by chairs and deans because they will have a context for the decision being made.

A key aspect of managing up and out involves framing issues in a way that reinforces the common ground among parties who may hold different perspectives on a particular issue. It is easier for individuals to be engaged in disagreement if they recognize that all share a common goal or purpose. With the common ground clearly understood, it is easier to listen to and weigh the relative merit of different views. Also, with the common ground clearly identified, it is more likely that the consideration of different views will improve decision-making and problem-solving.

Another important component of managing up and out is demonstrating respect for professional differences. When chairs and deans demonstrate that they appreciate and value views that are different from their own, they encourage more collaborative problem-solving and decision-making. They also model how diversity can benefit every aspect of campus life. When faculty and staff are free to express their views on issues without fear of retaliation or loss of professional respect, they will more quickly and freely contribute the best of their thinking to decision-making and problem-solving activities.

Developing a Fair and Effective Leadership Communication Style

This section of the text concentrated on leadership communication strategies that address the need to accurately assess the conflict issues and discuss the continued need to build credibility as an effective way to manage conflict. Here, the analysis and applications provided reinforced the need for a shared operational understanding of the mission and institutional priorities—essential elements of leadership communication strategies discussed in Part I. In addition, by working toward ensuring that your communication is sincere and honest rather than taking sides on an issue, your leadership credibility can be enhanced.

As you move to the final section of this book and its presentations on working with difficult people, it may be helpful to carry forward these thoughts:

- Effective leadership communication is both a skill and an attribute— an approach to managing people and the development of rapport and context. At times, sharing problems is the best way to develop a framework to support rapport and context.

- As an assigned trait, credibility is built through effective leadership communication with others and over time.

- Conflict is rarely managed through inaction or avoidance and the ability to manage conflict relies on leadership credibility.

Imagine yourself as a new department chair hired from outside the institution to lead a high-profile department. The department is comprised of 12 full-time faculty members who are all well known across campus. In addition, 10 of the 12 possess strong national reputations for their professional work. The two faculty members who do not enjoy the strong national reputation have much campus notoriety for their active participation and leadership in faculty shared governance and other campus work. While the department does not have formidable internal battles, the faculty members have traditionally functioned as individuals. Your predecessor served as chair for nine years, during which time he made no attempt to build consensus among the faculty, but rather led by giving each individual faculty member his or her voice.

The dean who hired you made clear his expectation that your leadership would be to help the faculty reach consensus on some significant departmental issues. In particular, the faculty members have not functioned well with regard to curriculum review and revision. Instead, the unwritten norm in the department is to support the changes each person wishes to make rather than seek compromise or consensus. With changes in institutional accreditation standards there is a greater need for faculty to share a common understanding about the department's mission and how it helps to advance the institutional mission.

Imagine how you might go about building leadership credibility with each faculty member in the department as well as with the dean and other relevant constituencies on campus. You will be carrying out an agenda set by the dean that is counter to what the department faculty members have practiced for many years. How you would persuade them to behave differently? Clearly, the faculty are likely to resist a change in practice unless they perceive a benefit to doing so. Consequently, you might give some thought to how to frame the advantage of reaching a common understanding about department mission and curriculum. A second source of resistance will be expecting faculty to behave in different ways. There is a freedom to acting individually, and it can be time consuming and frustrating to have to discuss matters as a whole department when the perception is that those matters were previously handled more efficiently as individuals. Hence, you will need to give some thought as to how you make the process of reaching consensus one that is perceived as advantageous by the department faculty.

Because this is not the only task you will need to manage, it will be important for you keep the primary objective in mind as you manage daily activity. Indeed, how you manage routine daily events can help to shape the faculty reaction to the expectation that they now collaborate on such departmental issues as curriculum. If, for example, in your daily work you can establish that you hear all perspectives and treat everyone fairly, it will be easier for the department faculty to consider a collaborative process. If, however, your routine decisions suggest that you favor some at the disadvantage of others, then faculty are more likely to be resistant to any overtures that they work collaboratively on the curriculum or any other issue.

Leadership credibility, however, is multidimensional, so you need to consider how you would go about enhancing your leadership credibility with the dean and other constituencies. The dean, for example, will need to know that you are making progress on the agenda for which you were hired. You might consider providing updates of the strategy being imposed and the progress made to inform the dean that you are taking the appropriate action. If, however, you just remain busy at the task without providing any update to the dean, it is likely that he will wonder if you are working toward the objective. Similarly, by intentionally working to build your leadership credibility with other constituencies on campus, you can indirectly influence the reaction of the faculty within the department to you and your leadership.

In many circumstances, griping can spread like wildfire, and so, especially as a new department chair, you will want to make a positive impression with every interaction possible. This does not mean that you will have the luxury of avoiding unpopular decisions while you enhance your credibility. Instead, you will need to make decisions that you recognize might be unpopular in ways that at least demonstrate your knowledge of the issues and your effective management of the people and perspectives involved.

Many of the routine activities that you will be expected to do as chair offer an opportunity for you to enhance your leadership effectiveness. For example, the way in which you manage conflict, the way in which you invest in the performance counseling of faculty, and the way in which you manage up and out can demonstrate your competence as well as leadership communication skill.

Part III

Using Leadership Communication to Manage Especially Difficult People

This section delves into the stickiest of subjects by addressing the most difficult types of individuals chairs and deans must manage and lead. To be effective and comfortable, chairs and deans must be able to manage conflict involving a variety of difficult personalities. The chapters offer insight and practical strategies for effectively managing such notable characters as the pot stirrer, the troublemaker, the prima donna, the drama queen (or king), and the confrontation junkie. This section also provides guidance for working with individuals resistant to change or intent on pursuing their own agenda. Because chairs and deans work with many constituencies, attention is given to managing conflict within and outside the department and institution.

Managing Personal Agendas

Personal agendas can undermine efforts to build consensus and thwart progress toward achieving common goals. Chairs and deans can limit the destructive impact of personal agendas by employing communication strategies that permit an objective review and assessment of individual goals and actions. This chapter offers ways to recognize and manage personal agendas that could undermine productivity and collegiality.

Many professionals have a personal agenda or individual goals for their professional development and achievements. This is not inherently harmful to department productivity or collegiality. Neither is the existence of a personal agenda inherently detrimental to chair and dean leadership. Personal agendas, however, can pose a challenge for chairs and deans when those agendas are inconsistent or in competition with departmental and institutional goals. For example, the faculty member who aspires to become the college dean will not pose a problem if he or she acquires experience and leadership skills in ways that are consistent with the existing institutional priorities. If, however, the faculty member pursues personal ambition by undermining the current leadership or by working actively to discredit others who may hold similar goals, the personal agenda will likely pose a challenge for chair and dean leadership and could threaten faculty morale and collegiality.

Personal agendas that are inconsistent with departmental and institutional priorities can jeopardize achieving the institutional and departmental mission, lower morale, and increase the potential for conflict. Personal agendas by definition are person specific and not community specific, so it is understandable that when personal agendas are not compatible with the departmental and institutional missions, conflict will inevitably develop

167

that can thwart progress in achieving departmental and institutional goals. Similarly, when faculty and staff perceive an individual as more committed to his or her own agenda than to the agenda shared by the department and the campus, morale and collegiality will suffer. The potentially negative ramifications of personal agendas that are inconsistent with shared objectives become clearer when one considers the leadership responsibilities assigned to chairs and deans. For an institution to advance its mission, chairs and deans must lead faculty and staff through continuous review of current practice and, when desirable, the design and implementation of new practices. Put more simply, chairs and deans are responsible for leading change. Change is not easy for many, and it seems to come particularly slow and hard at institutions of higher education. When individual faculty or staff members actively work to advance personal agendas that are inconsistent with departmental or institutional priorities, they thwart progress toward achieving the institutional mission and the department priorities.

The presence of a counterproductive personal agenda can also lower morale and increase the potential for destructive conflict. Faculty members who are committed first and foremost to their own agenda will inevitably lack commitment to the team or shared team objectives. This can fuel perceptions of inequity or favoritism. For example, when a faculty member regularly declines service assignments to invest more time in scholarship, it can appear to other faculty that this one faculty colleague is exempted from policy. This in turn can lower morale among faculty who will likely conclude that the faculty workload is not equitable and that certain faculty members operate with a different set of expectations. If the practice is permitted to continue, faculty morale will suffer and destructive conflict can erupt.

Chairs and deans must learn to recognize personal agendas if they are to manage those agendas successfully. This can be difficult because faculty members do not always volunteer their personal and professional goals. While there is often an annual mechanism for soliciting the achievements of individual faculty, there may not be a procedure that requests faculty to declare personal and professional goals. Even when faculty members are requested to submit their professional goals for the coming year or some prescribed period of time, they may not disclose objectives that might be perceived as inconsistent with departmental and institutional priorities. Hence, recognizing the existence of a personal agenda can be challenging for chairs and deans.

Perhaps the best indicator that a faculty member possesses a personal agenda is in how that faculty member invests his or her time and energy.

This assumes individuals spend time on those activities that matter most to them, and this is most often the case. Generally, when a faculty member is not making acceptable progress toward tenure or promotion, it is because that individual is spending more time on preferred activities which in turn causes the faculty member to be deficient in meeting the performance expectations in other less preferred activities. When this assumption holds true, then what faculty or staff members spend time on will provide chairs and deans with a glimpse of those faculty members' personal agendas. If, for example, a faculty member spends every spare moment on scholarship and writing, it is fairly safe to say that research holds more interest for that faculty member than other aspects of faculty work. Similarly, if a faculty member becomes absorbed in committee service and faculty governance despite a chair's caution that more time should be devoted to teaching and scholarship, it is typically an indication that the faculty member enjoys or values the service work more than other responsibilities assigned to faculty.

Chairs and deans can minimize the existence of personal agendas by building a shared vision. This is not accomplished in one meeting or even through annual retreats. To build a shared vision, chairs and deans need to help faculty understand how every decision and action supports the common departmental mission and the institutional mission. Chairs and deans are in a position to influence how faculty and staff interpret decisions made by the central administration and to help guide how they think about and view the institution's mission and priorities. A common understanding of the institution's mission is essential to developing a shared vision of how the department or college might work together to achieve that mission. The operational presence of a shared vision and agenda will help all recognize when a personal agenda exists that is not consistent with the shared purpose. Thus, essential to managing personal agendas is the need to cultivate a shared vision that supports the institutional mission.

A shared vision, however, is not by itself sufficient to stamp out all counterproductive personal agendas. Chairs and deans can help limit the negative impact of counterproductive personal agendas by establishing and sustaining clear policies and practices that treat all equitably and provide everyone with assurance that they are treated equitably. Although chairs and deans may treat all faculty members equitably, unless faculty members perceive this to be the case, the presence of a personal agenda can threaten faculty morale and spawn unhealthy conflict. A chair, for example, may require all faculty members to teach the department's 100-level introductory course. However, if it is not apparent to all department faculty that one faculty member meets this expectation by teaching the course at a satellite campus during the summer, then it could be perceived that the teaching expectation does not apply to all department members. Another key to managing personal agendas is to establish and sustain processes that are not only clearly understood by all but also offer everyone assurance of how all will be treated and how each decision will be reached. If, for example, faculty can count on a process that will ensure that all faculty members teach at least one section of the 100-level introductory course sometime during each calendar year, they will be less likely to conclude that the chair makes exceptions to policy for some faculty members.

Even when chairs and deans successfully create a shared vision that supports the mission and establishes clear policies and practices that assure all that everyone is treated equitably and that everyone will be held responsible for working toward the common purpose, unwarranted and unhealthy personal agendas can exist. In such instances, it is important that chairs and deans accurately discern the presence of potentially harmful personal agendas and manage those agendas individually. This can take time, and it demands strong leadership communication skills because it is not easy to persuade a person to place a greater priority on a shared agenda than on a personal one. Ideally, chairs and deans can help individual faculty and staff understand how advancing the shared agenda can help to fulfill a personal agenda, but this requires that faculty and staff be able to perceive themselves and their goals as part of a larger context and agenda.

THE CHAIR WITH AN AGENDA

Consider the example of a department chair who successfully persuades the dean of the need to retain a faculty member, Dr. Hamilton, who had been employed in a five-year, nonrenewable term position. Institutional policy makes clear that a faculty member hired in a nonrenewable term appointment cannot be retained. The faculty member can apply for an open position, but a contract cannot be extended to the individual unless that person, in this case Dr. Hamilton, surfaces as the preferred candidate in an open search. According to the chair, Dr. Hamilton is absolutely essential to the growing student enrollment in the department's newest program in educational leadership and strategy. The faculty member works well with students and has a wealth of experience which permits him to provide meaningful and rewarding connections for students. In addition to the faculty member who is nearing the end of a nonrenewable contract, there are two other faculty members who teach in the same program. The chair, however, points out that the institution stands to lose the faculty member who possesses the best connections, and these connections have helped to grow student interest in the program. But the institution does not have a faculty position and only has permission to fill the five-year nonrenewable contract with someone other than Dr. Hamilton.

Dean Sinclair finds the case persuasive and picks up the chair's cause by working with the advancement office to pursue external funding to support the creation of an endowed position so that Dr. Hamilton and his strong experience can be retained. Despite working against the calendar and some significant odds, the effort to secure funding to support an endowed position is successful. A private foundation is impressed with the program's focus on connecting students to the real world and agrees to fund an endowed position so that the institution is able to retain the faculty member who otherwise must leave the program. At the chair's urging, the grant application includes Dr. Hamilton's credentials to demonstrate the concrete advantage of creating the endowed position. The good news is shared with the chair and others in the department.

When the institution receives the first payment from the granting agency, the dean notifies the chair that Dr. Hamilton will be moved to the new position, which will have the effect of eliminating the otherwise mandatory termination. The dean is then surprised to receive a short note from the chair that reads, "Do not move Dr. Hamilton to the new position. Plans to grow the program require a different use of the endowed position." The dean indicates his surprise and confusion by replying, "What? I thought the entire purpose for securing the endowed position was to be able to retain Dr. Hamilton. His appointment at the institution will expire in 30 days if we do not move him to the endowed position." Imagine the dean's surprise when the chair responds, "You're right. We need to keep Dr. Hamilton, but it will be better for the program and the institution if we do not use the endowed position for Dr. Hamilton. I'll call your secretary to schedule a time when we can talk about this, but the success of the educational leadership and strategy program requires that you not move Dr. Hamilton to the endowed position."

Dean Sinclair has known the chair, Dr. Lane, for a long time. In fact, he considers him a friend as well as a bright and capable leader. In fact, Dean Sinclair hired Dr. Lane some 15 years ago for a staff position. Almost immediately, Dean Sinclair developed a high regard for Dr. Lane's ability, so when the education department developed serious problems, Dean Sinclair was pleased and grateful when Dr. Lane offered to jump into the hot seat and serve as department chair. Dr. Lane holds a doctorate, but his career path was nontraditional in that he lacked the typical teaching and research accomplishment usually expected. Although he has held the position of chair for nine years it is doubtful that his professional experience and record of scholarship would make him competitive for a nationally advertised department chair position. To help make Dr. Lane's appointment palatable to the other faculty, Dean Sinclair gave Dr. Lane professorial rank and appointed him to a full-time 12-month position with the understanding that Dr. Lane would not be eligible for tenure.

Assume the role of Dean Sinclair and decide what you would do next? Would you wait for the meeting that Dr. Lane promised to schedule, and if so, how might you prepare for the meeting? Would you take action sooner, and if so, what would you do? Clearly, Dr. Lane has an agenda that is not obvious to Dean Sinclair. Furthermore, the urgency expressed by the chair suggests that he does not perceive how his personal agenda may be problematic for Dean Sinclair and the institution. As dean, would you clarify the larger institutional agenda with Dr. Lane, and if so, how would you go about doing this? For example, the institution accepted funding from a granting agency to support a particular purpose. How might Dean Sinclair remind Dr. Lane that these are restricted funds and that the institution has an obligation to spend the money in accordance with the need articulated in the grant proposal?

How might you react if Dr. Lane explains that the endowed position should be used to support his idea to develop a Center for Education Strategy and Research? In making the case, the chair describes the relevance of the center's work to providing both experiential learning opportunities for students and research opportunities for faculty. Dr. Lane is enthusiastic about the benefits of such a center and proposes that he become the center's director, which would be the endowed position. Assume the role and perception of the dean and consider how you might perceive and react to Dr. Lane's ideas. Would you dismiss the suggestion and remind him that the funding was secured for different purposes? Or, would you consider Dr. Lane's proposal? If so, how might you assess the merit of the proposal without jeopardizing your credibility or the institution's position with the funding agency?

While Dr. Lane clearly has a personal agenda, that in and of itself may not pose a problem. As leaders, chairs and deans need to assess personal agendas and determine if they are counterproductive to the departmental and institutional objectives. Suppose in his role as chair, Dr. Lane explains that he is committed to the institution's goal to provide more experiential learning opportunities for students and that his proposal to create and chair the new center is important to this objective. Dr. Lane further contends that the center would advance other institutional priorities including, for example, making the program distinctive and enhancing professional mentoring opportunities for students. Even though the creation of a center may be consistent with the institution's mission and priorities, the plan could be disruptive to faculty morale and institutional success unless faculty and other constituencies support the plan and also perceive it as being consistent with the institutional mission and priorities.

Assume that as dean, you are persuaded that the center is consistent with the mission and establishing the center will reap the benefits described by Dr. Lane. Would you pursue the idea of creating the center and naming Dr. Lane as the its director? It is important to distinguish between an idea that may have merit and the immediate proposal. To rephrase this issue, the proposal to create a Center for Education Strategy and Research can be an excellent idea while the specific provisions in Dr. Lane's proposal may not be a good idea. For example, the benefits of developing the center may not require the conditions outlined by Dr. Lane. As dean, you might organize a group to develop the center concept, but resist using the endowed faculty position to fund the center director. Or, you might decide that Dr. Hamilton, whose five-year contract is at its end, should be the center's director because his credentials were part of the grant application that resulted in the endowed position.

What other options do you have and how would you decide on the best approach? In reaching a decision, you would want to consider the immediate and long-term context that surrounds the decision. For example, assuming the center is a good idea, how essential is Dr. Lane to its implementation? Or, would the center have more support if someone other than Dr. Lane served as director? You would also want to consider the campus culture and precedent. For example, are endowed chairs typically filled without a national search? How will the appointment of either Dr. Hamilton or Dr. Lane be perceived and will that perception thwart progress in advancing the institutional mission?

Now consider how your decision might be influenced by the fact that as chair, Dr. Lane has a history of making unilateral proposals. Suppose

Dr. Lane has also never lacked confidence and typically gives the impression that he believes those who disagree with him are slow to grasp what really needs to be done. Further, you know that Dr. Lane is quick to remind others of his long-standing friendship with you, the dean, and that he uses this relationship to gain support for his ideas. This attitude is evidenced in Dr. Lane's language as he talks about how others finally "come around" to his point of view, and that he demonstrates impatience with suggestions that he process his plan with faculty and staff or that he involve others in discussing a proposal before submitting it for approval. What does this information tell you about how the department and the campus will receive an announcement that the institution will now have a Center for Education Strategy and Research and that Dr. Lane will be appointed as the center's director? The anticipated reaction influences your decision as dean because these perceptions will have a direct impact on the center's success. Even the best idea can fail to produce the anticipated benefits if the immediate and long-range contexts pose an obstacle to its success and your leadership credibility as dean. In sum, no decisions are made in a vacuum, and even good ideas will fail if the context is not considered.

A Faculty Member With an Agenda

Consider a situation in which a department chair finds that one faculty member in the department offers reports on the activities of another faculty colleague. On a regular basis, the faculty informant reports on her colleague's activities to the chair. Although the reports are unsolicited, the information has been worrisome. It is through these reports that the chair has learned that the faculty member is having personal problems that might have an adverse affect on her teaching and other work at the institution. The chair is confident that the subject of these reports does not know that her colleague is filing them with the chair. At the same time, the reports are hard for the chair to ignore. Yet it is difficult to know how to respond without disclosing the source of the information. The faculty member offering the reports is careful to ask that the chair not say anything or let on that she knows what is happening. Hence, the chair is caught between the proverbial rock and hard place.

After several months, the chair has learned that the troubled colleague is headed for a divorce and dating an area business leader she met when arranging for professionals to speak to her class. The reports raise some concern because the informant describes how the colleague's boyfriend accompanies the class on field trips and how they freely demonstrate affection toward each other in front of the students and are very open about sharing a room when field trips require an overnight stay. The reports have not been confirmed by anyone else, and the chair cannot discern any noticeable change in the troubled faculty member. In fact, if it were not for the informant's report, the chair would not have any reason to be concerned.

Assume the position of chair and decide what, if anything, you would do. Would you pretend that you know nothing or would you take action? What responsibility do you have to the informant? What responsibility do you have to the troubled colleague? What responsibly do you have to the students? What responsibility do you have to the institution? Are there other constituencies to which you have a responsibility and which could be affected by the current situation? For example, what might happen if the dean learns of the situation from a student or a student's parent and you have not briefed the dean about the situation? If you take action on the information, you violate a confidence. However, if you do not take action on the information you have, you ignore a matter that many would believe warrants attention. At the same time, should you take action based on information from a single source? Is there any way to verify the reports without talking to the troubled faculty member about the information received? As chair, what would you do in this situation?

It may help to consider the informant's motive for filing the reports. Why would the informant request that you not act on the information? Does the informant, for any reason, have an axe to grind with the troubled colleague? Could there be a reason that the informant wishes to damage her colleague's credibility with you, the chair? You have been clear with the informant that there is little you can do unless you are given permission to share the information presented or act on it. Knowing that nothing can come of the reports, the informant continues to offer unsolicited information in strict confidence. As chair, it will be important for you to consider the informant's motives. You may wish to ask the informant faculty member what she expects to gain from forwarding information without granting you permission to use it.

It will also be important for you to consider both the immediate and long-range contexts. Would it matter if you knew that the informant is known to embellish the truth and revel in campus gossip? Would it influence your response if you knew that the troubled colleague has a history of inappropriate judgments? Such factors will (and should) inevitably influence your response. At the same time, it is important for chairs and deans to be able to discern fact from perception. It is human nature to incorporate what we know of a situation in deciding our response to a particular circumstance, but it is also easy to confuse fact and inference. In this situation, the chair would want to be sure that any perception of the troubled colleague having a history of exercising poor judgments is based on fact, not hearsay.

ANALYSIS AND APPLICATIONS

There is little room for shortsightedness or cowardliness in effective leadership. Chairs and deans will inevitably limit their own effectiveness if they ignore or surrender to personal agendas that are inconsistent with the departmental and institutional missions. Leadership inevitably comes back to the difficult task of keeping individuals with unique talents and contributions moving in a common direction in a collegial manner. Let's review the essential elements of each application:

- Create a shared vision.

- Establish and sustain processes that support the shared vision.

- Discern misguided motives.

- Consider the immediate and long-range context.

◆ Create a shared vision.

The existence of a shared vision helps chair and dean leadership in several important ways. A shared vision makes it easier for individuals to understand how a particular change will move the department or the institution in a desired direction. A shared vision can help chairs and deans manage the conflict that often grows out of resistance to change because the shared vision helps set priorities and create common perceptions about what needs to be done. Moreover, should differences exist about what should be done to realize the shared vision, the conflict will likely be easier to manage because it will be less personal—as everyone already agrees on the desired outcome.

Specific to the focus of this chapter, the presence of a shared vision helps chairs and deans manage personal agendas. First, a shared vision reduces the number of personal agendas because faculty members can more easily discern what needs to be done and which individual activities will be valued for their contribution to the shared vision. While as chair Dr. Lane demonstrates his awareness of some institutional priorities, this does not mean that he and Dean Sinclair have a shared vision of the institution's mission and priorities. Dr. Lane selects certain institutional priorities (building program distinction and enhancing mentoring opportunities for students) in support of his proposal, but this does not mean that the proposed creation of a Center for Education Strategy and Research derives from a common vision. When individuals share a vision, they have a common understanding of core and secondary priorities, the desired outcomes, and the parameters that guide specific action. Department faculty, for example, may possess a shared vision to become the region's primary supplier of graduates trained in a specific field, but they also recognize that certain strategies for achieving the mission might be beyond consideration because they are too expensive, impractical, or politically charged. While as chair, Dr. Lane relates his proposal to institutional priorities, he fails to demonstrate that he possesses a shared vision or that he understands the core priorities or the parameters that must be considered.

Second, the existence of a shared mission makes it easier to discern a counterproductive personal agenda because that agenda really stands out as being motivated by personal interest. A shared vision establishes a benchmark by which faculty and staff can separate good ideas from poor ideas. When a group or campus community lacks a shared vision, the dismissal of a poor idea will more likely be perceived as a personal affront toward the individual making the suggestion because there is not a commonly accepted basis for evaluating the merit of an idea. Such situations are more difficult to manage because the potential for conflict can involve hurt feelings and prompt defensive behavior. When faculty and staff possess a shared vision, an idea or suggestion can then be evaluated in terms of how well it advances the shared mission which in turn helps to depersonalize a decision or an outcome.

Third, a shared vision makes it easier for chairs and deans to check and interrupt a personal agenda without appearing to be singling out a particular person. It is infinitely easier to explain that someone's proposal will not advance the shared vision as well as another approach than it is to simply deny an individual's request. Without the framework of a shared vision, the denial of a request will more likely be perceived as personal rejection. Dr. Lane, for example, believes he has an excellent idea that will help both the education school and the institution. If the proposal is rejected, Dr. Lane is more likely to conclude that his efforts to help the school and the institution are not appreciated or valued. He is not likely to conclude that his idea fell short in meeting either the education school's or the institution's needs because, from his personal perspective, his is a good and right idea.

◆ Establish and sustain processes that support the shared vision.

Trust is enhanced when faculty and staff have confidence that everyone will be subjected equitably to the same policies and practices. Trust among colleagues and between the faculty and the central administration is important to managing personal agendas. When people are confident that policies and practices will be applied equitably to everyone, they have confidence that chair or dean leadership or "the system" does not advantage some individuals at the expense of others. This is important to preserving collegiality and faculty morale.

The perception of deal-making is also very costly to chair and dean leadership credibility because it suggests that some personal agendas are supported while others are not. Even a simple act of kindness can be perceived as evidence of favoritism. A department chair may, for example, assign a faculty member to class sections that meet later in the morning because the chair understands that the faculty member has young children and a long commute. The chair's action might be motivated out of consideration for the faculty member and a desire to avoid the need to find a substitute on short notice—all sound reasons for assigning later class times. Regardless of the reasons, the decision might be perceived as favoritism. If faculty can trust that the process of assigning classes and class times is fair and objective, they will be less likely to interpret the decision as an example of deal-making.

Clarity of purpose can also help build trust in chair and dean leadership. Trust grows when we can count on a leader to be competent and fair in exercising authority and in carrying out assigned responsibilities. When faculty and staff can trust the processes for considering individual requests, they are more likely to trust the chair or the dean. Some believe that the best way to build trust is to cultivate strong interpersonal relationships with faculty and staff, but it is impractical to believe that chairs and deans have the time needed to sustain close relationships with all faculty and staff. By establishing predictable processes, chairs and deans can earn the trust of faculty and staff.

◆ Discern misguided motives.

When a faculty or staff member pursues a personal agenda that is inconsistent with the mission, it can lower morale and spawn destructive conflict. As mentioned, faculty and staff are more likely to possess personal agendas when there is no shared vision of the mission or priorities. This is intuitive in that professionals typically have professional goals and objectives, so unless these goals are developed from a shared vision, the goals will inevitably be personal goals, not necessarily institutional ones. Further, the absence of a shared vision tends to increase the likelihood that a collection of personal agendas will be less compatible. The result lends some truth to the old adage that leading faculty is similar to herding cats or frogs. Most have observed departments, for example, in which every faculty member appears to be going in a different direction. This can be minimized, if not avoided, by creating a shared vision that sets parameters for personal goals that will be valued by both the department and the institution.

It is possible to have a shared vision and still need to manage personal agendas that are inconsistent with the shared vision. In the scenario of the informant faculty member, for example, it is difficult to understand how the informant faculty member's behavior supports a shared vision. If the informant faculty member's reports are intended to help the chair keep everyone on the same page in support of a shared vision, it is doubtful that the chair would be asked to keep the information confidential. Similarly, if the reports are intended to help the chair know how to best assist the troubled faculty member, it is pointless to ask the chair to not use the information. The insistence on offering negative information about a colleague without providing license to use the information in a constructive way suggests the existence of a personal agenda that may or may not be compatible with a shared vision. As is, the chair receives reports from the informant that call into question the credibility of the troubled colleague. The reports also suggest the occurrence of situations that the chair should not ignore. By insisting that the information be kept confidential, the reports are not helpful to any constructive resolution, so the actions of the informant faculty member cannot possibly support a shared vision. This in turn suggests that the reports may be motivated by a personal agenda. Perhaps the informant's reports are motivated by professional jealousy or by a desire to discredit the troubled faculty member. Or, the informant's reports might be motivated by a desire to become the chair's confidant. Regardless of the specific reason, the personal agenda can jeopardize the chair's leadership credibility, faculty morale, and department productivity. Time spent on a personal agenda that is inconsistent with the mission and shared vision is time lost to the task at hand.

Chairs and deans can discern misguided motives by assessing if the behavior supports or threatens the advancement of the mission and the department's ability to address recognized priorities. If the action threatens desired progress it is likely motivated by a personal agenda that is inconsistent with the mission and shared vision. Chairs and deans can reinforce the mission and shared vision by requiring faculty and staff to demonstrate that their actions support the accepted direction and priorities. For example, the chair might ask the informant faculty member to explain the purpose for the reports. This discussion would likely provide an opportunity to make clear that the reports are useless in helping reach a constructive resolution unless the chair can follow up with the troubled faculty member. Such a discussion would serve to remind the informant faculty member of departmental and institutional priorities. It would also establish the expectation that all actions should support the mission and shared vision.

◆ Consider the immediate and long-range context.

It is important to consider both the immediate and long-range contexts when assessing the potential harm of personal agendas. Chairs and deans should consider the long-term ramifications of possible alternatives before taking what appears to be the path of least resistance for the immediate situation. Dean Sinclair, for example, may appoint Dr. Lane as the director of the Center for Education Strategy and Research because it would be too uncomfortable to accept the chair's idea to create such a center and then name someone else the center's director. This reaction and subsequent decision derives in part from Dean Sinclair's long-time friendship with Dr. Lane. It would be understandably difficult for the dean to explain to his friend and colleague that someone else would be better able to lead the center.

However, should Dean Sinclair surrender to the path of least resistance without considering the long-range ramifications of naming Dr. Lane the center's director, Dean Sinclair will likely be setting himself up to manage other uncomfortable situations. At a minimum, Dean Sinclair would likely need to explain to others why Dr. Lane was handed the position without a search process. The action suggests that Dean Sinclair favors Dr. Lane and that the custom of posting available positions so all who are interested might apply can and will be short circuited whenever Dr. Lane covets a post. Such perceptions can undermine Dean Sinclair's leadership credibility with faculty and staff which in turn can diminish his ability to lead change or manage other responsibilities that require trust and credibility. Would these consequences be worth avoiding the immediate discomfort of naming Dr. Lane the center's director?

Some chairs and deans contend that without a crystal ball, it is difficult, if not impossible, to envision immediate reactions and long-term consequences of a particular decision or action. Typically, chairs and deans who hold this belief have not cultivated the leadership communication skill of anticipating responses. Chairs and deans can envision the long-range context by engaging in a systematic review of the potential ramifications of particular decision or action. This is done by listing the parties who will be directly and indirectly affected by the decision or action and imagining the response of each. Dean Sinclair, for example, could list all faculty and staff who might perceive themselves as contenders for the center's directorship and those who would need to work with the center's director. Once the list of individuals who would be affected by the decision is complete, Dean Sinclair would review each name on the list and anticipate what that person might say. This step is easier than you might expect, and chairs and deans who submit to this exercise typically relate that they are able to capture the anticipated responses—complete with precise wording and intonation. This envisioning practice can help chairs and deans weigh the pros and cons of a particular decision or action in advance of making the decision or taking action. Even when the exercise does not result in a changed outcome, the analysis will help chairs and deans gain insight into how best to present news of a decision or action.

SOME FINAL THOUGHTS

It takes time to manage personal agendas, but it is time well spent because a personal agenda that is inconsistent with the departmental or institutional mission can undermine effective chair and dean leadership. Specifically, the existence of a counterproductive personal agenda can thwart progress toward achieving a shared vision, undermine leadership credibility, lower faculty and staff morale, and increase the potential for destructive conflict. Consequently, chairs and deans cannot afford to ignore personal agendas that are inconsistent with the mission, even when doing so may seem counterintuitive.

Because an ounce of prevention is worth a pound of cure, chairs and deans will find it helpful to proactively work to discourage personal agendas that are inconsistent with the mission. Cultivating a shared vision among faculty and staff does much to discourage that counterproductive personal agenda because the shared vision helps individual faculty and staff recognize which behaviors will be valued for their contributions to the mission and shared vision. Similarly, when chairs and deans exercise predictable leadership that is grounded in clear policies and processes, they provide faculty and staff with assurance that all are treated fairly and equitably. The perception that some are favored will invite a competition and watchfulness that enhances the potential for conflict which will in turn undermine leadership success.

Even when chairs and deans take every possible precaution to prevent personal agendas that are inconsistent with the department's and institution's mission, they will at times need to manage the individual who places a higher priority on personal gain than shared vision. This requires that chairs and deans be able to discern misguided motives and be proactive in realigning the misguided personal agenda with departmental and institutional missions. Chairs and deans need to be ready to confront individual faculty and staff about their motives to help them see how some agendas can be hurtful to the shared vision and priorities. At the same time, chairs and deans need to be willing to take action that helps contain a counterproductive personal agenda when the individual is not willing to abandon that agenda in favor of one that supports the shared vision.

Finally, chairs and deans need to examine their own agenda and assess their motives and the anticipated consequences of a particular decision or action in terms of both the immediate and long-range contexts. This analysis will help to prevent chairs and deans from taking the immediate path of least resistance only to discover that the decision or action helped to create conflict or an obstacle in the future. Although this can be counterintuitive, it is essential to leadership credibility and success.

12

Containing the
Pot Stirrer/Troublemaker

Pot stirrers and other troublemakers thrive in environments that rely on one-on-one communication because statements that incite conflict and undermine the leadership typically remain unchallenged and therefore plausible in the minds of faculty and staff. Chairs and deans can limit the destructive influence of pot stirrers and troublemakers by nurturing open communication and structuring opportunities for collaboration. This chapter offers strategies for how to use leadership communication to inhibit individuals who are intent on stirring pots and causing trouble for and among others.

A *pot stirrer* spends time and energy raising issues without suggesting solutions. A pot stirrer uses language and takes action that fans the flames of conflict and plants the seeds of distrust. Pot stirrers actively work against resolution, clarity of purpose, and leadership credibility. Pot stirrers are not consensus builders, team players, or reliable colleagues. Consequently, pot stirrers thrive in department and campus climates that are characterized by distrust, competing agendas, conflict, secrecy, and fear. When the department or campus climates are characterized by open communication and mutual trust between and among faculty and between faculty and the central administration, pot stirring becomes a more difficult task. Pot stirring works best when individuals have reason to believe they do not routinely receive information that is relevant to their work or welfare in the department because this perception makes any assertion by the pot stirrer more plausible.

The best defense against pot stirring is to create and sustain a department and campus climate that is characterized by open and honest communication. More specifically, individuals must believe that important information is shared openly and that they will have an opportunity to voice concerns without fear of retaliation. Individuals must believe they can weigh in on significant issues and that their perspectives will be heard and considered. When individuals believe they are helpless in shaping a departmental or institutional response to changing conditions and their future in that department and at that institution is controlled by others, they will be more inclined to believe the worst about the leadership and their colleagues. Consequently, a departmental or institutional climate that is not characterized by honest and open communication and information sharing becomes fertile ground for the pot stirrer who wishes to undermine the leadership, plant seeds of distrust, create conflict, or increase resistance to change. However, when individuals have confidence that they receive honest information about relevant matters, they are better able to evaluate the messages promoted by the pot stirrer and the messages shared by the chair, dean, or others in the central administration. In a healthy department or campus climate, individuals are able to confirm the accuracy of statements made by a pot stirrer and this helps to contain the damage that might be done by pot stirrers.

Higher education has a number of stereotypes which, if perpetuated in a department or on a campus, can serve as fertile soil for the pot stirrer. Such stereotypes as the administrator who abuses faculty and the stereotype that suggests faculty will unilaterally resist all administrative leadership can become a backdrop and a springboard for creating distance between the faculty and the central administration. Similarly, stereotypes such as those that imply senior full professors represent deadwood or that the faculty perceive staff as second-class (or third-class) citizens contribute to the animosity among faculty groups and between faculty and staff. Such stereotypes open the door for the pot stirrer to use those stereotypes to plant seeds of distrust and close the door on collaborative decision-making or consensus building. If the faculty, for example, believe that the central administration cannot be trusted, the pot stirrer can more easily persuade faculty to interpret any communication from the administration in a negative way. Truth is interpreted through a lens shaped by stereotypes, and denying the negative interpretation often seems to perpetuate the stereotype. Consequently, the existence of such negative stereotypes creates a special leadership challenge for chairs and deans in managing the pot stirrer.

As this text is written for chairs and deans, both departmental and campus climate are discussed. It is possible to have a department with a healthy climate on a campus with an unhealthy climate, and vice versa. Climate is specific to the department or area that a chair or dean leads. Although a department chair may believe it is hopeless to create a healthy department climate because the campus climate is unhealthy, this is not true. Chairs and deans should work actively to promote a healthy climate within their area of responsibility because it will help enhance their leadership effectiveness and success. When chairs and deans ignore the need to create and sustain a healthy climate, they make every leadership task more difficult—and open the door for the pot stirrer.

Pot stirrers are motivated by a personal agenda, but the agenda may be promoting conflict or undermining leadership. This makes the pot stirrer different from the individual who has a personal agenda to advance certain professional interests that may or may not be consistent with the mission and shared vision. The pot stirrer's objective is most often to stir things up by casting doubt and/or by facilitating distrust and conflict. The motivation is specific to the person and the act of pot stirring can be habitual without a clear or discernable motive. Motives might range from a desire to be center stage to a desire to prevent change. Often pot stirrers recognize that the status quo is comfortable, if not beneficial, for them personally. Thus, pot stirrers are motivated to keep the world as it is because any change might require them to step up and perform in a different or new way.

Similarly, the department chair who attempts to dissuade an individual faculty member from pursuing a specific action by asserting that the action will upset colleagues will lose credibility and control if the individual faculty member talks directly with colleagues about the proposed action. Pot stirring is more effective when individuals do not compare notes or check perceptions. Pot stirrers present information in a way that will evoke a predictable (and typically less constructive) response that fuels a bias or a fear. In environments characterized by distrust, the pot stirrer appears credible because the negative interpretation of any message is believable as it confirms the worst. For some reason, it is often easier to believe the worst than to hold hope for the best. Pot stirrers prey on these human tendencies.

THE POT STIRRER VERSUS THE FACULTY COMMITTEE

Consider the example of the faculty member who, without fail, is able to cast doubt on any proposal brought before the department or campus faculty for a vote. Picture either a department meeting or a larger general faculty meeting that often occurs at smaller institutions. In this instance, the meeting is called for the purpose of reviewing and discussing a proposal formulated by a committee after several months of work. The committee presentation is concise but clear, listing the relevant findings and recommending a specific course of action. Faculty discussion is lively, and the questions and comments raised are motivated by a desire to understand the various aspects of the proposal. However, just as the group is nearing the point when someone might call the question for a vote, a faculty member seated in the back of the room or some other place that would require the majority of the group to physically turn around, interrupts the flow of discussion to raise a few questions that cannot possibly by answered definitively but which cast doubt on both the committee's work and the proposal.

Perhaps the faculty committee worked for months (or years) to review summer course offerings and is now ready to propose changes in those offerings that will better serve today's students and hopefully increase enrollment in summer courses. However, because it represents a change to the current structure, the proposal is subject to some resistance, and the pot stirrer can optimize both doubt (about everything from feasibility to management of the changes) and resistance to the faculty committee's proposal with a few strategic questions. Simple but nonspecific questions such as, "How would that work?" or "Will that really be better for the faculty member who is counting on summer pay?" can reverse the tone of the meeting and place the proposal (and months of work) in jeopardy. Sadly, the pot stirrer does not need to spend more than a nanosecond of preparation or thought to shoot down a proposal and preserve the status quo, even though the committee was charged to develop a proposal because there was general consensus that the status quo was not working and some change was needed.

Given the growing number of pressing issues that face departments and institutions, much of the preliminary work is typically done in committees and then brought to the full department, a faculty senate, or the campus for consideration and vote. This process is efficient in that it would be physically impossible and impractical to expect all faculty members to be involved in the study of every issue. At the same time, whenever an issue is sent to a committee, it creates a situation in which a group of faculty members and/or staff will be presenting their findings and recommendations to other faculty members and/or staff who most likely do not have a full understanding of the issue. Certainly the committee needs to present information clearly for others to understand, but accepting the committee recommendation involves both understanding and a certain amount of trust that the committee has done its work carefully and well. In short, the credibility of the committee influences how others perceive the committee's recommendations.

Assume the role of the dean who created the committee charged with reviewing the summer courses. You worked for almost a year with this hardworking group and helped them gather and interpret all relevant data. You supported their travel to a national conference on summer programs and worked with them to weigh the pros and cons of every conceivable model. You have as much confidence in their findings and proposal as they do. How might you react when, as the faculty are about to vote in support of the proposal, the pot stirrer asks, "Are you certain that faculty who count on summer pay will have work in the summer?" Do you as dean respond to the question or do you let the faculty committee field the question? What might you consider in making this decision? Your response might be influenced by whether or not it is important that the faculty perceive the proposal as authored by the faculty committee or by how much you had said during the meeting as faculty discussed the proposal. Context matters, so if it is important that the faculty perceive the proposal as the product of the faculty committee, you might remain quiet. However, since the question relates to a matter that only the dean can answer, you may need to respond. The question is a perfect example of what a pot stirrer can do to cast doubt on even the best proposal because the answers to the pot stirrer's questions likely exceed what the faculty committee controls in that they cannot make promises on issues such as whether courses may be canceled for low enrollment or pay issues.

Now consider what you might have done in advance of the meeting to help contain the pot stirrer. Pot stirrers are predictable and, with some forethought, it is possible to preempt and debunk the assertions that they are likely to make through their questions and comments. If, for example, you anticipate that the resident pot stirrer will wish to thwart any change to the current summer session for fear that it might reduce what he can earn teaching in the summer, you might encourage the committee to present some specific scenarios about how the proposed change would work. One of the examples presented needs to directly address the pot stirrer's situation. If the pot stirrer can be convinced that he has nothing to fear (or lose), he will be less likely to resist the change. If, however, you anticipate that the pot stirrer will resist any change simply out of principle, you might introduce and frame the committee's report by reminding all that the status quo is no longer feasible and the only remaining question is what should be tried next. While this may not silence the pot stirrer, it will hopefully help other faculty to resist the questions and comments made by the pot stirrer who seeks no change.

Finally, as dean, consider what you might do to influence the behavior of the pot stirrer in advance of the faculty meeting set to hear the committee's proposal. If you believe you can help to influence the thinking of the pot stirrer, while the committee is working to develop its proposal, you might engage him in conversation about the need to revise the summer session. You might also suggest that the committee pilot the proposal with a few faculty members invited to assume the role of devil's advocate. This can be a good way to discern in advance what issues might be heard at the larger meeting when a vote will be taken, and to learn about issues in time to revise the proposal in a way that addresses the legitimate concerns. While this will not likely silence the committed pot stirrer, it will steal much of his thunder because the committee will have addressed the legitimate concerns and will be able to say that the idea was reviewed and revised with the input of a few colleagues who were invited to be the strongest possible devil's advocates.

THE POT STIRRER VERSUS THE ADMINISTRATION

Consider Dr. Darrin, a faculty member who is very vocal about anything that displeases her. Moreover, Dr. Darrin's concerns seem far-reaching, so she often weighs in on matters that appear to have little or no direct influence on her work at the institution. Recently, Dr. Darrin got on her soap box about new plantings on the campus. While many registered their appreciation of the new plantings that replaced some overgrown bushes, Dr. Darrin wrote a memo to all faculty and staff questioning the new plantings. In her memo, Dr. Darrin challenges the wisdom of the administration for spending money on decorative landscaping when there are so many more pressing needs such as faculty salaries and improved benefits.

The dean and provost recognize that Dr. Darrin is unaware that a donor made a gift to the institution that was earmarked to improve the older landscaping and to create a garden area where students could sit and study. However, the dean also doubts that if she had this information that Dr. Darrin would alter her view, nor would she spare the campus one of her long emails bemoaning the administration. Dr. Darrin always appears to assume the worst and spends an inordinate amount of time alerting others to every negative thought she holds about the central administration. Dr. Darrin's note on the landscaping changes raises a red flag for other faculty members who wonder about the validity of Dr. Darrin's comments that the administration would place a higher priority on landscaping than faculty salaries—although most faculty members either would not have thought much about the money being spent on the landscaping or might have assumed the changes were because of a gift—had the issue not be raised by Dr. Darrin.

Assume the role of dean and consider what you would do to manage Dr. Darrin's pot stirring in both the short term and for the long term. For the short term, what can you do to balance the views espoused by Dr. Darrin? Would you talk directly with Dr. Darrin to correct her misperceptions? Would you send a memo to the campus that defends the administration's decision to spend money on the new plantings and explain that the project is being funded by a donor? How important is it that you persuade Dr. Darrin that her conclusions are inaccurate? As a pot stirrer, Dr. Darrin will not only be hard to persuade, but she will also be quick to move on to another issue. How important is it that you respond to Dr. Darrin's concerns? How important is it that all who received Dr. Darrin's memo are able to hear your response to her concerns?

Consider what you might do in the long term to manage Dr. Darrin, who genuinely seems to enjoy stirring pots. Would you talk with Dr. Darrin, and if so, what would you say? To select an appropriate and hopefully effective strategy, you would need to consider Dr. Darrin's personality and motive for stirring pots. Unless your appeal responds to Dr. Darrin's motive in a constructive way, anything you do will be ineffective. In fact, you run the risk of escalating Dr. Darrin's pot-stirring behavior. If, for example, Dr. Darrin's pot stirring is motivated by her perception that all administrators cannot be trusted, you might prompt her to be more diligent about watching every administrative decision should your long-term strategy attempt to persuade Dr. Darrin to demonstrate her support for the institutional mission by working collegially with the administration. This appeal is not likely to work because it would require Dr. Darrin to dismiss the perceptions that fuel her pot-stirring behavior.

As dean, would you solicit help or support from anyone else in managing Dr. Darrin's pot stirring? Would you, for example, attempt to contain Dr. Darrin's pot-stirring messages by talking with others? If so, who would you approach and what would you say? Because pot stirrers are often predictable, chairs and deans can contain the pot stirring by releasing information around any decision or action that curtails the opportunity for pot stirring. For example, if a chair anticipates that the department's resident pot-stirring faculty member will use the allocation of travel dollars to suggest that the chair plays favorites when responding to faculty requests, the chair might make clear the criteria for awarding travel dollars well in advance of making the individual allocations. Chairs and deans can limit the influence of pot stirrers by equipping faculty and staff with the information they need to appropriately evaluate the assertions made by those who wish to stir the pot.

THE POT STIRRER VERSUS THE DEAN

Consider the example of Dr. Ferris, who channels his civil libertarian, anti-administration perspective into successive messages that target and call to task virtually every administrative decision and action. Dr. Ferris is very serious and proud of his watchdog role on campus. As a tenured full professor with 35 years of service at the institution, Dr. Ferris believes he is the only one who is able to "keep the dean honest" and keep the faculty alert to "the dean's agenda." He takes this role so seriously that he acts as though he is not fulfilling his employment contract if a week passes without sounding an alarm.

Dr. Ferris's alarms are always public. His call to arms may be either written or oral, taking shape as proclamations at large (or modest) faculty meetings, social gatherings, or in email communication to the provost with countless faculty members copied (and blind copied) on the correspondence. For example, the dean recently received an abrupt email from Dr. Ferris. This communication was just three short sentences proclaiming that once again the dean was adding an administrative staff position without faculty consultation and this addition was at a time when many departments were in desperate need of a new faculty position. The note was particularly irksome because the new administrative staff position was developed from roughly eight months of review regarding institutional needs and all faculty had an opportunity to review the relevant data, offer their view of the data and institutional need, and respond to a list of alternative approaches as well as offer comment on the proposed reorganization and description for the new position. At each step of the process, faculty received updates on the review and an invitation to respond in writing or to attend a forum at which the data and alternatives would be discussed.

While the dean is gratified by the number of faculty who responded to the call for comment, he is also certain that a significant portion of the faculty did not see a need to spend time following and commenting on the initiative that spanned eight months. Or, rather, that was the sentiment until the faculty read the cryptic and accusatory note from Dr. Ferris. Assume the role of dean and consider what you would do. Would you ignore or answer the note from Dr. Ferris? If you ignore the note you might give credence to the charge made by Dr. Ferris. However, answering the note could appear defensive. Moreover, a response will take significant time to draft because you would probably want to detail the entire eight-month process to demonstrate the countless opportunities that faculty had to participate in the review and help generate the solution. What would you do?

It is virtually impossible to decide on the best course of action based on the information provided in this example because you would also need to consider other factors, including the credibility that Dr. Ferris has with other faculty. Will other faculty, for example, read his note and wonder why he is raising the issue given that you, as dean, faithfully provided updates and opportunities for comment and participation in the process? If Dr. Ferris enjoys high credibility with his faculty colleagues, you will need to answer but in a way that does not appear to attack him as a person or as a respected member of the faculty. One response you might consider is offering to meet with faculty members who have concerns about the new position. This demonstrates to all that you are willing to discuss the matter and places the more detailed response to Dr. Ferris in a discussion with only the faculty who care enough about the issue to attend such a meeting.

Imagine yourself holding such a meeting to respond to the accusatory note sent by Dr. Ferris. How would you structure the meeting? Would you, for example, say the meeting was called in response to the note sent by

Dr. Ferris? When responding to pot stirrers, chairs and deans need to temper their responses in ways that do not further embolden the pot stirrer. Imagine the satisfaction that Dr. Ferris might have if you as dean began the meeting by saying that it was called because of the note received from Dr. Ferris. Would this likely embarrass or embolden Dr. Ferris? To answer this question, you would need to know more about Dr. Ferris and what motivates him to pot-stirring activity. If part of the appeal is the pleasure of holding a spot on center stage, then such an opening could be counterproductive in that it might encourage Dr. Ferris to become even more aggressive about stirring pots.

ANALYSIS AND APPLICATIONS

Because the pot stirrer works to create a climate of distrust, fear, and conflict, effective leadership communication builds on the ability to analyze the motives behind the pot stirrer's desire to fan the flames of conflict. By broadly sharing the message, pot stirrers become accountable for their communication. Open communication goes a long way in silencing the pot stirrer's motives, which are often rooted in resistance to change and an interest in damaging leadership credibility—sometimes simply for the sake of derailing the issue and sometimes just for personal attention. Let's review the essential elements of each application:

- Practice open communication.

- Practice one-to-many communication.

- Make the context clear.

- Anticipate pot-stirring activity.

◆ Practice open communication.

The quickest way to rid the department and campus of pot stirrers is to practice open communication. When everyone can count on hearing relevant information directly from the chair or dean, they will be less likely to believe claims that are untrue and that undermine leadership credibility and program effectiveness. At the same time, by airing different perspectives and discussing issues openly, it is possible for the chair or dean to face the pot stirrer to explain and support ideas which if said in private would more likely promote distrust and lower morale. In the example of Dr. Ferris, the self-appointed watchdog, the chair can use open communication to lower Dr. Ferris's credibility with faculty colleagues. When others learn through open communication that Dr. Ferris has no basis for his claim, they will be less inclined to take seriously what Dr. Ferris has to say.

◆ **Practice one-to-many communication.**

Pot stirrers thrive when one-on-one communication is the primary method for sharing information because they are not held accountable for their communication. One-on-one communication can license multiple versions of the same set of facts. No one knows for certain if the messages are consistent from one person to another or over time. By practicing one-to-many communication, chairs and deans limit the ability of pot stirrers to say different things about the same event or issue to different people. In the example of the faculty committee that worked for months to develop a summer schedule proposal, one-to-may communication can be helpful in keeping the general faculty informed of major issues and decision points. This type of communication provides the essential background information needed by the faculty to resist the eleventh-hour shotgun attack by the resident pot stirrer.

◆ **Make the context clear.**

When faculty and staff understand the context, they are better able to assess the truth or falsehood of pot-stirring statements that, if believed, can discredit the leadership, fuel conflict, and thwart progress. It also prevents the pot stirrer from attributing false or personal motives to a particular administrative action. If, for example, the faculty understand that increasing enrollment is a pressing priority, they will more likely attribute the request for faculty to attend student visitation days to the need to increase enrollment. Understanding the context will make the faculty more resistant to a pot stirrer's claim that the administration is just passing their work to faculty. It is helpful if chairs and deans keep faculty generally informed about the larger context so that they are better prepared to hear and respond to the issues as they arise.

◆ **Anticipate pot-stirring activity.**

Persistent pot stirrers are predictable, and chairs and deans can reduce the conflict created through pot stirring by anticipating what the resident pot stirrer is likely to do. Dr. Ferris, for example, can be counted on to find fault with actions taken by the administration. Often it is possible to anticipate what pot stirrers will say, who they will influence, and the method or methods they will use to communicate their concerns. The dean working with Dr. Ferris, for example, might have anticipated the objection Dr. Ferris raised to creating a new administrative position and preempted the concern in any number of ways. One way would be to use the one-to-many communication discussed earlier, and the dean might have summarized the collaborative path to the final decision in the announcement of the new position. This would provide campus-wide information in advance to preempt the types of objections Dr. Ferris typically voices.

When managing a coalition of pot stirrers rather than an individual pot stirrer, chairs and deans might engage the group more formally to help think through the obstacles in advance of making a decision. For example, a chair or dean might help to manage the pot-stirring reaction to a proposal by holding a forum for the purpose of brainstorming pros and cons to a preliminary proposal, with the understanding that the comments will be used to improve the proposal before it is brought forward for a vote. This gives the pot stirrers their say, but in a controlled context that can be helpful and can work toward improving the final outcome rather than creating an opportunity for a more open-ended attack on the administration. In using this strategy, chairs and deans can even give credit to all who helped shape the outcome when announcing the finding or outcome. By crediting the pot stirrers publicly, their opportunities to raise more concerns after the fact are limited. This is an advantage because pot stirrers are inhibited by strategies that hold them accountable for their communication. By structuring an advanced opportunity for pot stirrers to raise every possible concern and help shape the outcome or final decision, they are accountable for having their last-minute concerns make sense and for raising their concerns in advance to inform the process and the outcome. This strategy makes any concerns raised after the fact more likely to be perceived as unhelpful to the outcome and as a personal attack on the administration.

SOME FINAL THOUGHTS

Chairs and deans will reduce the conflict associated with leading change if they effectively manage pot stirring. Fortunately, although pot stirrers can differ in their motivation, they are often predictable. Chairs and deans can contain pot stirring by practicing open communication that permits all faculty and staff members to be confident that they receive relevant information and that the decision-making process is open.

Chairs and deans can also limit pot-stirring activity by practicing one-to-many communication because this limits the opportunity for one-on-one communication. It is one-on-one communication that permits pot stirrers to adapt a message to a more inflammatory one that raises concern for individual audiences with little or no accountability for what they say. One-to-many communication preserves the integrity of the message because there are few opportunities to spin it in a way that tailors the message to one particular person. Similarly, keeping all informed of the context for decisions and actions will limit pot-stirrer activity because it prevents the pot stirrer from attributing false or personal motives to a particular action.

When managing pot stirring, the old saying about how an ounce of prevention is worth a pound of cure is significant. Chairs and deans will enhance their leadership communication and effectiveness if they analyze the motives and behavioral patterns employed by pot stirrers (the prevention) and use the information from their analysis to determine ways to keep pot stirrers accountable for their communication but allow them to contribute their concerns in ways that will enhance the final outcome (the cure). The objective is not to silence pot stirrers, but to silence their motives that are directed toward escalating conflict and fear and undermining the change and leadership credibility. Negative concerns are not harmful, and some devil's advocate thinking is essential to improving any outcome. The objective is not just to contain the unconstructive motives typically found in pot stirring, but to retain and learn from the concern and objections raised by pot stirrers who often have a more negative outlook on any change.

Working With the
Prima Donna/Drama Queen

Individuals who are quick to become emotional or melodramatic about issues can be difficult to manage because emotional reactions can divert the discussion from the issue and redirect attention toward responding to the emotion being expressed rather than responding to the issue. The prima donna/drama queen spends time and energy imposing his or her view and will on others and often takes credit for work done by others. The prima donna/drama queen is typically too self-absorbed to be a valuable or contributing team player. This chapter presents strategies for exercising leadership communication that keeps discussions focused on substantive issues rather than on personalities or emotions in ways that will prevent the prima donna/drama queen from derailing progress or thwarting the team effort.

The focus and examples in this chapter might seem far-fetched unless you have encountered a prima donna/drama queen in your leadership role. However, if you have ever had responsibility for managing a prima donna/drama queen, you will not be surprised to find a chapter devoted to this personality type. The prima donna/drama queen is a memorable personality who poses a unique leadership challenge for chairs and deans. Chairs and deans quickly learn that the prima donna/drama queen cannot be ignored. In fact, the prima donna/drama queen expects and even demands attention from the chair and/or the dean, and the way you choose to attend to the prima donna/drama queen can influence the department climate and productivity of both the prima donna/drama queen and those with whom this person works.

The prima donna/drama queen personality enjoys being in the spotlight. However, his or her ascent to center stage is not always through hard work or with popular support. One characteristic that distinguishes the prima donna/drama queen from other difficult personalities is the overt and often aggressive way in which this personality assumes center stage. The behavior exhibited by the prima donna/drama queen is often perceived by others as bullying. Consequently, what the prima donna/drama queen interprets as support from colleagues is more accurately described as fear. Faculty colleagues, staff, and even students avoid direct disagreement with the prima donna/drama queen, but instead seek constructive intervention from the chair and dean. Ego and emotion appear to limit the reasoning ability of the prima donna/drama queen, who is in his or her own view both passionate and always right. The prima donna/drama queen views disagreement with suspicion and disdain. Those who think differently are perceived by the prima donna/drama queen as having at best poor judgment and at worst an ulterior motive. The prima donna/drama queen not only seeks the spotlight, but he or she also actively works to push others (and especially leadership) off the stage.

In both word and deed, the prima donna/drama queen covets and protects the spotlight position. Words that can help chairs and deans identify a prima donna/drama queen in their midst include excessive use of the personal pronouns *I*, *my*, and *me*. Prima donnas/drama queens are unabashed about taking credit for virtually everything including, for example, vision, all good ideas, pivotal information, and positive outcomes. At the same time, they are resilient—almost Teflon-like—in refusing accountability for poor ideas, faulty information, or unsuccessful outcomes. If the outcome is successful, the prima donna/drama queen will remind everyone of the central role he or she played in producing the positive result. The prima donna/drama queen often asserts (and seems to truly believe) that success was realized only as a direct result of the contribution he or she made to the effort. However, should the results fail to meet expectations, the prima donna/drama queen will assert that the desired result could have been achieved had people only listened to his or her counsel.

In deeds, the prima donna/drama queen personality is easily spotted because he or she is quick to direct others and have both the self-professed wisdom to know what everyone else should be doing and the confidence to tell everyone else what to do. In short, the prima donna/drama queen is never wrong. Regardless of whether the prima donna/drama queen has responsibility for chairing a meeting or initiative, this personality will assume a position of authority and suggest who should do what, why they should do it, and when it should be done. At the same time, those with the prima donna/drama queen personality are slow to accept work assignments. Some with this personality perceive themselves as "idea" people and therefore reason that the work should be done by the less creative individuals. Other prima donnas/drama queens perceive the delegation of work to others as part of their calling. In words and deeds, prima donnas/drama queens perceive themselves as contributing to all that is positive, but they refuse responsibility when the outcome is negative.

It is possible to discuss the prima donna/drama queen as one personality because of the similarities between the prima donna and the drama queen. However, there are some subtle differences between them that warrant special mention and which can be explained by describing the drama queen personality in detail. Most notably, the drama queen typically expresses every emotion in the extreme. The drama queen reacts to everything with an emotional intensity that can include very melodramatic reactions to fairly routine events. The drama queen transforms worry into severe anxiety and good times into excessive elation. Consequently, the drama queen can transform a discussion intended to air differences into an ugly, unproductive emotional free-for-all. The drama queen is quick to interrupt others mid-sentence and escalate both the tone and intensity of the discussion. The drama queen is prone to answer reason with personal accusations about motives and process with such phrases like, "The chair (or dean) wants us to think that" or "That's just an excuse" or "This has got to stop." The rhetoric used by the drama queen asserts an unofficial position of power and knowledge that is intended to suggest to all who would listen that the drama queen is the department's or institution's only hope for righting the windmill.

At times, the drama queen will use emotion to control the actions and reactions of others. A drama queen might, for example, shift the focus of a discussion from the issue at hand to a discussion of hurt feelings and, as a result, derail the faculty discussion of the substantive issue. If the drama queen responds to a different perspective that is voiced with a statement such as, "That really hurts my feelings," or "You hurt my feelings," it can move the discussion from weighing the pros and cons of the substantive issue to assuring the drama queen that no one intended to hurt his or her feelings. Similarly, the drama queen often derails the constructive airing of differences by suggesting to individual colleagues that each needs to guard against ill will possessed by certain other colleagues. Concrete information and data are not welcomed by the drama queen because he or she needs emotional upheaval and personalized paranoia to persist in order to stay in the coveted spotlight.

The labels *prima donna* and *drama queen* involve societal stereotypes which might be considered to be descriptive of females, but males can also exhibit the personality traits associated with the prima donna/drama queen. Unfortunately, our language seems to lack parallel labels that carry a male connotation so we are left with using prima donna/drama queen to describe both women and men whose behavior fits this personality type. The particular expression of emotion, however, might change with the sex of the prima donna/drama queen in that the female prima donna/drama queen may be more prone to emotional outbursts involving tears while the male may resort to emotional outbursts of anger or rage. Of course, this distinction is not generalizable in that the male prima donna/drama queen can produce tears and the female can demonstrate rage. While the male and female prima donna/drama queen personalities might resort to different tactics, both seek the spotlight and enjoy being on center stage.

To understand the prima donna/drama queen, chairs and deans must look at issues and events from the perspective of the prima donna/drama queen. Prima donnas/drama queens view events and issues from a personal perspective and are not skilled in understanding attitudes and views held by others that differ from their own. Prima donnas/drama queens see the world clearly and are confident in their view. This confidence serves to make the prima donna/drama queen somewhat oblivious and often resistant to views espoused by others. Moreover, the self-confidence possessed by the prima donna/drama queen can give rise to a public intolerance of others and rash impatience with those who challenge his or her thinking. The prima donna/drama queen is quick to conclude (and exclaim publicly) that someone who thinks differently "doesn't get it." The prima donna/drama queen is impatient with anyone who doesn't immediately support what the prima donna/drama queen believes should be done. Consequently, while others are often stunned by the prima donna's/drama queen's apparent disregard for chair and/or dean leadership and the visible intolerance for views held by colleagues, the prima donna/drama queen truly believes that he or she has the best insight on virtually everything and is often visibly annoyed that others do not "get it" or understand what needs to be done.

The prima donna/drama queen typically operates from a personal agenda, but that agenda may be as simple as seeking attention or needing to direct the action. Frequently, it is less about seeking a particular outcome than it is more about controlling or directing the outcome. The prima donna/drama queen is motivated to remain in the spotlight. While the prima donna/drama queen enjoys having others solicit his or her ideas and opinions, he or she will also offer an opinion before being asked. Prima donnas/drama queens want others to hear them because they believe that they have vision, wisdom, and experience that are critical to the operation of the department and the campus.

THE PRIMA DONNA/DRAMA QUEEN AND THE CURRICULUM REVISION

Consider a faculty member, Dr. White, who reminds everyone of her 200% commitment to the department and the institution. Although Dr. White works hard, her contributions do not exceed the work done by her colleagues, but Dr. White's perception is that she works significantly harder than anyone else. Moreover, Dr. White believes that the department program is strong only because she works harder than everyone and, if it were not for her insight and dedication, the department would occupy a back seat on the campus.

While Dr. White spends full days on campus, she invests a considerable amount of time talking with others about what the chair and dean should be doing and watching what everyone else does. In a gossip-like manner, Dr. White offers unsolicited editorial comment on decisions and actions and is especially critical of decisions made or actions taken on which she was not consulted. Even when the chair discusses an issue at a department meeting before making a decision and while Dr. White contributes little if anything to the discussion, the chair can count on Dr. White to offer critical comment on the decision or outcome and to exclaim that "no one talked with me," or I "would have warned them about the obvious consequences." Dr. White prefers to offer advice in one-on-one conversations. She typically "advises" when the action being considered has a direct bearing on her work and life at the institution. When an action or decision will not likely affect her work or life on the campus, Dr. White is prone to save her counsel until after the fact, when she becomes the campus equivalent of the Monday morning quarterback and explains in great detail what should have been done. She is particularly fond of telling others that the department chair doesn't "get it" whenever the chair fails to take an action preferred by Dr. White.

Assume the role of department chair and consider how you would you manage the prima donna/drama queen personality who behaves this way. Would you make a point of discussing important issues directly with a prima donna/drama queen like Dr. White in advance of making important decisions? Doing this might befriend her in a way that causes her to become less critical of your leadership. At the same time, consulting with Dr. White individually might have a counterproductive result in that it might embolden her to believe that you check with her before taking any action, and it also might give her an opportunity to misquote you and tell others that before you make a decision or determine a course of action, you seek her counsel. It might also lower your credibility with other faculty who may perceive your solicitation of Dr. White's view as preferential treatment. Some faculty may perceive your need for her counsel as an indication that it is Dr. White who is the real department chair. One of the challenges of managing the prima donna/drama queen personality is that typically it must be done in a public setting because the prima donna/drama queen likes to be in the spotlight and on center stage. Hence, whether you attempt to placate Dr. White or opt to resist her expectation to be consulted in advance of decisions, your approach will likely be visible to others both in and beyond the department.

To illustrate the dynamic involved in managing the prima donna/drama queen, consider the situation of a department that worked for a full academic year to revise its curriculum. The department chair worked with the five faculty members who served on the department curriculum committee. At each step of the process, the committee consulted with other faculty members and invited comment at major decision points. At least once a month the curricular revisions that were being considered were discussed during regular department meetings so that every faculty member would be aware of the issues under consideration and have an opportunity to weigh in. Dr. White is not a member of the curriculum committee, but she repeatedly expressed her view that if the curriculum is to be revised then the result should be to create a truly innovative and distinctive program. She never offered any specific suggestions or commented on ideas presented throughout the year beyond admonishing the department chair and members of the curriculum committee that change for the sake of change would only cost the department majors. Work progressed and the department voted to approve the final proposal submitted by the curriculum committee. Even though Dr. White received the proposal in advance of the meeting and understood when the department vote would be taken, she did not attend the meeting. The department voted unanimously in favor of the proposed revision, but the outcome did not include Dr. White's vote.

Now, as the department begins to implement the approved change, Dr. White becomes more vocal about how the revision represents change for its own sake and does nothing to make the program distinctive. She openly criticizes the revision as being boring and lacking the innovation expected by today's students. The members of the curriculum committee are frustrated by her assertions, but they are not sure how to address them. Dr. White openly shares her view with anyone on campus who will listen. She tells faculty from other departments of her embarrassment over her department's "lame" attempt to have an innovative curriculum. She warns students to get requirements out of the way before the new program becomes effective so they don't "waste" their time and money taking the meaningless and trivial courses added as part of the curricular revision. This behavior angers virtually everyone in the department, but no one wishes to confront Dr. White because doing so only ever seems to produce negative results. In fact, once during a department meeting when Dr. White was ranting about the "miserable" proposal that took the committee a full year to develop, a member of the committee reminded her that she had passed on every opportunity to offer comment as the proposal was being developed. Without hesitation, Dr. White snapped, "I shouldn't have to do your work for you. I wasn't elected to the curriculum committee and I have my hands full managing the department personnel committee."

Assume the role of department chair and decide what you might do. Would you ignore Dr. White and hope that she moves on to other issues or would you address the negative statements that she is making about the approved curricular revisions? If you believe you should address the potentially harmful comments being made by Dr. White, how would you approach her and what would you say? Would you, for example, attempt to persuade her that she is wrong to dismiss the curricular revisions as lame and unimportant? Or, would you attempt to reason with Dr. White by reminding her that, like it or not, the department has voted and the revisions will be implemented? Or, would you point out that she is risking her credibility and rapport with department colleagues by making statements that do not help improve the revised curriculum, but only criticize it? Given what you know about the prima donna/drama queen personality, how might you expect Dr. White to respond to each of the three appeals? Are there other appeals that you might make?

Assume that you decide to reason with Dr. White by reminding her that the department has voted and that she missed her opportunity to persuade the faculty to reach a different outcome. You point out to her that she can still exhibit constructive leadership and collegiality by offering specific suggestions that might improve the revised curriculum. Can you anticipate how Dr. White, a steadfast prima donna/drama queen personality, might respond? Assume that she replies, "I know that you have to defend the sorry revision, but don't expect me to support this baloney. If you are half as smart as I hope you are, then you know I'm right. These changes aren't going to make the program distinctive." Again, put yourself in the role of department chair and consider how you would respond to Dr. White.

Remember that the prima donna/drama queen sees the world from a self-centered perspective. The prima donna/drama queen enjoys the spotlight and center stage, so initiatives that deny her this role will likely receive instant and contentious disapproval. In managing Dr. White, you would want to consider and distinguish between the things that cannot be changed and those that might be altered. For example, there is no way that she can assume the coveted center stage spot for the curriculum revision approved by the department. Dr. White was not a member of the curriculum committee, and she elected to pass on the opportunities for input that might help shape the outcome. You might consider if there is a constructive center stage role for her at this point in the process. For example, might Dr. White be assigned a role in implementing the approved curriculum revision? Is there a particular course that she might work to develop? This strategy only works if there is a legitimate role for the prima donna/drama queen personality. It would not, for example, be helpful to give Dr. White a center stage role in implementing the curricular revision if it would not produce the desired outcome. You might also assess the merit of the statements she made and debunk the arguments being made. While this may not persuade her, it can help to solidify the understanding and support of others in the department. For example, perhaps Dr. White's claim that the curricular revisions will not make the program distinctive is irrelevant because the revision was made to keep the program in compliance with accreditation criteria. Curricular revisions that are made to demonstrate that the program satisfies accreditation criteria yield compliance and will not, by themselves, yield distinctiveness. You might, however, suggest that she bring to the next meeting of the curriculum committee her thoughts on how the program might move from compliance to being distinctive. This put-up-or-shut-up approach will change the dynamic in that Dr. White will now be forced to demonstrate before her colleagues how the program might be made distinctive instead of asserting that it was someone else's failed job. What other alternatives might be used to manage this prima donna/drama queen?

THE CHAIR AS PRIMA DONNA/DRAMA QUEEN

Consider the example of the department chair, Dr. Klein, who was hired from outside the institution when the department needed structure and organization. As department chair, Dr. Klein has done a remarkable job bringing order to what was described as planned chaos. Almost immediately, he attended to every detail and demonstrated patience for personally monitoring every aspect of the department's work. Now, six years later, his personal control and scrutiny over every aspect of the department continues, even though the department is now well organized and the faculty collaborate often and well on virtually all matters. With the immediate need to instill order and stability in the department addressed, faculty members are becoming more vocal about their unhappiness with Dr. Klein's leadership. The faculty perceive Dr. Klein as controlling and manipulative. They complain that he only supports initiatives that are his ideas and that he is quick to claim credit for ideas offered by others. The faculty also bemoan that too much time is spent reporting back to Dr. Klein for no apparent purpose other than to permit him to be a controlling gatekeeper on all department matters. In addition, Dr. Klein prefers to communicate using email or one-on-one conversation.

The dean has noticed a growing discontent with Dr. Klein's leadership from both within and outside the department. The dean has also listened to Dr. Klein's more frequent laments about the "problem" faculty in the department and the "ineffective" leadership in other offices at the institution. It seems that nothing pleases Dr. Klein. He complains that faculty members do not keep him properly informed of their whereabouts and activities and that those in leadership roles in other offices do not consult him on all matters involving or impacting "his" department.

According to Dr. Klein, even students believe they can act unilaterally. Last semester, students from the department petitioned the student government for funds to bring a speaker to campus. While the speaker was admittedly a "big name" in the discipline, Dr. Klein forbid any publicity about the speaker's lecture or presence on campus. It was months later that the dean learned of the speaker's visit to the campus. When asked why the event was not publicized, Dr. Klein explained that he needed to do damage control to protect the department and institution from negative press. According to Dr. Klein, the students' plan for the speaker was so disorganized that he needed to "sit on this powder keg" to prevent it from exploding. The dean learned about the speaker after the fact when faculty members in the department complained that they understood that the dean's office and the institution's public relations office would not agree to publicize the event. Without exception, the faculty bemoaning the lack of support for the event recounted that Dr. Klein had told them of the institution's refusal to provide publicity.

Assume the role of dean and consider what you might do in this situation. Would you forget the matter since the event has passed and there is nothing that can be done? Would you try to gather more information about the speaker's invitation and visit to the campus? If so, what information would you seek and how might you gather it? Would you confront Dr. Klein about what the faculty told you? If so, how would you approach Dr. Klein and what would you say? For example, would you call him? Email him? Meet with him? Think through what might happen if you used each of these communication channels and how your approach might change with each channel of communication. In each format, how would you raise the issue and what would you say? Would you involve anyone else in this discussion? If so, who would you include and why?

Let's assume that you decide to talk with Dr. Klein. In a one-on-one meeting with him, you express surprise that you were unaware of the speaker's visit to campus. Dr. Klein assures you that "you didn't miss anything." He adds that the event was controlled totally by students who "literally threw the event together at the last minute" so it was, of course, poorly attended. Dr. Klein adds, "I was able to predict the outcome from the moment I learned of the students' half-baked scheme." You press on, adding that you understand that the speaker is a prominent person in the discipline who might have netted the department and the institution some favorable publicity. Dr Klein replies, "Precisely. I told you that the students exercised poor judgment in not seeking my leadership of the event before they contacted the speaker and sought funding support from student government. I could have transformed the event into a golden opportunity for the department and the institution." Without hesitation, he adds, "It is incredible that the speaker accepted the invitation since it was not extended by me. This really makes me wonder what the students told the speaker to get her to come."

Put yourself in the role of dean and consider where you might lead this conversation. Would you conclude that it is pointless to pursue the matter with Dr. Klein, or would you press on? What is your primary objective for raising the issue with Dr. Klein, and has the conversation thus far caused you to revise your objective? What are the potential risks and benefits of aborting the conversation? What are the potential risks and benefits of pursuing the conversation? To put this in other terms, what are the short-term and long-term issues at stake in your management of Dr. Klein? For example, does his behavior have implications for the management of the department and for your leadership credibility with the department faculty and students?

Let's assume that you decide to continue your conversation with Dr. Klein. You disclose that some of the department faculty members have complained about the lack of administrative support for publicizing the event. He dismisses the concern with a curt, "You know how faculty can be, especially the group that I have to manage." Sensing that Dr. Klein is not hearing your concern, you ask how the faculty got the idea that you and the public relations staff refused to publicize the event when neither office was aware of the event. Dr. Klein replies, "Don't give them a second thought. You know how melodramatic my faculty can be. I suppose that a few of them think we should have permitted the students to fail publicly, but you should be grateful that I know better." You again ask how the faculty drew the conclusion that support for publicity was refused. He begins to appear more impatient with your inability to grasp the fact that he was doing what he needed to do to spare the department and institution negative publicity, but adds somewhat indignantly, "Well, I may have said that I was certain that you and the institution would not provide publicity. You wouldn't want me to have them think you are stupid or reckless with resources, would you?" As dean, how would you respond? Has this conversation served the purpose you intended? Does the conversation cause you to reconsider your primary objective in working with Dr. Klein? Where would you go from here? What observations have you made that might inform your leadership communication with Dr. Klein and the faculty in the department? At a minimum, this exchange might help you understand why faculty members complain that Dr. Klein is controlling and manipulative and why several refer to him as a spin doctor.

ANALYSIS AND APPLICATIONS

Responding to raw emotions can quickly sidetrack any discussion, and because the prima donna/drama queen personality uses emotional issues to create flashpoints, chairs and deans can better contain and even reverse the damage by using effective communication strategies to stay focused on the issues rather than the behaviors. Given the desires of the prima donna/drama queen to be the center of attention, understanding how to use the audience to create public communication and to manage this personality's need for attention can create greater accountability for the prima donna/drama queen. Let's review the essential elements of each application:

- Stay on the issue.
- Time your intervention well.
- Play to the audience.
- Assess underlying motives and statements of fact.

◆ Stay on the issue.

When dealing with the emotional responses of a prima donna, and especially those of a drama queen, it is important that chairs and deans stay on the issue and resist responding to the emotion as you run the risk of excluding the issue. It is natural to respond to the emotion, but doing so can derail the discussion of the issue and cause chairs and deans to abandon their leadership responsibility, which is to help faculty and staff reach constructive solutions. Getting off topic can also cause chairs and deans to sacrifice their leadership credibility with others as it can mean that important issues are left unresolved or unaddressed in order to soften or placate the emotional response of the prima donna/drama queen. For example, an untenured faculty member who cries during an annual performance review might prompt a chair to become supportive when he or she really needs to focus on clarifying how the faculty member is not meeting performance expectations and what must be done to secure a favorable tenure review.

Sometimes it is impossible to ignore the emotional response or the persistent quest to claim the spotlight and be on center stage. In the example of Dr. White, the chair cannot ignore her persistent claims that the revised curriculum is "boring" or her attempts to sour students to the revision. But leadership intervention will only be effective if the chair stays on the issue and is not drawn off into the more personal accusations being levied by Dr. White. For example, ensuring that the focus is on the issue might be done by building an informed context for the new curriculum with all members of the department. This strategy can allow other faculty and students to dismiss Dr. White's rhetoric as uninformed. The department chair might also structure an opportunity for the department to hear Dr. White's concerns with the express purpose of letting all understand and evaluate the merit of them. Because prima donnas/drama queens are seldom motivated to gather information or data (after all, they don't need facts to be certain of their position), this can be a powerful leadership communication strategy for containing Dr. White's negative influence. While such strategies may not stop her, they may empower Dr. White's audience to separate the reasonable argument from the unreasonable assertion. Also, these strategies allow for any positive thoughts expressed by Dr. White to inform and improve the outcome.

◆ Time your intervention well.

Most people are uncomfortable managing tears, excessive anger, or other forms of emotional outbursts, and it is not easy managing the prima donna/ drama queen who is quick to become emotional and even melodramatic. While it is intuitive to avoid emotional outbursts because they can be very unpleasant, it is important for chairs and deans to manage emotional outbursts. If emotional outbursts are left unmanaged they can have a counterproductive affect. Managing an emotionally charged conflict can be a chilling prospect to even the most competent chair or dean and with good reason. When a prima donna/drama queen personality is building emotional steam, it is difficult to believe that anyone could succeed in having the prima donna/drama queen hear reason or be persuaded to a different view. Chairs and deans, however, must realize that there is a difference between aborting inappropriate behavior and managing emotional outbursts. In fact, the very worst time to attempt to manage conflict is when emotions are at their peak. Similarly, it is most difficult to manage the prima donna/drama queen when he or she is basking in the glow of the spotlight and is center stage. There is, however, a practical and significant difference between managing emotionally charged conflict and aborting inappropriate behavior. By aborting inappropriate behavior and postponing discussion of the conflict until emotions are more balanced, the issue of contention can then be framed objectively and embedded in the presentation of reasoned perspectives and data, chairs and deans will be able to deny the prima donna/drama queen the attention that typically follows an emotional outburst—which most often derails discussion of the substantive issue.

Both Drs. White and Klein seek to persuade others of their points of view by making unsupported assertions. Dr. White's claim that the new curriculum is "boring" and lacks distinctiveness is comparable to Dr. Klein's claim that the students' invitation to a prominent member of the discipline was a "half-baked scheme" that threatened to bring negative press to the program and the institution. It is impossible to assess these claims as true or false based on information obtained from Dr. White or Dr. Klein. Without gathering more information and other perspectives, it becomes virtually impossible to break through the circular reasoning asserted by each. Consider Dr. Klein's claim that he knew the speaking event would be poorly attended because the students had not consulted him and such consultation would have meant proper planning. It may be that the event was poorly attended because it was not publicized. A key aspect of timing one's intervention is gathering relevant facts and other information that permits a more informed discussion of the conflict. It is unlikely that chairs and deans can manage the prima donna/drama queen in one meeting. Instead, chairs and deans should take the time needed to truly understand the issue and to have assembled all of the relevant facts which will equip them to manage the difficult personality of the prima donna/drama queen.

◆ Play to the audience.

Remember that the prima donna/drama queen enjoys being in the spotlight and on center stage. The prima donna/drama queen relishes attention and seeks validation from others. This need for external validation makes it possible for chairs and deans to use audience response to help manage the prima donna/drama queen. Despite possessing excessive self-confidence, the prima donna/drama queen also needs to know that others recognize the contributions made by the prima donna/drama queen. Chairs and deans can use audience response to help manage the prima donna/drama queen by involving others in the conversation with the prima donna/drama queen. When chairs and deans discuss differences with the prima donna/dram queen in a one-on-one communication, it is easy for the prima donna/drama queen to dismiss the chair or dean as "not getting it." If, however, the prima donna/drama queen is permitted to observe that others agree with the chair or dean, it is more difficult to dismiss the leadership.

In the example of Dr. White, it is important that the department chair helps other faculty members sustain their support for the revised curriculum. Similarly, it is important that the chair prevents students from becoming disenchanted with the curricular revisions. Consequently, communication with faculty and students is at least as important as communication with Dr. White. In managing the prima donna/drama queen, chairs and deans need to realize the importance of communicating with the various audiences and that there is likely more than one audience that should be considered. The word *audience*, in this sense, is synonymous with *constituency*. In the situation involving Dr. White, the significant audiences include, for example, other faculty members, current and prospective students, and the central administration, especially if she enjoys any credibility with the dean and other administrators.

◆ Assess underlying motives and statements of fact.

A leadership strategy is only as good as the leader's assessment of the situation. Key to managing the prima donna/drama queen personality is to give some thought to his or her motive and to discern facts from inference or fiction. Even when the prima donna/drama queen is motivated merely to remain in the spotlight, this difficult personality will likely exploit issues that evoke reactions because the view expressed attacks or threatens motives held by others. Claims made by Dr. White about the revised curriculum, for example, threaten the very motivation that spurred the curriculum change. Faculty in the department worked hard over several months for the express purpose of developing a more distinctive curriculum. Hence, Dr. White's conclusion that the revised curriculum is "boring" hits a nerve, which helps to fan the flames of her emotionally laden accusation. Dr. Klein, in contrast, might be motivated to retain ultimate control and decision-making authority. If initiatives that are done independent of Dr. Klein fail, then faculty members and students will be more inclined to seek his involvement early—increasing his control as chair beyond what it would be if faculty and students were empowered to take independent action.

Understanding the prima donna's/drama queen's motives offers insight into how to manage this difficult personality. If Dr. Klein seeks control, a discussion about what did or did not happen in the instance of the student-sponsored speaker will not help. Similarly, it will do little good to insist to Dr. White that the revised curriculum will bring distinction to the program, especially since it will take time to realize the anticipated benefit of implementing a new curriculum. In fact, prima donna/drama queen personalities thrive on confusing the situation and ultimately have greater influence over outcomes when their personal motives are not detected and challenged. Dr. Klein, for example, will gain more control over the department faculty if the dean believes that the speaker event might have been a disaster and does not question Dr. Klein's motives for killing the event rather than helping it succeed.

Knowing the prima donna's/drama queen's motives will help chairs and deans to discern the relevant facts and perspectives. The management of this difficult personality requires that chairs and deans distinguish between assertion and fact. If the dean, for example, knows that Dr. Klein's motivation is retaining unilateral control, it becomes easier to understand which of his statements represent assertions or inferences derived from his perspective. Most often, the prima donna/drama queen personality views events from a personal perspective and thus is not able to separate fact from fiction and instead interprets statements and events in ways that support a previously held theory or perspective. Chairs and deans will be better able to manage this difficult personality if they take the time to assess motive and distinguish between fact and fiction.

SOME FINAL THOUGHTS

Prima donnas/drama queens are one of the more challenging, difficult personalities to manage because they are motivated by personal agenda and rely on emotion rather than reason. Chairs and deans need to resist the temptation to be drawn off the issue of substance and into the realm of emotion, even when the intuitive reaction is to assuage the emotional appeal. This requires patience, timing, and effective leadership communication. It can be counterintuitive to remain focused on facts and issues when confronted with an emotional outburst, but doing so is the only way to effectively manage the prima donna/drama queen. Chairs and deans can enhance their efforts by taking time to carefully and systematically assess the motive(s) of the prima donna/drama queen and to discern between fact and fiction. This analysis will help chairs and deans identify the data and perspectives needed to more fully understand the substantive issue which in turn can be used to help hold the prima donna/drama queen accountable for reasoned and responsible claims and communication. Recognizing that it is unlikely that even the most knowledgeable and skilled chair or dean will be able to persuade this difficult personality in private one-on-one communication, chairs and deans need to make full use of public conversations and settings in order to hold the prima donna/drama queen personality accountable for more reasoned and accurate communication.

14

Managing the Confrontation Junkie

People who thrive on confrontation can thwart consensus building because their goal is not to reach agreement. Confrontation junkies thrive on conflict and sometimes enjoy the battle more than winning. They work to both create and then fuel conflict rather than resolve it. Their presence can also threaten collegiality, department or campus climate, and morale. Chairs and deans can exercise specific leadership communication strategies that permit the constructive airing of different views while minimizing confrontational behavior that intensifies hostility or destructive conflict. This chapter presents strategies for exercising leadership communication that helps chairs and deans manage the confrontation junkie.

The confrontation junkie marches to a different drummer. Whereas the overwhelming majority of individuals prefer to avoid or ignore conflict, the confrontation junkie thrives on it. This basic personality trait gives life to specific behaviors that can be difficult to manage in the workplace. The confrontation junkie is typically looking for a fight, and this means that he or she interprets the actions and statement of others in the most divisive way possible. The confrontation junkie does not give others the benefit of the doubt, but instead will typically rely on literal interpretations that offer reason for the disagreement. The confrontation junkie can transform a simple request for information into something akin to a personal insult. For example, a routine request to have absences from work reported can cause the confrontation junkie to come out swinging with claims that his or her integrity is being called into question for no apparent reason. Even when campus policy clearly stipulates that employee absences are to be approved in advance by an employee's supervisor, the confrontation junkie will likely respond to such a request with anger and indignation.

The confrontation junkie is always ready to pick a fight because he or she enjoys the battle. The confrontation junkie does not lose sleep or become uncomfortable in the face of hostility, and therefore is more likely to make the conflict personal. The confrontation junkie will intentionally confuse the issue with the person presenting the idea or making a request for information. The confrontation junkie can transform the chair's or dean's request to report absences into evidence that supports his or her claim that the chair or dean is at best being unreasonable and at worst prejudiced toward the confrontation junkie. This tactic often leaves the chair or dean on the defensive because the successful confrontation junkie will have shifted the issue from the need to report absences to whether the chair or dean is being mean and vindictive. This ability to twist the real issue helps to explain how and why the confrontation junkie can undermine leadership credibility and effectiveness.

Unless you have had experience managing the confrontation junkie, this may be hard to believe. It might be difficult to imagine how a simple request for information covered by campus policy can be turned into a situation that places the chair or dean on the defensive. Remember, the confrontation junkie seeks rather than avoids conflict. Conflict does not embarrass or stress the confrontation junkie, and consequently he or she typically invites an audience. Instead of responding to a seemingly simple request for information, the confrontation junkie shifts the issue and raises the stakes by replying with an accusation about the motive of the person making the inquiry. Also, the confrontation junkie's reply is seldom a one-on-one communication, but is instead a form of one-to-many communication where he or she copies other people so that the chair or dean finds himself or herself in the position of needing to explain the initial request to others who would normally not be involved in such routine matters.

True confrontation junkies do not give much thought to keeping the peace or even to phrasing their comments and concerns in a way that would reduce defensiveness. Instead, a confrontation junkie will make his or her critique on the views held by others in ways that might appear to be an attack on those holding a different view. Typically, a colleague who is seeking to provide constructive feedback might preface a critical comment about someone's viewpoint with a qualifying comment such as, "I can understand why you might believe this, however . . ." or "It's obvious that you have given this much thought, but . . ." The confrontation junkie, how-ever, is prone to making personal comments when registering an objection to a different view, such as, "Why can't you see how stupid that is," or "Your ideas never work," or "And you wonder why no one listens to you." Because confrontation junkies work at making disagreements personal, they inhibit consensus building, constructive change, teamwork, and effec-tive communication. Instead, the behaviors of the confrontation junkie can lower morale and increase paranoia among others, which also under-mines leadership credibility and effectiveness.

The confrontation junkie will also create divisiveness between and among others by intentionally sharing information that promotes ill will or distrust. The confrontation junkie will attribute statements to others that may be very different from what was actually said. Confrontation junkies contribute to conflict by repeating partial or false information. They are particularly skilled at asserting "facts" that are not easily confirmed and which, over time, can lower trust between and among colleagues. These tac-tics permit the confrontation junkie to create conflict and then fan the flames of that conflict without being directly involved. A confrontation junkie, for example, might invoke needless fear and anxiety about a search for a new dean by calling into question the central administration's use of a search firm. Claims about search firms not understanding the campus or working only to please the administrators who pay them can taint the entire search process and make every candidate interviewed for the position sus-pect of being an ill fit for the position or at least in terms of what the faculty would want in a dean. Such negativity can have an adverse affect on the outcome of the search and on morale, even when there is no truth to the claims asserted and perpetuated by the confrontation junkie.

Ironically, the confrontation junkie may or may not believe what he or she insists is the truth. A confrontation junkie, for example, may or may not believe that a search firm cannot identify candidates for the deanship who would be able to meet the needs of the faculty. While confrontation junkies typically sound passionate, and even desperate, about the views they espouse, it is not always the case that they believe what they profess. The confrontation junkie thrives on turmoil, so the rhetoric he or she uses is often a means to an end and not a message of conviction. Or, it is also possible that the confrontation junkie has a strong desire to create turmoil around the search for a new dean (or chair) as part of a larger desire to fuel animosity between the faculty and the central administration.

The confrontation junkie does not worry about being held account-able for making inaccurate statements. Instead, he or she assumes responsi-bility for sounding alarms. Even when an alarm is unfounded or false, the confrontation junkie will take a bow for raising the issue that kept things "honest" because it made everyone watchful. Being combative is part of the confrontation junkie's identity, so there is a sense of not doing one's job unless people and issues are stirred up. The confrontation junkie is fulfilled by the presence of conflict because he or she is gratified by turmoil and up-heaval. Absent conflict, the confrontation junkie is out of business, and harmonious relationships do not provide the same satisfaction for the con-frontation junkie as they do for others.

Chairs and deans often find it difficult to restrain the confrontation junkie whose fearless (and often personal) approach to conflict can alienate everyone else. Left unmanaged, the confrontation junkie can leave col-leagues battle worn, with wounds that never heal. Yet if others are not will-ing to challenge the incomplete and inaccurate statements made by the confrontation junkie, it will be difficult to build and sustain a campus en-vironment that permits honest discussion, consensus building, and collab-orative problem-solving. Chairs and deans must manage the confrontation junkie effectively in order to preserve a collegial climate in the department and on the campus. Because the confrontation junkie plays to an audience, chairs and deans will not be able to manage the confrontation junkie pri-vately. As a general rule, all difficult personalities require some public man-agement to curtail the damage they might cause and to hold them accountable for their actions. Appealing to the confrontation junkie will not likely influence his or her behavior. It is preferable to manage the con-frontation junkie by publicly holding him or her accountable for commu-nication. Accountability need not be a negative confrontation; however, it must model for others the importance of assessing the merit of the con-frontation junkie's statements. Remember, since the confrontation junkie feeds on missing or inaccurate information in order to prey on others' inse-curities and fears, chairs and deans can help check the influence of the con-frontation junkie by listening carefully to what he or she asserts and publicly asking for reasoned substantiation. Thus, if the confrontation junkie asserts that a curricular change being considered by the department will cause the program to "lose all of its majors" or "jeopardize its accredi-tation," the chair would be well served to ask why the confrontation junkie believes this to be true. If there is truth to the statement, it is important to know and to consider this information. However, if the confrontation junkie has no basis for the assertion, asking the question will hurt his or her credibility which in turn will limit the confrontation junkie's influence on halting the curricular revision.

Ironically, a campus climate that encourages the honest airing of different views is typically problematic for the true confrontation junkie, so chairs and deans must realize that the true confrontation junkie will work against such efforts. Consequently, when chairs and deans are successful in building and sustaining a collegial environment marked by a climate where individuals can air different views without fear of retaliation or humiliation, they do a lot to contain the harm that can be done by the confrontation junkie. By reviewing some specific instances of the confrontation junkie in action, it may be easier to recognize why and how chairs and deans need to exercise leadership communication that limits the destructive influence of this difficult personality.

MANAGING THE CONFRONTATION JUNKIE AT MOMENTS OF DECISION

Consider the confrontation junkie Dr. Faulkner, who, at a department meeting, is determined to control through intimidation and wishes to abort his colleagues' consideration of curricular revisions that could alter what Dr. Faulkner teaches. The proposal being considered at the department meeting was developed over several months by the department's curriculum committee and, as chair, you know that the faculty presenting the proposal have worked hard and have much invested in the proposal. You also know that the department curriculum committee made a point of inviting all faculty members to hear and respond to preliminary ideas. They were careful to consider all suggestions made, and the final proposal represents almost a full academic year of conscientious and deliberate work.

Nonetheless, the committee is nervous about presenting the curriculum proposal at the full department meeting for a vote. You understand that the committee would be confident in their work and more comfortable presenting the proposal to the department if it were not for Dr. Faulkner. Dr. Faulkner has passed on all opportunities to offer his views to the committee, but the committee fears he will move to sabotage the proposal at the department meeting and get it voted down. The committee's concerns would have them sounding paranoid to anyone who does not know Dr. Faulkner. Sadly, your experience as department chair gives you reason to believe that Dr. Faulkner will do precisely what they expect him to do at the department meeting.

You need to use your leadership role as department chair and your experience working with Dr. Faulkner to change the anticipated dynamic at the department meeting. What might be done in advance of the meeting to alter the discussion? Would you have a conversation with Dr. Faulkner? Is there any special guidance that you might offer to the curriculum committee? The complexity of the conflict dynamic involving this particular confrontation junkie will be more fully realized if you think in concrete terms about what you might do in advance of the meeting. For example, if you elect to talk with Dr. Faulkner before the meeting, it is possible that he might interpret your efforts to persuade him as an indication of the power he holds over the final vote. And if so, your attempts to reason with him could backfire. Similarly, all the advice you might give the committee might serve to reinforce Dr. Faulkner's image and power in altering the outcome because the advice would likely be perceived as confirming the fear that the committee holds.

Pre-meeting intervention will only be helpful if it alters the anticipated dynamic with Dr. Faulkner. Depending on what you know about his perception of the curriculum proposal, you might offer to defuse the potentially sensitive issue. If, for example, the collective wisdom is that Dr. Faulkner will oppose the proposed revision because it moves the upper-division courses he teaches from required to elected course status, you might defuse this sensitive issue by making clear to him why this change could be advantageous for him. Dr. Faulkner might worry that making his course an elective would hurt the enrollment, when it could increase the enrollment by making it open to nonmajors. If Dr. Faulkner is motivated by self-interest, you might be able to defuse the sensitive issue that will fuel his objection by persuading him that the proposed curricular revision could advantage the very outcome he wishes to protect.

Even if you have viable options for defusing the sensitive issue in advance of the department meeting, you will need to give some thought as to how you might conduct the meeting to permit a reasoned consideration of the curriculum proposal. This means you must also give some consideration as to how you might contain or limit any destructive communication that might curtail productive discussion. As chair, you have some opportunity to structure the process used during the department meeting. By this, we do not mean that you would structure the decision, but you could structure how differing views would be aired to permit the faculty to reach a decision. Especially when a confrontation junkie (or any other difficult personality) will be at the meeting, it is best to give some forethought to how to structure and manage the discussion. "Winging it" seldom works because in taking the whatever-will-be approach, you surrender an important advantage—the ability to anticipate in advance what Dr. Faulkner might do and say. A little forethought can prevent you from feeling stuck or outwitted in a meeting that you are responsible for chairing.

The benefit of this leadership communication strategy will be easier to see by imagining the department meeting at which the curriculum committee presents the proposal for faculty discussion and vote. Imagine a meeting with about 20 faculty members. The curriculum committee presents the proposal and fields a few questions. The faculty members seem generally supportive of the proposal, but as you contemplate calling a vote, Dr. Faulkner stands up and says, "Nothing surprises me anymore. There was a day when you could count on faculty to recognize a dangerous change when they heard one proposed."

This is enough to halt all other conversation as heads turn toward Dr. Faulkner and he continues: "This proposal will cost us all our majors and jeopardize our accreditation. Since no one else is being realistic, let me remind you that a drop in major headcount will likely cost the department several faculty positions." He then turns to the untenured faculty in the room and continues, "Are you willing to put your job on the line for some creative mumbo jumbo that will scare students away from tried and true programs?" Dr. Faulkner now turns to the tenured faculty in the room and asks, "Are you willing to jeopardize an accredited program we know works? How can you possibly doubt that an unaccredited program will have an adverse affect on student recruitment and enrollment?" With full crescendo, he closes his remarks by adding, "Who among you is so stupid and idiotic that you would vote for a change that will ruin a strong program?" People turn to look at you because, as chair, you are conducting the meeting. What do you say or do next?

If you have had experience managing the confrontation junkie, you know full well what this moment feels like. It is frustrating but pivotal in that in addition to the curriculum proposal, your leadership credibility also hangs in the balance. What do you do? Would you, for example, attempt to discredit Dr. Faulkner and point out that he had ample opportunity to raise his concerns earlier? While some faculty, especially those serving on the curriculum committee might appreciate your pointing this out, such a response will likely have little impact on Dr. Faulkner, who might shoot back, "I'm too busy to watch all of your incompetent moves, but I cannot sit quietly by during a meeting when you are trying to brainwash those with less experience into voting in favor of something that could cost them their jobs. Someone has to care about the health and future of this department." Again, if you have had experience managing the confrontation junkie, you will recognize that such rhetoric is typical of this personality type. It also escalates the discussion unfolding in front of the department from consideration of a curriculum proposal to an attack on your leadership credibility as chair of the department. What do you do next?

One way to return discussion to the substantive issue and to limit the negative influence of the confrontation junkie is to not respond in kind, but to reframe the issue before the department. You might, for example, point out that Dr. Faulkner has raised some very serious concerns about the curriculum proposal under discussion. You might assure everyone that you and the curriculum committee wish to hear and consider all possible pros and cons and invite Dr. Faulkner to share with the department the basis for his conclusion that the proposed curriculum would produce a drop in enrollment and jeopardize the program's accreditation.

This put-up-or-shut-up reply to Dr. Faulkner has several advantages. First, it refocuses the discussion on the substantive issue. Second, it debunks his effort to call to question your leadership credibility. Third, it gives Dr. Faulkner every benefit of the doubt while forcing him to do more than issue unfounded assertions. Should he have valid reasons for his conclusion, the faculty should hear and consider them. If, however, Dr. Faulkner is attempting to increase paranoia and damage your leadership credibility while killing a change he does not support, it will become more obvious when he cannot substantiate his assertions as you invited him to do. When this happens, you will have succeeded in discrediting Dr. Faulkner without attacking him. You will permit others in the department to form their own conclusions about Dr. Faulkner's knowledge of the issues being discussed and his motives for objecting to the proposed curricular review. This leadership communication strategy permits you to curtail the damage that Dr. Faulkner might cause without permitting the conflict to become something others perceive as a conflict between you as the chair and Dr. Faulkner.

MANAGING THE CAMPUS WATCHDOG

Consider the confrontation junkie, Dr. Beacon, who enjoys the role of campus watchdog and believes that if it were not for her scrutiny the faculty would be passive pawns in the administration's plan to deny faculty their rightful authority. Dr. Beacon does not limit her involvement to faculty and curricular issues. She is known to call out any and every example of mismanagement in a spirited and combative manner that all have come to expect.

Her most recent missive to the entire campus community called into question the administrative wisdom of cleaning the exterior of a sandstone building on the campus when there were so many more pressing needs. In a two-page, single-spaced electronic memo to the campus, Dr. Beacon was openly critical of the administrative decision to place "cosmetics ahead of education." In the memo, she asserts that the faculty and students do not matter to the central administration or the "astronomical sum" being spent on this "purely cosmetic" renovation would be redirected to more pressing priorities such as faculty salaries or instructional support. The memo is addressed to the entire campus community so it is not clear that Dr. Beacon expects a reply. She is merely sounding an alarm and calling attention to "this newest evidence of administrative mismanagement."

Dr. Beacon's distrust of the administration is implied in the memo, and the fact that she is not seeking a response from the administration indicates that her primary objective is to sound the alarm. Assume the role of dean of the faculty at a small institution and decide what you would do in this situation. Would you reply at all? If so, would you reply privately to Dr. Beacon or would you use the "reply to all" email option to have the entire campus read your response? Though this memo is what you have come to expect of her, it is frustrating because Dr. Beacon refuses to gather the facts before sounding such alarms. In this instance, the work being done on the old sandstone building is not at all what Dr. Beacon believes.

You surmise that she has concluded that the sandstone building will be cleaned because of the scaffolding in front of the structure. Similar scaffolding was used several years ago when the sandstone exterior of another building was cleaned. However, there is an entirely different reason for the scaffolding, and the work is not cosmetic. While doing routine roof inspections, workmen discovered that metal clamps used to affix the top tier of the heavy sandstone blocks to the roof had rusted through and that the sandstone blocks were inching their way forward. If not repaired, continued freezing and thawing would eventually cause the blocks to break loose and fall. The administration deemed the repair essential to the safety of all who walk in and out of the building on a daily basis.

Would you explain this to Dr. Beacon? You might like to think that doing so would embarrass her such that she would begin to gather facts before assuming the worst, but you know that confrontation junkies do not feel such embarrassment. Instead, Dr. Beacon is likely to take the position that it was "stupid" of the administration to begin the work without notifying the faculty of what would be done. This, by the way, is not a bad idea. One way to help curtail the negative influence of the confrontation junkie is to make information openly available to all. With the scaffolding up and Dr. Beacon's alarm sounded, it seems that little will be gained by taking the facts directly to her. You might, however, share the facts of the safety renovation with the entire campus. This will help to quiet Dr. Beacon's alarm. In doing so, however, it is helpful to take the high road and resist any temptation to make a statement that might be viewed by her or others as intended to discredit her or, worse yet, suggest that she does not have a right to ask questions. Anything beyond a straightforward presentation of the facts to explain the work being done on the sandstone building might open the door for Dr. Beacon to switch issues and sound different alarms.

Suppose that in answering Dr. Beacon's memo to the campus, you express your regret that she opted to reach conclusions without first gathering the facts and you assert your willingness to supply any and all information that would promote understanding. This sounds reasonable and even magnanimous, but it opens the door for the true confrontation junkie to move the public exchange to other matters. Dr. Beacon might, for example, offer no apology for jumping to the wrong conclusion about the repair of the sandstone building, but instead take credit for pushing the dean into "living in the sunshine on all matters." Dr. Beacon might reply by writing, "I am pleased that the dean has finally acknowledged the importance of being truthful with the faculty. If he is sincere in making this offer, he should not mind answering the following questions: 1) Why has the number of staff hired in student affairs increased while the number of faculty has remained the same? 2) Why has the number of administrative positions increased at the college?"

The list of questions could be much longer, but these two illustrate how the confrontation junkie tends to frame questions. Notice that both questions make some assumptions which may or may not be true. It can be time consuming and exhausting to answer such questions because while these questions can be framed with virtually no preparation, they can take an enormous amount time to form a thoughtful response that is clear to all who may not understand the issues. Hence, as tempted as you might be to make a statement that puts Dr. Beacon in her place or points out that she wrote without gathering the facts, yielding to this temptation can cost more time in the long run. Sometimes it is better to resist taking the bait.

Consider how your response to Dr. Beacon might vary if you recognize that this confrontation junkie has alienated many of her faculty colleagues. Dr. Beacon tends to view the world from a very personal perspective and has been quick to seek justice when events do not suit her. She has, for example, filed complaints of sexual harassment against several colleagues and has filed complaints against various members of the administration. None of the complaints filed have resulted in a formal finding that supports the charges made by Dr. Beacon. Would (or should) your response to Dr. Beacon's newest missive about the sandstone building be different if she had in the past filed charges against you as dean? Would (or should) your response to her newest missive about the sandstone building be different if she had charges pending against you as dean? It would, of course, depend to some extend on the nature of the charges, but the bigger concern would be that any response you might make would need to be such that Dr. Beacon and others would not perceive it as retaliation toward her. When under direct attack from a confrontation junkie, it is best to take the high road and to do so publicly. Ideally, chairs and deans want others who observe the communication between them and the confrontation junkie to perceive the confrontation junkie as unfair in his or her communication.

With each new episode demanding more time, chairs and deans can become battle worn managing the confrontation junkie, who may seem to have lots of time to sound alarms and fan the flames of conflict. Some time can be saved by building a firewall. In this sense, a firewall serves to buffer you from the confrontation junkie. Colleagues of Dr. Beacon make the best possible firewall because as a confrontation junkie, she does not wish to lose her audience of peers. The dean can help build a firewall around Dr. Beacon by engaging other faculty in the response to her. If, for example, the safety renovations done on the sandstone building were considered by a faculty committee, your reply might encourage Dr. Beacon to check with her faculty colleagues for more information. This strategy has the effect of demonstrating that her missive was aimed at faculty colleagues and not merely the dean or the central administration. The creation of an effective firewall will spare the dean because faculty members who have been involved in decision-making will begin to respond to Dr. Beacon. This strategy has the effect of limiting Dr. Beacon's negative influence in seeking to undermine the dean's leadership credibility.

ANALYSIS AND APPLICATIONS

Chairs and deans can limit the negative influence of the confrontation junkie by refusing to respond to every utterance he or she makes. When chairs and deans do offer a response, it must be well thought out. It is also essential to reply to those issues that help keep the larger campus community informed, or issues that serve to enhance leadership credibility. Similarly, chairs and deans can limit the negative influence of the confrontation junkie by structuring the process of communication around central issues in ways that promote a responsible and open airing of different views. Community expectations for responsible speech curtail the ability of the confrontation junkie to stir things up by making unfounded assertions. Let's review the essential elements of each application:

- Resist taking the bait.
- Defuse sensitive issues.
- Build a firewall.
- Structure the process.

◆ Resist taking the bait.

Chairs and deans can defuse the confrontation junkie by discerning when and when not to respond. Simply put, it is not a good idea to answer every shot fired by the confrontation junkie. It is physically impossible to keep up the pace that would be required to respond to every statement or charge make by a true confrontation junkie and still fulfill other assigned leadership responsibilities. The confrontation junkie can provoke something by uttering a top-of-the-head thought or question, but a good reply takes much longer to generate and disseminate. When chairs and deans fall prey to taking the bait and attempting to answer every statement made by the confrontation junkie, they permit the confrontation junkie to set the agenda and control the communication. In the example of Dr. Beacon, should the dean respond in a way that invites her to pursue other issues in this campus-wide electronic forum, the dean will find it difficult, if not impossible, to keep up the debate.

First, it is more dangerous to respond when the reply will permit the confrontation junkie to take the conflict to a new level or to stir up more anger. Second, it is dangerous to reply when any response made will be perceived as attacking the confrontation junkie rather than as responding to the issue. Finally, there is no need to respond if the confrontation junkie is raising an issue of little significance to others. However, a response is helpful when it clarifies an issue that is on the minds of others. A response is also helpful if it contributes to understanding and if it enhances leadership credibility.

◆ Defuse sensitive issues.

Confrontation junkies are often predictable. They enjoy stirring things up and are motivated to protect self-interest. Chairs and deans should be able to predict with some degree of certainty when the resident confrontation junkie will speak out. The negative influence of the confrontation junkie can be limited by debunking the anticipated rhetoric in advance. In the instance of Dr. Faulkner, one might be able to predict that he would oppose any curricular change that will have an impact on the courses he teaches. Leadership communication strategies that successfully alter how Dr. Faulkner views the proposed change will have the benefit of altering his public reaction to it.

◆ Build a firewall.

Chairs and deans are helped when more people are willing to challenge the often unsupported rhetoric of the confrontation junkie. It is more difficult for the confrontation junkie to undermine or discredit chair or dean leadership if others recognize his or her attempts to discredit the leadership and help to limit the confrontation junkie's tactics. Chairs and deans can construct effective firewalls around the confrontation junkie by building bridges with other constituencies. The more isolated the chair or dean is from other constituencies, the more vulnerable that chair or dean is to the discrediting tactics of the confrontation junkie. Perhaps the single best defense against the confrontation junkie is any and all leadership communication strategies that help chairs and deans build rapport and work collaboratively with various constituencies. When chairs and deans enjoy positive and productive working relationships with various constituencies, they will have a firewall between them and the confrontation junkie.

◆ Structure the process.

Chairs and deans can limit the negative influence of the confrontation junkie by structuring the opportunity for him or her to weigh in on an issue or decision. When the confrontation junkie (and everyone else) has an opportunity to offer views in an open discussion, it limits his or her influence. The rhetoric of the confrontation junkie is more powerful and persuasive when it is uncontested or when there is the perception that the chair and dean does not wish to hear or consider it. As described in the example of Dr. Faulkner, it is possible to limit the destructive influence of the confrontation junkie by using leadership communication that structures the conversation to keep attention focused on the substantive issues that warrant careful discussion and consideration. The objective is not to structure a prescribed outcome, but to structure the process to ensure an informed outcome.

SOME FINAL THOUGHTS

The confrontation junkie can be a difficult personality for chairs and deans to manage. Unlike many other challenging people and situations, the confrontation junkie embraces rather than avoids conflict. The confrontation junkie does not seek understanding or resolution, but instead enjoys the chaos—meaning that the confrontation junkie is typically working at cross purposes with the chair and/or dean. But to be effective in fanning the flames of conflict, the confrontation junkie must have an audience. The best defense that chairs and deans have is to curtail the audience that might be willing to listen to assertions made by the confrontation junkie. The best strategy to limit such influence is to keep faculty and staff informed. When the prospective audience can dismiss the comments of the confrontation junkie as ranting, they serve as an effective firewall to surround the confrontation junkie and limit the damage that might otherwise be done. When others hold the confrontation junkie accountable for his or her statements, it is easier for everyone to discern and dismiss the unsubstantiated claims that are often presented by the confrontation junkie as facts.

It is helpful to remember that the confrontation junkie is often motivated by a personal agenda. If chairs and deans are able to predict the perspective held by the confrontation junkie, this insight might be used to defuse a sensitive issue. By removing the perceived threat, it is possible to minimize or halt the confrontation junkie's otherwise destructive behavior that is designed to protect the status quo or persuade people to come to a particular outcome—an outcome that is perceived by the confrontation junkie as personally desirable and not an outcome that will strengthen relationships and the department.

Engaging the Passive and Indifferent Soul

Some individuals not only resist change, they resist taking any action. Left unengaged, passive and indifferent individuals pose obstacles to positive action, contribute to workload inequity, and threaten department and campus morale. Unless they are helped to reengage, passive and indifferent souls have effectively renegotiated position duties that are lighter than those assigned to their peers. This chapter presents communication strategies for engaging passive and indifferent individuals so they become positive contributors rather than obstacles to positive action.

After considering such difficult personalities as the pot stirrer/trouble-maker, the prima donna/drama queen, and the confrontation junkie, you may wonder why we would devote a chapter to the passive and indifferent soul. However, this individual also poses a conflict for the chair and dean, albeit a very different one. While this personality type does not create an in-your-face conflict as some we have discussed, the passive and indifferent faculty or staff member can undermine leadership credibility in significant ways. Consequently, it can be a big mistake for chairs and deans to ignore or try to work around passive or indifferent souls. When chairs and deans ignore passive and indifferent faculty or staff members, they legitimize their behavior, and this behavior can threaten the climate and productivity of the department or campus.

An academic department or campus is only as strong as its weakest link. Passive and indifferent faculty or staff members represent weak links because these individuals do not contribute to the overall success of the department or campus. Instead, passive and indifferent souls rely on others to fill the void they create by their passivity and indifference. Not only do they fail to make a positive contribution to the overall productivity and success of the department or the campus, but their lack of participation creates several conditions that can pose significant leadership challenges for chairs and deans. One challenge includes sustaining morale among those who pick up the slack despite inequitable workloads. For example, on a campus where students are advised by faculty and students can select the faculty member they want to be their advisor, it typically follows that faculty members who work hard to be strong advisors have more advisees. The passive faculty member who is seldom on campus and appears indifferent to students is actually rewarded with less work to do because students seldom request this faculty member to serve as their advisor. Passive individuals can also adversely affect the department climate and morale. As the traditional role of faculty expands to absorb responsibility for assessment, student recruitment and retention, mentoring, service-learning, and other initiatives, chairs and deans find it more difficult to work around the passive and indifferent faculty member because doing so spreads the work across fewer faculty members. The inequitable distribution of work can cause morale issues that threaten the department and campus climate and take a toll on leadership credibility. Consequently, individuals who are passive or indifferent pose a special leadership challenge for chairs and deans.

Passive and indifferent faculty and staff members have an adverse affect on productivity. They can disrupt change and thwart consensus building though their inaction. All the decisions and initiatives that require input from everyone are jeopardized when a passive or indifferent individual fails to comply with a request or is very late in complying with a request, which might be anything from supplying information needed for a reaccrediation review to completing one's assigned work regarding the department's assessment plan. At a minimum, the initiative moves on without all the information requested or the work is reassigned and completed by someone else. Depending on the issue and the nature of a request made to a passive or indifferent individual, the targeted deadline might be missed while chairs and deans wait for a reply from the passive or indifferent individual. Unless chairs and deans are able to extract the work requested from a passive or indifferent faculty or staff member in a timely way, the tardy and noncompliant behavior will threaten productivity and consensus building in the department or on the campus.

When chairs and deans ignore the passive or indifferent faculty or staff member, they run the risk of increasing resentment among those who must make up for the missing participant. Hardworking faculty and staff will eventually resent a chair or dean who permits passive individuals to remain disengaged and underworked. It can be counterintuitive for chairs and deans to fail to pick up the challenge of engaging the passive and indifferent faculty and staff member. Lack of attention to this personality type results because some chairs and deans conclude that passive or indifferent souls are a lost cause. Or, chairs and deans might decide that the passive or indifferent department member is not worth the time and energy it would take to reengage that person. This decision can undermine one's leadership credibility. Even when faculty colleagues declare passive or indifferent faculty members deadwood and wash their hands of them, faculty members will still expect chairs and deans to manage passive and indifferent souls. Failure to manage these individuals will likely be viewed as a cop-out with unfair consequences (usually in the form of additional work) for the other hardworking and engaged individuals.

Passive individuals are not all the same. Some may actively seek to avoid participation while others who appear to be passive may simply not know how to participate. Chairs and deans need to recognize these differences among the passive and indifferent because they cannot be managed the same way—one size does not fit all. Some may need a pep talk while others need concrete direction on what to do to become engaged. Some may need to be helped past an old wound created by a decision that was made well before you joined the institution. Still others may require a clarification of performance expectations, and some may require clear measures of accountability. Chairs and deans must accurately assess the reason a faculty or staff member is disengaged in order to have an opportunity to reengage this individual. A pep talk, for example, will do little to motivate those who remain disengaged because they are not certain how to become active participants.

Engaging the passive or indifferent soul requires persistent and consistent communication. Pep talks seldom have long-lasting or positive results without a clear assessment of the motives that fuel the passive or indifferent behavior. Once the motives are assessed, chairs and deans need to begin by engaging the passive or indifferent individual in regular and frequent conversation. Sometimes this requires clarifying performance expectations. For example, if a passive faculty member has become accustomed to missing department meetings, the chair will need to establish the expectation that all faculty members are expected to attend department meetings. It is unlikely that one memo from the chair will change behavior, so the chair will need to follow up and clarify the expectation every time a meeting is missed. To avoid the charge of picking on one faculty member, performance expectations should be clear and public, and chairs and deans must be consistent in holding all to the common performance expectations. If the goal is to have the passive or indifferent faculty member meet the performance expectations placed on every faculty member, then reminders and other consequences must be applied equitably for all faculty members.

REENGAGING A FACULTY MEMBER

Consider the example of tenured full professor Dr. Ford, who teaches his courses but does little else at the institution. The institutional policy on faculty workload sets specific expectations for teaching load and mentions that scholarship, service, and academic advising are also assigned work responsibilities for all tenure-track and tenured faculty members. As a new dean, you recognize that many faculty members carry enormous workloads and are stretched too thin, while others, like Dr. Ford, appear to get by teaching a full load (and sometimes overload for extra compensation) without being asked to do more. It seems clear that the quickest and most affordable way to provide relief for the overworked faculty is to amortize committee service and academic advising equitably across all faculty members. Where would you begin? Would you, for example, broach the issue from an institutional perspective or would you delegate the responsibility to each department chair?

Many factors should be considered when selecting the best approach, including the campus culture, the locus for personnel decisions, the provision for merit pay, the role responsibilities for chairs and deans, and faculty perceptions and expectations. In order to focus on the management of passive or indifferent faculty, assume that institutional policy makes you, as dean, accountable for all faculty personnel decisions. This helps to explain why the faculty seem convinced that the dean should assume responsibility for lightening the heavy faculty workloads. Would you still involve department chairs, and if so, how? Or, would you direct some change initiative from the dean's office directly to faculty? These are not insignificant decisions because engaging the passive or indifferent soul requires a mix and balance of authority and knowledge of the individual and the campus culture. While institutional policy might place the authority for faculty workload with the dean, any dean, especially a new dean, will need to involve others to more precisely develop and implement a strategy that will be effective. Furthermore, a campus-wide strategy will not likely be an effective means to engage each passive or indifferent faculty member given that the motivation for each person's behavior is potentially different. The most helpful strategy is one that is a combination of campus-wide performance expectations and an individualized appeal to each passive or indifferent faculty member.

To illustrate what is involved in managing the passive or indifferent soul, let's focus for a moment on Dr. Ford. From conversations with his department chair and file information, you know that Dr. Ford was tenured and promoted on time and that his teaching evaluations have been consistently solid throughout his 14 years at the campus. At the same time, Dr. Ford has consistently declined all opportunities to serve on committees outside his immediate department. Although the department staffs one of the larger enrolled programs, Dr. Ford advises only two or three students, while his department colleagues each advise an average of 25 to 30 students.

It is clear that the chair holds Dr. Ford in high regard and emphasizes that he has published more than any of his department colleagues. The department chair adds that this is especially impressive since the institution is not a "publish or perish" type of institution. When you share with the chair that other faculty in the department have complained that Dr. Ford does not pull his weight, the chair seems comfortable dismissing those concerns as typical for a busy time of year and hints that the complaints might be motivated by some professional jealously, pointing out that Dr. Ford is not to blame for either condition. What would you do? As dean, would you let the matter rest and redirect your attention to other more pressing maters? Or, would you pursue the matter, and if so, how would you proceed?

Before moving on to other issues, you might learn what you can about what motivates Dr. Ford to behave in ways that are passive and indifferent. How might you do this? Your approach will likely take into account your role and experience at the institution. As a new dean, you have the advantage of fresh perspective. You do not need to perpetuate habits or old perceptions. You might, therefore, ask to meet with Dr. Ford for the purpose of offering him a particular service assignment. You might explain to him that you seek someone with his record of scholarship and effective teaching to help design and lead a professional development program for new faculty. Most likely, Dr. Ford's response will tell you much about what motivates his passive or indifferent behavior. Are there other approaches that you might use to learn more about Dr. Ford's reasons for remaining on the sidelines?

Suppose that when you offer the leadership opportunity to Dr. Ford, he volunteers that it is hard for him to make commitments beyond his classes. Or, he expresses discomfort in assuming a leadership role that sets him up as an expert. Either response offers more insight into Dr. Ford and an opportunity to learn more about the factors that have limited his involvement in institutional work. For example, when he discloses his discomfort in assuming the "expert" role, you might point out that the activity could be structured in a way that eases such discomfort. Having a discussion about how to structure a professional development program for new faculty represents progress when talking with a faculty member who previously has been disengaged from all such initiatives.

Even if Dr. Ford responds to your invitation with a polite "No thanks," you have an opportunity to learn more about what motivates him. You might, for example, respond to his "No thanks" with praise and sincere surprise, commenting on how someone with his record of scholarship and teaching effectiveness is precisely what is needed. Depending on the dynamic of the conversation, you might add that you were especially hopeful that he would have time to serve in this important way because you noticed that he is not currently occupied with any other service assignment at the institution. Regardless of the outcome, the conversation serves to signal Dr. Ford that, as dean, you have performance expectations that are consistent with institutional policy, although your expectations may differ from those held by your predecessor.

Engaging the passive or indifferent soul seldom happens in one meeting, but it can happen if chairs and deans first take the time to learn more about the motivation of the passive or indifferent behavior. It would be a mistake to assume that the passive and indifferent personality type resides only among faculty and staff. This challenging personality type can also be found in individuals who hold important administrative positions at the institution. Regardless of the position held, chairs and deans can use the same leadership communication strategies to make performance expectations clear and to assess how best to reengage the passive or indifferent soul.

MANAGING THE WAYWARD CHAIR

Consider the department chair at a large institution who consistently misses deadlines and passes on any opportunity to represent her faculty and programs at the institution or within the community. The chair, Dr. Collins, has served at the institution for roughly 30 years. She is well liked across campus and possesses a charming interpersonal communicative style. Many years ago, Dr. Collins was very active on campus and has served more than once as the elected president of the faculty senate. When the previous chair retired 12 years ago, her faculty colleagues elected her chair of the department. Her selection was expected, especially since Dr. Collins is also known for her work at the national level with the discipline's professional accrediting body. It seemed to all who know her that Dr. Collins was the only responsible choice for chair. As dean, you too were elated with the department's choice and looked forward to an informed and cordial working relationship with Dr. Collins in her new role as department chair.

Almost immediately there were problems. Dr. Collins frequently missed or came late to meetings. This surprised you, but she was quick to explain that she needed some time to extract herself from other commitments and transition into her new role. Many of these commitments were off campus and included tasks such as serving as a reviewer for the discipline's accrediting body. Now, 12 years later, things are not better, and a good case could be made that things are worse. What would you do? Would you talk with Dr. Collins about your assessment, and if so, how would you structure the conversation? Since Dr. Collins was a popular choice for the position she holds, she will likely be surprised and possibly defensive to learn that you believe her work does not meet performance expectations. You would want to consider how others perceive her work because, if others are not in a position to realize that Dr. Collins is not meeting performance expectations, you might be perceived as picking on a person that others like and respect.

Would your response change if the consequence of Dr. Collins's indifferent behavior as chair was becoming more harmful? For example, what if the institution is now busy preparing for accreditation and you recognize that her performance record is not one that will responsibly prepare the department for the review. Would your response differ if the department chaired by Dr. Collins is among the largest enrolled at the institution? Part of managing the passive and indifferent soul is taking stock of the cost for the passive and indifferent behavior. Especially when the passive or indifferent person occupies a leadership position, there is a cost to all who count on that person's leadership.

If you decide that you must talk with Dr. Collins, what would you say? Assume that you explain in some detail what you have observed and that you are concerned that this practice will not ready the department for the upcoming institutional accreditation review. You are careful to remind Dr. Collins that you hold her in high regard and even appeal to her knowledge as a nationally recognized expert with her discipline's accrediting body. You appeal to her professional pride and explain that the institution is counting on her to model for other chairs how a department or program should prepare for the upcoming review. Does this seem like a reasonable approach or is there another tactic you would try? If not, think through how you would handle your conversation with Dr. Collins. How would you phrase the purpose for the meeting? Would you meet over lunch or in the office? How would you present the situation so that she has no doubt that you value her ability and, at the same time, believes that the institution needs for her to contribute more of her expertise and talent in how she manages her department chair duties and responsibilities? You've enjoyed such a positive relationship with Dr. Collins for so long that you anticipate that she might be embarrassed by the conversation, and you want to be certain to assure her that she is valued and held in high regard.

Assume that in meeting with her, you said everything as well as it might be said, but Dr. Collins becomes defensive and indignant that you would suddenly "turn" on her. What do you do? When caught by surprise with an unexpected view, it often pays to not offer comment but to simply listen. Understanding how another is viewing the situation is absolutely essential to managing it effectively. In this instance, Dr. Collins did not respond as you anticipated, so it will be helpful to learn more about how she views the situation and your account of it. In your conversation, she continues by reminding you that she never kept her work at the national level a secret, and further, she believes that all who wanted her to serve as department chair understood that she would accept the chair role only if it did not interrupt her work at the national level. Dr. Collins also contends that if she had not been successful in managing the chair's role, things would have crumbled long before now. How do you respond? Her perspective places you between the proverbial rock and hard place in that to make your case you must demonstrate that things have not been going well for some time, and this will likely increase Dr. Collins's anger. Also, it will likely be more difficult to obtain her cooperation if she hears you attacking her performance as department chair. What do you do?

How might you have altered your approach to Dr. Collins had you known how she would view the situation and hear your comments? Assume the full benefit of hindsight and think how you would manage the conversation with Dr. Collins if you knew that she believes she has your support for managing chair duties around her work at the national level, which often takes her off campus. Knowing her perspective helps you define the issue that needs attention in a way that Dr. Collins can understand. Especially if she believes that she has your support to manage department chair duties around her commitments at the national level, there is little to be gained by talking about unfulfilled responsibilities from earlier years. Similarly, there is nothing to be gained by airing the misunderstanding around her appointment.

Given Dr. Collins's perspective, you might instead focus on changes in higher education that must be addressed. This conversation need not be combative in that you can acknowledge her passion for her work at the national level and express concern for whether it is fair to expect her to manage both when external conditions have altered the demands on department chairs. This approach offers Dr. Collins the option to select one or the other job while making clear that keeping both will require some change in how she carries out the department chair responsibilities. This tactic has the advantage of shifting the burden to Dr. Collins to demonstrate how she might successfully manage both roles while meeting new performance expectations for department chairs. As her supervisor, you have clarified the current performance expectations in a way that does not provoke anger or defensiveness.

ANALYSIS AND APPLICATIONS

Effective leadership brings together the various members of the community. Chairs and deans will help maximize the strengths of a campus if they take time to learn and understand the reasons some people may be disengaged. When people know and understand performance expectations and how their contributions are valued, it is possible to change behavior. Let's review the essential elements of each application:

- Assess the motivation for indifference.

- Make expectations clear.

- Be transparent.

- Value participation.

◆ **Assess the motivation for indifference.**

The strategy of reengaging a passive or indifferent soul will only be effective if it incorporates the motive for the disengagement. This assessment may not be easy to make. Do not rely on department or campus lore. Conclusions should be tested and chairs and deans should adjust their conclusions as appropriate. It might take several meetings over a period of time with the passive or indifferent faculty or staff member. The time spent, however, is worth it because absent an accurate assessment, it is virtually impossible to develop or execute an effective leadership communication strategy.

In the example of Dr. Ford, it was easy to hypothesize several plausible scenarios for why he has not engaged in campus work. Knowing the precise reason helps to bring the best approach into focus. In other words, chairs and deans will be more effective in engaging the passive or indifferent soul if they address the reason for the passive or indifferent behavior. This also makes the management of a difficult personality type more comfortable because it does not attack the person, but instead invites that person to work with the chair or dean in managing the reason for nonparticipation. By addressing behavior, it is possible to discuss inadequate performance without attacking the person because the approach assumes the passive or indifferent individual can and will meet performance expectations once those expectations are made clear. Hence, the approach does not imply some inherent deficiency in the person. This approach may seem counterintuitive to chairs or deans who would prefer to assume a more authoritative posture, but getting to the root of the issue can obtain faster results without inciting messy or uncomfortable confrontations.

Knowing Dr. Collins's perspective is an enormous advantage in knowing how to proceed with what might be a very ticklish situation. Especially when working to engage a long-time and well-liked employee, it is preferable to proceed in a manner that does not invite defensiveness or anger. One key component to managing these types of situations resides in understanding how the person will view the situation and then structuring the choices that the person has in order to continue. Dr. Collins, for example, needs to decide if she wishes to continue to serve as department chair in light of the increased role responsibilities and performance expectations. If she does, then she has made her own decision to accept the responsibility for meeting performance expectations that have changed and may intrude on her work at the national level.

◆ Make expectations clear.

No faculty or staff member can be held accountable for meeting performance expectations if the performance expectations are unclear. Hence, a logical way to begin working with a passive or indifferent soul is by clarifying performance expectations. This discussion of expectations need not be combative or confrontational. Instead, such a conversation can be both supportive and constructive if the chair or dean approaches the task assuming that the passive or indifferent soul does not know or understand the performance expectations. The inevitable task of engaging the passive or indifferent faculty or staff member will be more confrontational if the approach assumes that the person is intentionally escaping work. When chairs and/or deans start by pointing out that a person's performance does not meet expectations, they are more likely to put that person on the defensive. This in turn reduces the opportunities for collaborating on a solution that would create a win-win outcome for everyone involved. What gain would the dean realize, for example, if Dr. Ford is told that he is not meeting performance expectations and needs to do more? Dr. Ford might sign up for some committees, but it is difficult to imagine that he would faithfully attend meetings or make a significant contribution to the committee's work. It is more likely that he will resent needing to "play the game" or put up with "busy work" that is to him pointless. Indeed, if Dr. Ford just joins a committee to get the dean off his back, nothing is gained. However, more could be lost if Dr. Ford alienates more faculty who perceive him as being among the deadwood on campus.

Dr. Collins became defensive and believed that the dean had "turned" on her because she did not perceive a problem with her behavior. Dr. Collins believed that she was managing both her department chair duties and her work at the national level. She did not perceive a problem because she held fast to her understanding of performance expectations, which represented the understanding she initially had when she assumed the department chair position some 12 years earlier. Conditions change over time, and chairs and deans should review and clarify performance expectations of those they supervise on a regular basis. This might be done as part of an annual meeting to discuss one's goals for the coming year. It can also be done through ongoing discussions of current issues that permit chairs and deans to relate individual performance expectations to the larger context and changing conditions.

◆ Be transparent.

When chairs and deans are transparent, others can predict their actions and reactions in ways that help guide performance. If, for example, everyone knows that the chair will not say anything to faculty members who miss department meetings, the behavior communicates that the chair doubts the importance of the meeting or at least does not mind if people miss them. It is virtually impossible to persuade others, especially passive and indifferent souls, to take seriously something that the chair or dean appears to take lightly. This is true for the simplest behavior, such as arriving promptly at meetings as a courtesy to colleagues. Transparency is also critical to the perpetuation of professional values, such as communicating accurately or placing the institution's welfare ahead of personal welfare.

Chairs and deans can model professionalism and what it means to meet performance expectations in their own behavior. The department chair, for example, who believes that faculty should inform him of all absences, will be more effective in gaining faculty cooperation and compliance if he too informs others of his absences. The perception of a double standard, no matter how small, does not help a chair or dean to engage passive or indifferent faculty and staff in meeting performance expectations. If anything, such double standards license and embolden others to not worry when they fail to meet performance expectations.

◆ Value participation.

There is no substitute for having the chair or dean note and recognize good work. This affirms performance expectations and shows appreciation for those who meet them. This recognition can be informal, but it must be sincere. It is a mistake to believe that the only recognition that matters to faculty and staff is merit pay or some other tangible reward. A kind and sincere word from the chair or the dean lets an individual know that his or her work was noted and valued. If Dr. Ford assumes responsibility for structuring a professional development program for new faculty, the dean can do more than say thanks. The dean might, for example, write a letter to Dr. Ford's chair or feature the professional development program and his work in a campus newsletter. The dean might also host a thank-you luncheon for Dr. Ford that is attended by all the new faculty members who were helped by him during the program.

Similarly, there is no need to have Dr. Collins believe that her work has been substandard for more than a decade. The dean will more likely get the desired change by appreciating all work done to date while explaining why current conditions require some change and inviting Dr. Collins to consider what might be best in meeting the new and increased performance expectations for a department chair. It is important to remember that the objective is to reengage the passive or indifferent soul, not to convince them how poorly they have performed. It is infinitely easier to get a person to work differently than it is to get that person to accept a poor assessment of his or her performance.

SOME FINAL THOUGHTS

There is enough work to go around. Given the myriad issues facing higher education, institutions of all types and sizes need every faculty and staff member fully and productively engaged in work that will advance the institutional mission. Passive and indifferent souls jeopardize institutional effectiveness and success because when even one person is not engaged in the work of the institution, the campus is operating at a disadvantage. Not only do passive and indifferent individuals represent a loss of man hours, they represent loss of brainpower. At the most basic level, this means that the institution is paying for services that it is not realizing. Part of effective chair and dean leadership must be about the business of engaging the passive and indifferent souls.

Some chairs and deans may believe it is preferential to ignore and work around passive and indifferent faculty and staff. In particular, chairs and deans who understandably dread managing conflict may conclude that it is better not to poke the sleeping person with a stick, but just to let him or her be. Though counterintuitive for some chairs and deans, the better long-term conflict management strategy is to engage the passive and indifferent souls in the life and work of the department and the campus. To do otherwise can escalate conflict among the engaged faculty and staff members who will typically hold chairs and deans accountable for equitable workloads or exhibiting preferential treatment for some.

Chairs and deans can engage passive or indifferent souls without invoking defensiveness or inciting unnecessary conflict. Obtaining involvement does not need to be a battle. It needs to be professional, and the very best of being professional is assuming that others will respond positively and constructively when treated professionally. To do this, chairs and deans need to give careful consideration to how the passive or indifferent individual perceives the situation. This will offer insights into the motive for the passive or indifferent behaviors. Similarly, it is fair and professional to make performance expectations clear. A person has little hope of doing well or being recognized for good work if he or she does not understand the performance expectations. Chairs and deans owe it to all faculty and staff to make performance expectations clear, but this practice may be especially helpful to the passive or indifferent soul. Finally, chairs and deans will enhance their ability to engage passive and indifferent souls if they are transparent in showing what behaviors are valued and go the extra step to express appreciation for the changed behavior when a passive or indifferent faculty or staff member becomes more engaged.

Using Leadership Communication to Manage Especially Difficult People

The final section of this book provided examples of how to apply leadership communication strategies when working some of the most difficult people. From the analysis and application of basic skills to create shared understanding and context for decisions to developing sincere, honest communication as a means of building credibility, we hope the practical leadership communication strategies you have developed allow you to take the counterintuitive stand when managing personal differences and difficult personalities.

As institutional expectations increase and higher education continues to change, the ability to consider conflict or situations of potential conflict from both first-person and third-person perspectives should ease some of the discomfort in dealing with difficult situations and people. To assist you with continued development of this leadership communication skill, it may be helpful to remember the following:

- It is possible to anticipate and preempt the destructive reactions of difficult personalities.

- It becomes easier to manage difficult personalities if you first try to perceive the world from their perspective.

- A strategy for managing conflict is only effective if the basis for the conflict is first accurately assessed—the third-person perspective is absolutely essential to developing an accurate assessment.

Imagine yourself as the new chair of a mid-size department, and among your faculty you have a pot stirrer, a prima donna/drama queen, a confrontation junkie, a few passive or indifferent souls, and several who seem intent on pursuing personal agendas that jeopardize the departmental and institutional missions. All is not lost in that you also have several very strong faculty who contribute much to the department and the institution. Having been promoted to the position of chair from within the institution, you know all the faculty well and consider yourself successful in working with a full range of personalities and temperaments. At times, it has been difficult, but for the most part you have managed to get the department work done. However, you recognize that not all contribute equally to the outcomes achieved by the department.

Each achievement has carried a cost. For example, to reach consensus on the last curriculum revision, you spent hours in one-on-one conversations with many of the faculty to seek their support of the cooperative effort and to secure approval for the proposal developed by the department's curriculum committee. Worse yet, the difficult personalities in the department now seem to believe that you are somehow indebted to them in return for their support of the curriculum proposal. Ironically, those who appear to believe that they have some collateral are the ones who contributed least to the development of the new curriculum. In a few instances, the difficult personalities act put out because the new curriculum requires them to teach new content—for which they have assumed a martyr status.

Although for the most part you have been successful in making things work despite some difficult personalities, you now face some leadership challenges that exceed anything you have previously handled. In particular, your institution is preparing for its next accreditation review and the regional accrediting body has issued new criteria that place greater accountability at the department and program level. This new task is so comprehensive and massive that it will take every member of the department to pull it off. Even if the bulk of the preparation might be done by a subcommittee of the department, the full department will need to be up to speed before the site visit because the new criteria established the need for all faculty and staff to know how their individual work advances the institutional mission. As you think about some of the difficult personalities in your department, you know that some will see the preparation for institutional accreditation as the central administration's problem while others will assert that the institution should take a stand and not permit any outside agency to set the campus agenda. You recognize that there is a mountain of work to be done and little time for theatrical denials or indifference toward the task.

You are reasonably certain that it will be important to get all the difficult personalities to cooperate and work together in the same direction. Knowing what you now know about managing conflict and working with difficult personalities, how might you approach this task? You will want to begin by informing the faculty of the upcoming accreditation review and the new criteria to be used for the review. In addition, you will want to build a common understanding among the members of your department about the importance of accreditation to both the institution and the department, the new criteria, and how this review will differ from others they may have experienced. Ideally, this should be started long before the department must begin the actual task of gathering data and preparing self-study information on the department's programs because a common understanding about the task will help to contain those who might approach this activity with a personal agenda. Also, with everyone fully informed about the process and expectations, it will be more difficult for the pot stirrer, prima donna/drama queen, or confrontation junkie to derail constructive activity for the review. However, failing to inform all department members of the task and how this task is different from before will pave the way for these difficult personalities to disrupt productive efforts.

As you prepare for this initial phase, you will want to anticipate how each of your difficult personalities will react so that you can give some thought to how you might respond to them when they behave predictably in department meetings. The objective will be to help others perceive their antics for what they are and to be able to distinguish between constructive thinking that aids the task and rhetorical tactics intended to derail the department's work. When others are able to more accurately assess the motives and contributions of the more difficult personalities in the department, your leadership challenge becomes easier. At the same time, it will be important that you not be perceived as waging a personal attack against any of the more difficult personalities in the department. Instead, you will want to engage them in discussion of the issues and hold them accountable for explaining or supporting statements they may make. This allows you to demonstrate that you believe they are capable of making a valued contribution, and they will be less likely to become defensive or, if they do, their defensive behaviors will more likely seem unreasonable to others in the department.

Managing difficult personalities takes patience and time. But, if you exercise the leadership communication strategies offered in this book, you should be well on your way to more effective and more comfortable conflict management. To achieve this level of proficiency and comfort, however, you will sometimes need to resist your first impulse and communicate in ways that may seem counterintuitive. You may, for example, need to be more public in your management of difficult personalities in order to hold them accountable for their actions, even though the temptation might be to let them alone in hopes that they do not raise a ruckus. Or, you may need to take the time to inform those you lead of the larger context when your first impulse is to just get a task done as quickly as possible. However, knowing the context is the only way that others can possess shared understanding from which they can work to reach consensus about issues and options. Such principles of effective leadership communication may sound reasonable, but they can be hard to implement when chairs and deans face tough issues and conflict. For this reason, we recommend in closing that you revisit this text as needed—like one might require a booster shot to sustain a vaccine inoculation against a disease. In this instance, the disease is the stress that often accompanies the management of conflict.

Annotated Bibliography

General References

Bennett, J. B. (1998). *Collegial professionalism: The academy, individualism, and the common good.* Phoenix, AZ: American Council on Education/ Oryx Press.

The author presents a philosophical model to define the current state of the academy and then defines an alternative, relational model for higher education. John Bennett explores how a sense of faculty individualism, increased competition for funding and students, and departmental separatism contribute to the current state. In addition to a new model, he also offers some specific suggestions for how chairs and deans can work against individualism, foster relationships, and engage in a true collegial community.

Bergquist, W. H. (1992). *The four cultures of the academy: Insights and strategies for improving leadership in collegiate organizations.* San Francisco, CA: Jossey-Bass.

Drawing on more than 20 years of research and experience, William Bergquist delineates four distinct cultures that exist in higher education. The first two, collegial and managerial, Bergquist traces back to the beginning of U.S. higher education. These campus cultures are marked by deriving meaning from the academic disciplines that the faculty represent (collegial) and creating meaning from the implementation and evaluation of the institution's goals and purposes (managerial). The remaining two cultures are marked by how programs and activities further personal and professional growth (developmental) and how meaning is derived primarily in establishing equitable policies and practices (negotiating). Bergquist presents case studies to illustrate how these cultures interact with institutional values, leadership, and criteria for performance.

Chu, D. (2006). *The department chair primer: Leading and managing academic departments*. Bolton, MA: Anker.

This book's scenarios, concepts, practical tips, and questions for reflection are primarily drawn from the experiences of current and former chairs. Divided into three sections, this primer begins with an orientation to chairing, moves to a discussion of essential topics for chairs, and concludes with thoughts on leading and changing a department.

Coffman, J. R. (2005). *Work and peace in academe: Leveraging time, money, and intellectual energy through managing conflict*. Bolton, MA: Anker.

Former department head and dean, James Coffman served as a provost for 17 years. Among his professional accomplishments, Coffman's systematic approach to resolving disputes recognizes the value of understanding institutional context while acknowledging that unproductive disputes can be managed through a foundation of trust and integrity.

Collins, J. (2001). *Good to great: Why some companies make the leap . . . and others don't*. New York, NY: HarperCollins.

Using companies that were able to sustain outstanding results for more than 15 years, Jim Collins, a former faculty member in Stanford University's graduate business school, and his research team developed a schematic of distinguishing characteristics that move an organization from merely being good to achieving greatness. Among the organizational elements Collins examines are the type of leadership, the role of dialogue and debate, and a strong understanding of organizational strengths. The framework and research process for selecting the great organizations highlighted is also discussed.

Dickenson, R. (1999). *Prioritizing academic programs and services: Reallocating resources to achieve strategic balance*. San Francisco, CA: Jossey-Bass.

Vice president for an organization that serves higher education, this former president's work focuses on the internal and external pressures for quality and accountability that lead to over-programming and disconnected institutional planning. Robert Dickenson presents scenarios from various colleges and universities that analyze programs and engage in resource reallocation to create institutional program reform.

D'Souza, D. (1991). *Illiberal education: The politics of race and sex on campus.* New York, NY: The Free Press.

The focus of this book is the author's contention that those institutions that seek to promote diversity on campus are really thwarted efforts that continually reinforce the structures that permit bias. Dinesh D'Souza asserts that the institutions most vocal in seeking a "multicultural community" are those that experience the worst tensions.

Gappa, J. M., Austin, A. E., & Trice, A. G. (2005, November/December). Rethinking academic work and workplaces. *Change, 37*(6), 32–39.

Adapted from a forthcoming book, the authors examine how external pressures—including fiscal constraints, new educational technologies, increased specialization, and changes in the student body—have significant impact on the academic workplace. In addition to the changing demographic of today's faculty, the authors argue that when the academic environment respects each faculty member, both the institution and its faculty will fully reap the benefits of the essential elements (balance and flexibility, academic freedom and autonomy, employment equity, professional growth, and collegiality and community involvement) and have policies and practices to improve the workplace.

Gladwell, M. (2002). *The tipping point: How little things can make a big difference.* Boston, MA: Little, Brown and Company.

Malcolm Gladwell, a staff writer for *The New Yorker*, presents examples of how ideas, behaviors, products, and other social phenomena can sometimes behave just like epidemics if they have the right combination of contagiousness, people to spread them, and a receptive social context.

Green, J. S., & Levine, A. (Eds.). (1985). *Opportunity in adversity: How colleges can succeed in hard times.* San Francisco, CA: Jossey-Bass.

The authors build on the premise that institutions facing fiscal challenges have opportunities to turn themselves around. A collection of chapters written by experts with various levels of institutional authority, this book focuses on institutions that have maximized their financial and academic resources to develop into stronger organizations based on their own understanding of institutional purpose.

Heifetz, R. A. (1994). *Leadership without easy answers.* Cambridge, MA: Harvard University Press.

Organizing his view of leadership by distinguishing first between routine and innovative problems and then whether one has authority in a situation, psychiatrist and professor Ronald Heifetz uses example cases to illustrate his theory of leadership. The book moves from developing an understanding of leadership to exploring individual strategies of leadership in historical situations, concluding with thoughts on how to balance the competing values inherent in leadership.

Holton, S. A. (Ed.). (1998). *Mending the cracks in the ivory tower: Strategies for conflict management in higher education.* Bolton, MA: Anker.

As a professor of communication studies, former department chair, and assistant to the president, Susan Holton brings together a collection of models for managing conflict. The book reviews conflict in general and its theoretical underpinnings and examines specifically the reasons, types, and manifestations of conflict on campuses. Each chapter presents instructional approaches for successfully managing conflict to create greater institutional and personal effectiveness.

Kouzes, J. M., & Posner, B. Z. (1993). *Credibility: How leaders gain and lose it, why people demand it.* San Francisco, CA: Jossey-Bass.

Because leadership is a relationship, the authors set credibility as the foundation of that relationship. Credibility is defined as the trust and confidence leaders earn from their constituents. The trust that credibility generates encourages initiative and risk-taking, increases productivity, and lends itself to resolving conflicts using principles, not positional authority.

Kouzes, J. M., & Posner, B. Z. (1995). *The leadership challenge: How to keep getting extraordinary things done in organizations.* San Francisco, CA: Jossey-Bass.

The authors surveyed more than 60,000 leaders and constituents across all organizational levels. Drawing from this research base, they offer five basic, fundamental leadership practices: challenge the process; inspire a shared vision; enable others to act; model the way; and encourage the heart. Complementing these practices, they share actual case studies to highlight how these practices work.

Messick, D. M., & Kramer, R. M. (Eds.). (2005). *The psychology of leadership: New perspectives and research.* Mahwah, NJ: Lawrence Erlbaum.

A blend of scholarship and practical examples, this work includes chapters on the diversity of leadership books on the market, an examination of the psychological exchange between leaders and followers, the role of cooperation, and a reframing of thoughts on team leadership.

O'Toole, J. (1995). *Leading change: The argument for values-based leadership.* San Francisco, CA: Jossey-Bass.

James O'Toole argues in favor of values-based leadership, through which he says trust and respect for followers can overcome the powerful forces resistant to change. Using the U.S. presidents depicted on Mount Rushmore as examples, O'Toole shows how leadership that is principled yet practical, and marked by integrity, trust, listening, and respect, creates a moral symmetry among those with competing values.

Sykes, C. J. (1988). *ProfScam: Professors and the demise of higher education.* Washington, DC: Regency Gateway.

According to the author, the culture that exists among the professoriate is corrupt and the reason for the collapse of the American higher education system. Charles Sykes describes a culture that creates rewards for publication, no matter how trivial the findings, communicates via jargon because substance is lacking, and devalues education by destroying coherent curriculum and good teaching.

Tucker, A. (1992). *Chairing the academic department: Leadership among peers* (3rd ed.). New York, NY: American Council on Education/Macmillan.

A former academic vice chancellor in a state university system, Allan Tucker based this book on training materials created by a grant-funded project to develop a model for enhancing the leadership skills of department chairs. The first edition was published in 1981. This third edition presents broad-based categories of issues department chairs deal with, along with illustrative examples and questions designed to facilitate the application of the issues and suggestions to one's own institutional context.

Tucker, A., & Bryan, R. A. (1988). *The academic dean: Dove, dragon, and diplomat.* New York, NY: American Council on Education/Macmillan.

Recognizing that roles vary based on institutional context, this book offers advice for deans with jurisdiction over budgets, faculty, and curricula. Drawing on their own professional experiences and the experiences of others, the authors explore topics such as assessing program viability, evaluating performance, dealing with students, and creating relationships with others within the campus community.

Warren, C. O. (1990). Chairperson and dean: The essential partnership. In J. B. Bennett & D. J. Figuli (Eds.), *Enhancing departmental leadership: The roles of the chairperson* (pp. 30–35). New York, NY: American Council on Education/Macmillan.

Charles Warren focuses on the roles and responsibilities of both the dean and the department chair in creating and nurturing a positive, supportive professional environment. Specific elements of effective communication, including the role of the sharing of information between the dean and the chair, are discussed.

Part I • Establishing a Foundation for Effective Leadership Communication

Bennett, J. B. (1998). Professionalism: Academic or collegial? In *Collegial professionalism: The academy, individualism, and the common good* (pp. 42–72). Phoenix, AZ: American Council on Education/Oryx Press.

In this chapter, Bennett engages the fundamental question of the ways in which academics can claim to be professionals. He moves from the theoretical to the practical by examining the problematic behaviors that can come from insistent individualism—behaviors that work against the common good and that can lead to relational difficulty, polarization, and a sense of disconnectedness.

Coffman, J. R. (2005). Policy and procedure: Development and implementation. In *Work and peace in academe: Leveraging time, money, and intellectual energy through managing conflict* (pp. 47–59). Bolton, MA: Anker.

With institutional context as a framework for exploring policy differences, Coffman offers examples of how policy and procedures can create or fuel conflict in the promotion and tenure process and in the filing of grievances.

Dickenson, R. (1999). Reaffirming institutional mission. In *Prioritizing academic programs and services: Reallocating resources to achieve strategic balance* (pp. 29–42). San Francisco, CA: Jossey-Bass.

This chapter explores the tensions that exist among the power of institutional legacy, market realities, and the quest for excellence. Dickenson's perspective uses institutional mission as a way to plan while acknowledging the balances that exist on campuses involving continuity, stability, and responsiveness. The institutional mission is the academic grid within which to evaluate all programs.

Greenberg, M. (2002, March 8). An administrator's guide to how faculty members think. *The Chronicle of Higher Education.* Retrieved September 28, 2006, from http://chronicle.com/jobs/2002/03/2002030801c.htm

Milton Greenberg presents five lessons he learned about perceptions faculty have of administrators and the role of communication in fostering those perceptions.

Higgerson, M. L. (1996). Structuring the mission. In *Communication skills for department chairs* (pp. 2–35). Bolton, MA: Anker.

Using case study analysis, Mary Lou Higgerson provides a sense of the process department chairs might employ to help them understand their role in building consensus around shared values by offering opportunities to work through various scenarios. In addition, she defines elements of an effective mission statement and relevant communication strategies to enhance participation.

Leslie, D. W., & Fretwell, E. K., Jr. (1996). Mission and organization. In *Wise moves in hard times: Creating and managing resilient colleges and universities* (pp. 77–105). San Francisco, CA: Jossey-Bass.

Mission plays a powerful role in focusing the community's energies and creativity on the qualities that make a college or university unique. However, one challenge in establishing a clear mission is the multiplicity of stakeholders in a college community, from faculty to students to legislators and more. An institution that deals successfully with increasing complexity, diverging interests, and multiple ownership will be able to define and control its identity and will succeed by filling a need that other institutions do not.

Martin, W. B. (1985). Mission: A statement of identity and direction. In J. S. Green & A. Levine (Eds.), *Opportunity in adversity: How colleges can succeed in hard times* (pp. 40–61). San Francisco, CA: Jossey-Bass.

Warren Martin contends that a good mission statement is as important to an institution as good management. He discusses the role of values in guiding institutional development, quality, planning, and relationships and offers some thoughts for those institutions engaged in defining mission.

Sturnick, J. A. (1998). And never the twain shall meet: Administrator-faculty conflict. In S. A. Holton (Ed.), *Mending the cracks in the ivory tower: Strategies for conflict management in higher education* (pp. 97–112). Bolton, MA: Anker.

A consultant and former faculty member and campus president, Judith Sturnick offers a series of simple and direct statements aimed at working toward developing a common understanding of issues, depersonalizing the issues, and establishing ground rules for behavior. These principles are illustrated in a case study of successful conflict management.

Tucker, A. (1992). Leadership and decision making. In *Chairing the academic department: Leadership among peers* (3rd ed., pp. 56–72). New York, NY: American Council on Education/Macmillan.

Several models of chair behavior are described in this chapter. In addition to reviewing overall leadership styles, Tucker presents a list of questions designed as an assessment of how a person perceives the directive and supportive nature of his or her own leadership style. Complemented by case study examples, the chapter suggests criteria for evaluating faculty involvement in decision-making.

Tucker, A. (1992). Power and authority of a chair. In *Chairing the academic department: Leadership among peers* (3rd ed., pp. 44–55). New York, NY: American Council on Education/Macmillan.

In this chapter, Tucker explores the role of positional and personal power in relation to the ability to influence change. Among the discussion points offered are thoughts on daily decisions about things like how to communicate good and bad news, how to present the department, and the role of serving as the primary liaison for external communications. A primary element of the chapter is the recognition that knowledge must be shared and how that influences department members' perception of chair authority.

Tucker, A., & Bryan, R. A. (1988). Department chairpersons and the dean. In *The academic dean: Dove, dragon, and diplomat* (pp. 25–54). New York, NY: American Council on Education/Macmillan.

This chapter is devoted to a discussion of effective communication between the dean and the chair, the characteristics of a good chair, and the role of the dean in the various institutional chair selection processes.

Part II • Developing a Fair and Effective Leadership Communication Style

Berstene, T. (2004, Summer). The inexorable link between conflict and change. *Journal for Quality and Participation, 27*(2), 5–9.

Thomas Berstene draws on his more than 21 years of experience in the fields of quality and organizational assessment to explore the differences between constructive and destructive conflict, how social factors can affect conflict, and how to manage conflict constructively within a group.

Birnbaum, R. (2000, January/February). The life cycle of academic management fads. *Journal of Higher Education, 71*(1), 1–16.

Robert Birnbaum's study proposes that management fads can be traced from creation to eventual abandonment, and that they diffuse between nonacademic and academic systems. Specifically, he asserts that there is a five-stage cycle: creation, narrative evolution, time lag, narrative devolution, and dissonance resolution. The author points out management fads are imported from business rather than exported from higher education, and within the realm of higher education, business management fads have not had the positive outcomes promised by proponents.

Cloke, K., & Goldsmith, J. (2003). *The art of waking people up: Cultivating awareness and authenticity at work.* San Francisco, CA: Jossey-Bass.

The authors discuss the importance of cultivating authenticity, which requires more courage and a greater energy expenditure in the short term but yields long-term benefits. They also offer some probing questions aimed at helping people think more deeply about how to be more authentic in their work.

Cornwell, G. H., & Stoddard, E. W. (2001). Toward an interdisciplinary epistemology: Faculty culture and institutional change. In B. L. Smith & J. McCann (Eds.), *Reinventing ourselves: Interdisciplinary education, collaborative learning, and experimentation in higher education* (pp. 160–178). Bolton, MA: Anker.

Chronicling the struggles and changes associated with interdisciplinary faculty and curriculum development at St. Lawrence University, the authors discuss the shift from departmental autonomy to a core curriculum that demanded team teaching and the introduction of university-wide considerations into departmental staffing decisions. Across the institution, old structures still remain, and there is a familiar tension for junior faculty caught between the cultures; however, the authors conclude that the university has undergone a radical change in its faculty culture as a result of the interdisciplinary emphasis.

Engelkemeyer, S. W. (2005, November). *Navigating the whitewaters of departmental change.* Paper presented at the meeting of the American Council on Education on Chairing the Academic Department, San Antonio, TX.

Currently serving as the dean of the School of Business at Ithaca College, Susan Engelkemeyer's presentation looked at the vision, skills, incentives, resources, and plans needed to implement change. All five of these elements are necessary, because without any one aspect, an organization will experience confusion, anxiety, frustration, or false starts rather than the transformation that comes from change.

Ewell, P. T. (1999, November/December). Imitation as art: Borrowed management techniques in higher education. *Change, 31*(6), 10–15.

Peter Ewell explores the academy's reaction to imported management techniques and suggests some reasons institutions might want to ponder using at least some form of management borrowed from business.

Gaff, J. G. (1985). Faculty: Ongoing development and renewal. In J. S. Green & A. Levine (Eds.), *Opportunity in adversity: How colleges can succeed in hard times* (pp. 137–163). San Francisco, CA: Jossey-Bass.

Although the statistics are dated, Jerry Gaff presents a strong case for the role of faculty development and how it must go beyond creating just expertise to helping faculty help the institution. This pattern of faculty and institutional renewal can help an institution transform its curriculum in ways that meet evolving and ever-changing student needs.

Guskin, A. E., & Marcy, M. B. (2003, July/August). Dealing with the future now: Principles for creating a vital campus in a climate of restricted resources. *Change, 35*(4), 10–21.

Codirectors of the Project on the Future of Higher Education, the authors offer a comparison of the assumptions and actions of various institutional responses to severe fiscal problems. Many institutions muddle through fiscal crises, but the authors suggest that the institution that takes transformative action, using its vision of the future to create a collective recognition of fiscal realities, will be in the strongest position to restructure for its fiscal health.

Higgerson, M. L. (1996). Conducting performance counseling. In *Communication skills for department chairs* (pp. 106–138). Bolton, MA: Anker.

Using performance counseling as an opportunity to accrue benefits for all involved, the case studies presented in this chapter allow the reader to put the notion of counseling into practice with insights into various approaches to talking with untenured and tenured faculty.

Higgerson, M. L. (1996). Implementing change. In *Communication skills for department chairs* (pp. 169–200). Bolton, MA: Anker.

Working from the premise that change is essential for department survival and growth, the author addresses the need to identify the people and pressures that influence the change process. Complete with scenarios, the author walks the reader through questions and tactics for effective change implementation.

Higgerson, M. L. (1996). Managing conflict. In *Communication skills for department chairs* (pp. 139–168). Bolton, MA: Anker.

There is a difference between resolving conflict and managing it, and conflict resolution is often an impossible task. This chapter and its case scenarios focus on strategies for reducing destructive conflict while allowing for the existence of constructive conflict.

Higgerson, M. L. (2006). Building a climate for faculty evaluation that improves teaching. In P. Seldin & Associates, *Evaluating faculty performance: A practical guide to assessing teaching, research, and service* (pp. 35–49). Bolton, MA: Anker.

This chapter provides several strategies for shaping the communication about teaching evaluation in ways that reduces faculty resistance to being reviewed and optimizes the benefit for the individual faculty member, students, and the institution. Among other practical tips, the author discusses how to reconceptualize evaluation to create a conversation about performance counseling rather than performance evaluation and how to discuss performance expectations in clear, concrete behavioral terms.

Higgerson, M. L., & Joyce, T. A. (2004, February). *Strategies for succeeding with limited resources: Why the department should not attempt to do more with less.* Paper presented at the 21st Annual Academic Chairpersons Conference, Orlando, FL.

Tight budgets pose a serious challenge for chairpersons who find themselves accountable for maintaining quality instruction and encouraging innovative instruction, which is often more expensive to deliver. The authors present specific strategies that enable chairpersons to optimize department performance despite limited resources.

Jourdain, K. (2004, Summer). Communication styles and conflict. *Journal for Quality and Participation, 27*(2), 23–25.

Drawing from the ancient work of Hippocrates and Galen, Kathy Jourdain, a facilitative coach and consultant, describes four primary communication styles: the expressive/spirited style; the technical/systematic style; the considerate/sympathetic style; and the direct/bold style. She proposes that a well-functioning team needs members with each communication style and that individuals have the ability to develop flexible styles to enhance conflict management skills.

Kezar, A. (2005, November/December). Moving from I to we: Reorganizing for collaboration in higher education. *Change, 37*(6), 50–57.

Based on her study, Adrianna Kezar delineates eight key organizational features conducive to collaborative work with mission, networks/coalitions/alliances, and integrating structures serving as the most salient features for an exemplary, collaborative campus.

LaNoue, G. R. (1990). Ethical issues in faculty evaluation. In W. May (Ed.), *Ethics and higher education* (pp. 133–153). New York, NY: American Council on Education/Macmillan.

George LaNoue discusses the role of individual attributes and performance and group membership (race, gender, etc.) in evaluation. He presents four aspects to define a well-functioning evaluation system that provides a level of protection while maximizing the exchange of relevant information and serving to create an ethically sensitive system essential for good morale.

Leslie, D. W., & Fretwell, E. K., Jr. (1996). Decisions and conflict. In *Wise moves in hard times: Creating and managing resilient colleges and universities* (pp. 107–133). San Francisco, CA: Jossey-Bass.

This chapter focuses on decision-making in times of fiscal crisis, and the authors found that although open and honest communication may move people toward a common understanding, it can also lead to more conflict. They determined that a fiscal crisis can put a tremendous amount of pressure on an institution to centralize its decision-making processes. In their assessment, however, centralized decision-making did not necessarily produce better decisions, nor did it make those decisions easier to accept. The authors ultimately recommend that institutions proceed with a process whereby groups can work separately but simultaneously toward solutions.

Mills, D. Q., & Pumo, J. M. (1999). Managing change in higher education: A leader's guide. In D. G. Oblinger & R. N. Katz (Eds.), *Renewing administration: Preparing colleges and universities for the 21st century* (pp. 288–301). Bolton, MA: Anker.

The authors posit that the information age has changed higher education. The changes wrought by technology include the increased need for operational efficiency, the changes in students and their learning styles, the internationalization of educational material, and the growth in costs. These factors mean the demand for organizational change will continue for some time, and the authors advocate applying change management principles to foster a campus culture that can adapt to technology-enabled education practices.

Sorenson, N. L. (1998). The cutting edge: The dean and conflict. In S. A. Holton (Ed.), *Mending the cracks in the ivory tower: Strategies for conflict management in higher education* (pp. 81–96). Bolton, MA: Anker.

For the new dean or provost, Nancy Sorenson, who has held numerous deanships, offers general guidelines for managing conflict in the face of competing expectations. To meet the challenge the dean needs to remember that conflict is neutral, its causes are complex, and, because it is impossible to predict the responses of others, in managing conflict one must know how to manage oneself. The chapter then presents a series of common situations that create tension, along with situational analysis strategies.

Tucker, A. (1992). Faculty evaluation. In *Chairing the academic department: Leadership among peers* (3rd ed., pp. 216–245). New York, NY: American Council on Education/Macmillan.

The evaluation of faculty may be the most difficult and yet the most important aspect of a chair's job. The author states that a necessary condition for effective evaluation is clear, specific criteria coupled with reasonable, definitive assignment of activities. This chapter offers thoughts on elements of the process and examples of performance ratings.

Tucker, A. (1992). Performance counseling and dealing with unsatisfactory performance. In *Chairing the academic department: Leadership among peers* (3rd ed., pp. 246–259). New York, NY: American Council on Education/Macmillan.

Effective performance counseling requires a comprehensive under-standing of departmental and institutional goals, objectives, and mis-sion. The author reviews the characteristics of performance, tactics for initiating conversations about poor performance, and ways to encour-age appropriate performance. The chapter concludes with a case study and exploratory questions about handling performance counseling.

Tucker, A., & Bryan, R. A. (1988). Dealing with the faculty. In *The aca-demic dean: Dove, dragon, and diplomat* (pp. 81–100). New York, NY: American Council on Education/Macmillan.

Recognizing that chairs and deans frequently come from the faculty ranks, the authors move from the nature of communication with the chair to focusing on one-on-one dealings with individual faculty members in matters of promotion, salary adjustments, and conflict be-tween a faculty member and the department chair.

Part III • Using Leadership Communication to Manage Especially Difficult People

Bennett, J. B. (1998). Creating and nourishing communities of hope. In *Collegial professionalism: The academy, individualism, and the common good* (pp. 131–161). Phoenix, AZ: American Council on Education/Oryx Press.

This chapter explores academic leadership skills for incorporating di-verse ideas and individuals and handling tendencies toward self-indul-gence. Although the author recognizes that some complaining is normal and natural, he points out that the best antidote for indiffer-ence is promoting communication through a variety of public means of discourse.

Bryant, P. T. (2005). *Confessions of an habitual administrator: An academic survival manual.* Bolton, MA: Anker.

In Paul Bryant's 46-year career in academe, he held numerous faculty and administrative positions. This book offers insights drawn from his experiences across multiple campuses, distilled into practical principles for survival. His lessons run the gamut from discussions about working with staff, students, and faculty to accountability and institutional governance and the various human elements that play out around an administrative role.

Chu, D. (2006). Challenging personnel. In *The department chair primer: Leading and managing academic departments* (pp. 75–82). Bolton, MA: Anker.

The author notes that difficult people come in many forms—from the faculty members too involved in issues that don't concern them to those who are not involved enough in issues that do. He offers chairs a series of tips to consider when working with challenging people, based on responses he solicited from current and former chairs about best practices.

Coffman, J. R. (2005). Some best practices. In *Work and peace in academe: Leveraging time, money, and intellectual energy through managing conflict* (pp. 121–131). Bolton, MA: Anker.

This chapter is a summary of the former provost's tips for gaining perspective, developing trust grounded in fairness, and creating an environment that avoids chronic conflict.

Higgerson, M. L. (1998). Chairs as department managers: Working with support staff. In S. A. Holton (Ed.), *Mending the cracks in the ivory tower: Strategies for conflict management in higher education* (pp. 46–59). Bolton, MA: Anker.

The author, who has served in various roles from faculty senate president to vice president for academic affairs, presents a step-by-step approach to managing conflict. While the chapter focuses on examples of conflict among support staff, the three-step process of minimizing the potential for conflict, setting the right tone for airing disagreements, and managing (not necessarily resolving) conflict are applicable strategies for all types of conflict.

Olson, G. A. (2006, March 31). A culture of openness. *The Chronicle of Higher Education*. Retrieved September 28, 2006, from http://chronicle.com/jobs/2006/03/2006033101c.htm

As the dean of arts and sciences at a public university, Gary Olson writes about how a campus culture of secrecy breeds mistrust and paranoia, while a climate of openness and transparency allows existing injustices to be corrected.

Paradise, L. V. (2004, June 29). The provost as gatekeeper. *The Chronicle of Higher Education.* Retrieved September 28, 2006, from http://chronicle.com/jobs/news/2004/06/2004062901c/careers.html

The former provost discusses personal experiences in evaluating promotions and tenure recommendations. Louis Paradise offers lessons including reading between the lines, reading credential packets closely, and being diplomatic as essential elements in the decision process.

Tucker, A. (1984). Dealing with conflict and maintaining faculty morale. In *Chairing the academic department: Leadership among peers* (2nd ed., pp. 217–237). New York, NY: American Council on Education/Macmillan.

This chapter's focus on departmental conflict suggests the need to transform conflict into opportunities for problem-solving. Particularly salient to the management of difficult people, the author discusses the need to determine what conflicting values are held by those involved in the conflict, clarify misconceptions about issues, and communicate clearly.

Tucker, A., & Bryan, R. A. (1988). Relations with presidents, provosts, vice presidents and other deans. In *The academic dean: Dove, dragon, and diplomat* (pp. 113–134). New York, NY: American Council on Education/Macmillan.

Because not all relationships on a campus are contained within an academic unit, the authors present some of the ways chairs and deans interact with other administrative offices across campus in their daily and institution-wide responsibilities.

Index